TRIAL WITHOUT END

TRIAL
WITHOUT
END

A Shocking Story of Women and AIDS

JUNE
CALLWOOD

Alfred A. Knopf Canada

Published in Canada by Alfred A. Knopf Canada
Copyright ©1995 by June Callwood
All rights reserved under International and Pan-American
Copyright Conventions. Published in 1995 by Alfred A. Knopf, Canada.
Distributed by Random House of Canada Limited, Toronto.

Canadian Cataloguing in Publication Data

Callwood, June
    Trial without end : a story of women and AIDS

ISBN 0-394-28033-4

1. Ssenyonga, Charles – Trials, litigation, etc.
2. AIDS (Disease) – Patients – Ontario – London.
3. AIDS (Disease) – Ontario – London.   4. Women –
Ontario – London – Crimes against.   5. Women –
Diseases – Ontario – London.   1. Title.

RA644.A25C35   1995   364.1'42'092   C95-930453-3

First Edition
Printed and bound in the United States of America

for Cheryl Wagner

INTRODUCTION

I WAS HAVING MY so-called annual medical checkup, which happens every two years or so, when it struck me that my doctor, Cheryl Wagner, was telling me something for the second time. She was going on about some man who had infected several of her patients with the AIDS virus. She had notified public health authorities repeatedly and now was dealing with the attorney-general's office, but so far nothing had stopped him from infecting others.

"Is this the same man you told me about last time I was here?" I asked.

"Yes," she said, wrapping the blood-pressure cuff around my arm. "Only now we know of three more women he has infected."

In 1991, when this exchange occurred, Canadians had only begun to appreciate that even single occurrences of un-protected sex could cause women to be infected with HIV, the human immunodeficiency virus that leads to the cata-strophic physical collapse known as acquired immunodefi-ciency syndrome, or AIDS. When AIDS first emerged in North America in 1982, it was seen as a disease that almost exclusively affected homosexual men, intravenous drug users who shared needles, and babies born to infected women. Until nearly the end of the eighties, the received wisdom from experts was that North American women could get HIV infection from heterosexual sex only after years of exposure to the semen of an infected man.

A haemophiliac who testified in February, 1994, before Mr. Justice Horace Krever during the investigation into Canada's tainted blood scandal told the hearing that he was infected with HIV in 1985 and married a year later. When he asked his doctor if his bride was at risk from the infection, he was assured that she was not. They had unprotected sex, and she died three years later of AIDS.

By the nineties the world knew how wrong the experts had been. In 1994 the World Health Organization estimated that seventeen million men and women worldwide were infected with HIV, the AIDS virus, most of them through heterosexual sex. Three million contracted the infection in 1994 alone, half of them women.

By a series of coincidences, it happened that Cheryl Wagner, a slender woman with a mane of unruly dark hair and huge shy eyes, was one of the first women family doctors in Canada with experience in treating AIDS. She chose family medicine as her specialty and expected a career of "babies and Pap smears." Instead, in 1986, a mature student who entered medical school in her early thirties, she stepped almost straight from graduation into the practice of a doctor who had died of a fast-spreading and baffling new disease, AIDS. She inherited from her predecessor a caseload of gay men with AIDS. Very soon she was one of a handful of downtown Toronto general practitioners, and almost the only woman, with expertise in the appalling new infection.

In the fall of 1988, she had her first woman patient with the AIDS virus. Only days later, she had her second. Both women were infected by the same man; a third infected by that man was not far behind them, and then Cheryl learned of more.

She prodded public health authorities to stop the man. They warned him not to have unprotected sex, but soon after the warning he infected another woman. At Cheryl's insistence, public health officials issued the man with a restraining order not to have sex at all. He then infected another woman. The doctor, frantic and furious, insisted that it was now a matter for the criminal law.

The problem for police and Crown prosecutors was that what the man was doing, namely wantonly infecting women with a fatal virus, was not a crime. No law exists in the Canadian Criminal Code expressly to punish a person with a sexually transmittable disease who knowingly infects others. The reason such a law does not exist is that it would be almost unenforceable. The state would have to prove that only the accused, and no one else, was the source of the infection — nearly impossible in a society of adults who are sexually active with multiple partners.

Ironically, an old law in the Canadian Criminal Code that prohibited careless transmission of a sexual disease was rescinded in 1985, just as AIDS began to explode. The law was intended to control the spread of syphilis and gonorrhoea, but in the sixty years of its existence there had never been a conviction.

In the United States, more than twenty states have enacted special legislation designed to punish HIV-infected people whose sexual behaviour puts others at risk. By 1993 the new statutes had resulted in more than two hundred convictions, mainly by allowing a loose standard of proof. The sentences have been severe. California, for instance, has a law against HIV-infected people soliciting sex: a prostitute convicted under that law received a twenty-year sentence. In Oregon an HIV-positive man was charged with putting at risk five children, three of them sodomized. None was infected. The man was sentenced to sixteen years in prison. An infected soldier in Virginia got a sentence of fifteen years and was dishonourably discharged for not wearing a condom when he had sex with another man. In Georgia an HIV-infected man was sentenced to ten years in prison for biting a police officer, although biting is not considered a method of transmitting HIV.

More than a year after my checkup, sometime in January, 1993, Cheryl Wagner left a message on my answering machine. She said she had an idea for a book I should write. When I called back, she told me that the man with HIV had been arrested and was going to trial in the spring. By her count, he had infected at least ten women, five of whom had agreed to testify against him. A sixth, who had appeared at his preliminary hearing, was in a coma and would die in a few days.

"I think this story has to get out so women will start protecting themselves," Cheryl said. "One of my patients infected by him has agreed to talk to you."

The meeting with Cheryl's patient, who did not give me her full name, was very moving. She was a distraught young woman, a social worker with a cosily furnished apartment and the face of an angel. Weeping much of the time, she told me about this "charming, intelligent man," Charles Muleka Ssenyonga from Uganda, with whom she had had an affair lasting over a year. She had loved and trusted him, she said, and he knowingly had infected her with the AIDS virus. Her immune system was collapsing and she had maybe a year to live.

I went to see Louise Dennys, publisher at Knopf and a friend. She was interested in the subject, so I launched the research with a visit to Cheryl Wagner at her home. Cheryl produced voluminous files: the case had become an obsession. The papers she gave me included the judge's decision at the man's preliminary hearing, medical reports on the soaring incidence of AIDS among North American women, articles on the ethical and legal issues surrounding this

unusual case, and a great deal of material on a Florida
dentist whose patients became infected. This case was relevant, Cheryl explained, because of an amazing development.
Using the same esoteric technique that matched the DNA —
the unique genetic fingerprint — of the virus of the Florida
dentist with that of his victims, a young Canadian scientific
whiz had succeeded in matching the DNA of the virus infecting Cheryl's patients. He would testify that all the women
were infected by the same source. Without that evidence, the
Crown's case would be much more vulnerable.

Cheryl also gave me newspaper clippings describing the
man's arrest and his preliminary hearing in London,
Ontario. Photographs of him accompanied some of the stories. Charles Ssenyonga appeared as a stocky, muscular,
black man in his mid-thirties with close-cropped hair and a
rounded forehead and faint, arched eyebrows. In the pho-
tos, he wore a bewildered expression.

Cheryl said, "There have only been a handful of criminal cases in Canada involving AIDS. Since the accused person usually pleads guilty, there isn't a full trial, but Charles
Ssenyonga says he is innocent. No one knows how this will
turn out, but we do know it will be our biggest AIDS trial
yet."

One of the previous criminal trials involving AIDS happened in 1991 and centred on an Ottawa man who gave a
blood donation to the Canadian Red Cross Society knowing that he was infected. He was charged with committing
a common nuisance and admitted guilt. The sentence,
which he appealed as too harsh, was fifteen months in
prison. The Ontario Court of Appeal ruled that the sentence was appropriate and added that the man's conduct
"verges on the unspeakable. It cries out for a sentence that
would act as a deterrent to others and which would express
society's repudiation of what he did." In 1993 the Supreme
Court of Canada agreed with the Ontario decision.

Another AIDS-related case concerned an HIV-infected man in Calgary who pleaded guilty to a charge of criminal negligence causing bodily harm after having sex with two women, neither of whom, fortunately, was infected. The third was William Wentzell of Halifax, who pleaded guilty in 1989 to criminal negligence causing bodily harm after infecting his pregnant girlfriend with the virus.

Charles Ssenyonga was only the second person in Canadian legal history to plead not guilty to an AIDS-related criminal offence. The first was a Toronto man, Denver Lee, twenty-one, a bisexual and an intravenous drug user who shared needles. He had not been tested for HIV but had reason to suspect he was infected following unprotected sex with an HIV-infected man. In March, 1990, he had unprotected sex with a thirty-four-year-old woman and subsequently he was tested and found positive for HIV. The woman was not infected. The Crown, testing the waters for an appropriate charge, decided on aggravated sexual assault and prepared arguments that the woman's consent to sex had not been obtained in the legal sense, since Lee's failure to warn her that he might be infected was an act of fraudulence. Lee was brought to trial in April, 1991. The Crown argued that consent was obtained by fraud and Lee's lawyer maintained that an assault did not take place because the sex was consensual. The judge declared that he saw no evidence of fraud and acquitted Lee, though he added that with a "so-called friend such as Mr. Lee," the woman had no need of any enemies.

Charles Ssenyonga's case, however, was unique in several ways. Unlike Lee, he knew for certain that he was infected when he had unprotected sex with numerous women; in fact, he was defying a public health order that he remain celibate. Ssenyonga faced trial on two charges: criminal negligence causing bodily harm and aggravated sexual assault. Neither charge against him described the real reason he was in court, which was for the crimes against humanity and common decency of failing to wear a condom during sexual intercourse and not informing his sexual partners that he was infected with HIV.

The Ssenyonga case could have been exceptional for another reason: the accused was a black man. Though relations between the races in the nineties are at a sensitive stage, and police often are accused of prejudice against blacks, the long investigation, the arrest, and several trials and hearings involving Charles Ssenyonga seemed to most observers to be mercifully free of racism. Given the wave of patients infected by the same man, Cheryl Wagner could not do otherwise than plead with authorities to take action, and because she assembled such convincing evidence, officials in charge of public safety were obliged to proceed as best they could against him. Public health and law-enforcement people moved to stop Ssenyonga because of his behaviour, not his colour. Ssenyonga was a scoundrel who happened to be black; later, in Newfoundland, another scoundrel, Raymond Mercer, also infected many sex partners with the AIDS virus, and he happened to be white.

The Ugandan community in Canada understandably was rattled by the media attention Ssenyonga attracted. While deploring the man's behaviour, Ugandans would have preferred that less notice had been taken of it. Many of them wondered if there would have been much public interest in the case had Charles Ssenyonga been white. No one can deny that their experiences in a white-dominated society would justify such suspicions, but the Ssenyonga case would have made prime media copy whatever his colour. It was unique in that it brought together all the explosive elements of AIDS in the nineties: the spread of HIV to heterosexual women, the emergence of technology to match the genetic makeup of viruses, and the manifest failure of public health authorities and the law to control sexual behaviour.

Charles Ssenyonga's trial began in London, Ontario, on the morning of April 5, 1993. It opened with a reading of the charges. Ssenyonga, standing beside his lawyer, Fletcher Dawson, said he was not guilty. Then Bruce Long, regional Crown attorney for southwestern Ontario, a man who had spent two years preparing for this moment, rose to his feet, settled his court gown on his shoulders with a tug, and began to outline the case of Her Majesty the Queen against the man who would not wear condoms.

I was there with my notebook. After months of research, during which I interviewed many of the women Ssenyonga had infected, I came to the same conclusion that Cheryl Wagner did. It is important to tell the story of Charles Ssenyonga and of the frustration that met every effort to stop his behaviour. Many women — intelligent, educated, self-reliant women — were fooled by Ssenyonga and it has or will cost them their lives. Women are still being fooled by charming sexual predators. I hope that this book will help spread the word that AIDS can happen to anyone.

AUTHOR'S NOTE

The identities of all the women infected by Charles Ssenyonga are protected by a court order, as is the name of a male relative of one of them. It is not likely that any of the women would have testified against Ssenyonga without assurances of anonymity. In some cases, even their parents do not know that they are HIV-infected. All agreed to be interviewed by me on the understanding that I would use pseudonyms and alter such identifying information as physical description and employment. In every other respect, their stories are true.

I

A WOMAN WE WILL CALL JENNIFER ANDERSON made an appointment with Dr. Cheryl Wagner on the afternoon of September 21, 1988, and went to the doctor's small office in an unprepossessing medical building on the corner of Sherbourne and Bloor Streets, which is on the fringes of Toronto's gay community.

"I think I have AIDS," Jennifer said to the doctor.

She was not the first woman in Cheryl's office to make that statement. That summer several women in a state of panic had come to Cheryl Wagner with the same concern, seeking her out because she was almost the only woman doctor in Toronto who was treating AIDS. When blood tests were done, each patient had proved to be negative for HIV. Jennifer Anderson was different: her blood had already tested positive, twice.

Jennifer explained to the doctor how she came to know of her infection. A friend had persuaded her to donate blood to the Canadian Red Cross, which subsequently notified her that her blood was unacceptable. Her physician received the report from the Red Cross and informed Jennifer she had AIDS. Hoping the Red Cross was wrong, Jennifer went for another test, which confirmed the presence of HIV in her blood.

Cheryl studied her new patient. Jennifer was a slender, quiet-spoken, affable young woman with long red hair and a calm manner. Well-dressed in the style of a business-woman on the executive track, she had the easy poise that comes from a fond upbringing in a privileged home. She represented a new face for AIDS, and Cheryl's heart sank. Epidemiologists had been warning the public that the AIDS virus was not selective, that anyone could get it, but the message had not been received. Jennifer Anderson symbol-ized the next wave of the disease: women.

"Do you have any idea how you might have become in-fected?" Cheryl asked.

"Yes, I do," Jennifer replied promptly. "In the past year and a half I had sexual relations with only one person, a man from east Africa. In fact, he may be in two high-risk categories. I suspect that he is bisexual. I am certain that my infection came from him."

Cheryl didn't ask for the man's name. Most doctors spe-cializing in HIV have the same protocol: if they are confident that their patients will act responsibly and notify all sexual contacts, they don't press them for embarrassing informa-tion. Public health authorities recognize that the situation is a delicate one and sheer numbers make it impossible for them to trace all contacts of every infected person. Doctors therefore are given leeway to use their judgement.

"You should notify your contact that he should be tested," the doctor advised Jennifer.

Jennifer looked worried. "I have already done that. I'm afraid he didn't take it seriously."

"Keep at it," Cheryl told her. "This is important."

Jennifer Anderson's first meeting with the man who in-fected her had taken place in the fall of 1986 at a small din-ner party given by Jennifer's cousin, John Webster. A handsome, dashing gay man, John held a prominent posi-tion in an Ottawa lobbying firm. He and Jennifer were raised in the same affluent suburb of Montreal, where the family ethic was based on responsible behaviour and good manners.

She was in Ottawa on business when John invited her to the party and she accepted gladly. A striking Ugandan was there: Charles Ssenyonga. Though John Webster clearly adored Charles, who had been his house guest for several months, Jennifer gathered that the African was heterosexual and the two were not having an affair.

Jennifer was fascinated by Ssenyonga, who held the floor that evening. He was eloquent and knowledgeable about politics, African customs, the law: topics she found absorbing. She liked the look of him: his proud carriage, the haughty, classical features, a quick, infectious smile. Moreover, her interest was returned with an intensity that took her breath away. Ssenyonga's most compelling feature was the powerful sexuality he projected. At first Jennifer was disconcerted by his blazing focus on her. Sitting close to her as if to drink her in, he seemed unaware of anyone else in the room. After a few uncomfortable minutes, she was intrigued. He seemed to be dazzled by her wit and good humour; she felt clever and beautiful.

Ssenyonga explained that he was on the point of moving to Montreal. In Ottawa he had been selling African crafts at a kiosk in the market area but business was poor; Ottawa already had a boutique that was selling African artifacts and there were not sufficient customers for two outlets. To make ends meet he was working as a night watchman.

Jennifer leaped at the hint that he needed a ride to Montreal. He accepted her offer to drive him, and she arranged to pick him up the next day. When she did, the poverty of his possessions touched her heart. Ssenyonga could put everything he owned into two suitcases and a box or two. She reflected that the work he had been doing was at odds with his qualifications. Ssenyonga was a cultivated, intelligent man with a degree from McMaster University in Hamilton, Ontario, and five years of law school in Uganda and Kenya. Jennifer suspected his lack of significant employment owed much to racism.

Jennifer's friends considered her something of a sexual prude. One serious relationship in university ended about the time she graduated and she had not found anyone else who attracted her. When she met Charles Ssenyonga, she had been celibate for more than six months. But when she and Ssenyonga reached Montreal, she went to bed with him at once. She admits, though she finds it difficult to be so frank, that she was expecting the sex to be great, and it was. Along with dexterity and gentleness, the man had amazing stamina.

They had sex without a condom. No harm could come from that, Jennifer reasoned, because she was taking birth control pills.

After she returned to Toronto, they talked on the telephone a few times and exchanged fond letters once or twice. He made trips to Toronto to spend the weekend in her apartment.

A few weeks after the affair began, Jennifer became ill with what seemed a severe case of flu accompanied by a slight rash on her chest. "It was the worst flu of my life," she recalls. "I thought I had been run over by a truck."

She visited her doctor, who found that Jennifer had generalized enlarged lymph nodes consistent with a viral illness, but "nothing to worry about." On an impulse, Jennifer asked if it was possible that she could have AIDS. She said she was having a sexual relationship with a man from east Africa where, as she understood it, the incidence of AIDS was very high. The doctor gave assurances that her fears were groundless. AIDS, she said, was a rare disease and women didn't get it.

A week later, restored to her normal robust health, Jennifer decided the doctor was right.

Jennifer Anderson is an analytical person and the long stretches between Ssenyonga's visits gave her time to consider what she was doing. She was not in love with him, she decided; she was merely attracted. He was the most exciting and mysterious man she had ever known. She could be sure of Ssenyonga's good character because her cousin John had been close to Ssenyonga since his arrival in Canada, and John had fastidious taste in friends.

She was piecing together some sense of Ssenyonga's background. He was the oldest of a family of eight children, his position of firstborn son counting for much in Africa. He was born on June 14, 1957, and his parents expected greatness of their handsome son. Both parents were Roman Catholic, as are many Ugandans, and both were teachers. Ssenyonga's father, Murekwa, was a highly respected man of stern bearing, and his mother, considered a beauty, had a more easy-going nature. The family lived on a sizable estate near the village of Kanyeguyero in the southwest of Uganda near the Rwandan border, home of the Banyankole tribe.

Ssenyonga's name, in keeping with African tradition, differs from his parents' names and the names of his siblings. It means "father of the egret," an auspicious name, the egret being the clan bird. But the children were raised to shun tribal festivals and customs, which their father believed to be primitive and backward. Instead, Ssenyonga's family embraced the style of English gentry. The language of the home was English, though when the father was absent their mother spoke to her children in Runyankole, one of the Bantu family of languages, and cooked African dishes for them.

Charles was a charismatic and brilliant child, but feckless. His younger brother John was the studious, reliable one, yet it was fun-loving Charles who carried his father's ambitions. A rigid, obsessive man, the father pushed Charles to read English books and encouraged him to be a lawyer.

Education was a passion in the household. The children could see the helplessness that resulted from illiteracy: people came to their home from miles around to ask their parents to read instructions for them or to write letters. When it came time for Charles to go to high school, he was sent to a Roman Catholic seminary to be taught by the priests called White Fathers, some of whom were Canadian.

After that he went to Kampala, capital of Uganda, to study law at the country's only university then, Makerere, where Uganda's elite is educated. He fell immediately into the thick of student politics. From John Webster, Jennifer learned that Ssenyonga was lucky to be alive. He fled the country in 1981 during a bloody attack on the university by soldiers hunting down student rebels. With Milton Obote in command of a dictatorial Ugandan government, Charles was a refugee in Kenya for two years, attending law school at the university in Nairobi, until it became clear that he could not go home again. In 1983, with the cooperation of Canadian Employment and Immigration, External Affairs, and World University Service of Canada, he was among many Ugandan university students in the same distressed condition who in the eighties were given refugee status and scattered across Canadian campuses. The one chosen for him was McMaster University, which has no law school. He obtained a degree instead in political science, graduating in 1986.

Jennifer's relationship with Ssenyonga began to develop some strains. She was a punctual person but Charles was indifferent to time. He would phone to say he was coming on a Friday night but would not turn up until Saturday, if at all. When they argued, she told him that she expected him to be dependable and he told her she was too uptight.

Though annoyed, she continued in the relationship. She wasn't dating anyone else and, besides, the sex was wonderful. Ssenyonga was an attentive lover and seemed to adore her. He had no qualms about having intercourse with her while she was menstruating.

John Webster worried about his cousin. He talked to her about Ssenyonga. "He's seeing other women, you know," he said. "Don't get in too deep."

She asked Ssenyonga about the other women the next time she saw him.

"Well, sure, that's true," he acknowledged easily. She was left speechless for the moment but then she decided it didn't really matter. Her emotions were not so involved that she needed fidelity.

Ssenyonga hated Montreal, which he said was racist. Public transit drivers insulted him openly, and employers curtly dismissed his applications. A job as a door-to-door encyclopedia salesman quickly fell apart. He returned to Ottawa early in 1987 and found work as a security guard, but he was fired a few months later for making long-distance calls on the company phone.

In the spring of 1987 Ssenyonga moved to London, Ontario, where he and a Ugandan friend, Chris Karuhanga, rented space in the London Mews, a downtown mall, to open a boutique they called The African Store. They chose London after some study of the market possibilities, taking into consideration that London had a thriving Ugandan community and Ugandans are intensely loyal to one another. Jessica Msamba Lewycky, a Ugandan university student and jewellery maker living in Ottawa, invested some money she borrowed from a friend. John Webster, always a figure in Ssenyonga's life, loaned the partners $10,000 for start-up costs. Charles and Chris had little money of their own, but they obtained a bank loan. They stocked the shop with costly and tasteful drums, ivory and ebony carvings, jewellery, mud paintings, children's toys, and ornate wooden furniture.

Jennifer and Charles lost touch that summer, but the relationship resumed in the fall when she went to London on business and called him. Over the next five months she drove to London from time to time, staying the weekend in the basement apartment Ssenyonga shared with Chris. Jennifer was shocked by the poverty of the apartment. Ssenyonga's bedroom contained nothing but a second-hand mattress on the floor and a few law books.

Her health was fine, except for rather frequent colds and flu, but Ssenyonga was suffering a series of excruciating headaches. At her urging he saw a doctor. The doctor, he told her, wanted him to be tested for the AIDS virus; Charles didn't elaborate on the doctor's reasons. Charles was insulted. He told Jennifer indignantly that the doctor would never tell a white man to be tested. Jennifer had heard this before. Every time the subject of AIDS was mentioned, Ssenyonga reacted the same way, exploding with anger at what he saw as a form of racism aimed at Africans. "This whole thing about AIDS in North America is just a conspiracy to discredit blacks, especially blacks from Africa," he would complain.

Ssenyonga was not being entirely truthful about his visit to the doctor. The doctor he saw about his headaches was a family physician, Dr. Nancy Reid. She found that Ssenyonga had swollen lymph glands, indicating the presence of an infection. In contrast to his bluster with Jennifer Anderson, with the doctor he behaved in a rational, concerned manner. To her, he conceded that it certainly was possible he had the AIDS virus.

This was a side of Ssenyonga that all his doctors were to see: an alert, informed, intelligent man who understood perfectly that he was in a high-risk group and that he very likely was infected. What none of the doctors suspected was that outside their offices Ssenyonga always denied that there was the slightest possibility he was infected. He seemed to feel that HIV infection was demeaning.

Ssenyonga most certainly knew, in some part of him, that there was a good chance he was infected. When he left Africa in 1983, AIDS was well-established in his homeland. By the nineties, Uganda had one of the highest concentrations of AIDS in the world: twenty-five to thirty percent of all sexually active adults have the virus. In one village an old woman is raising seventeen grandchildren: all the parents are dead. By 1993 the small country of only seventeen million people had one and a half million orphaned children; by the end of the century it is estimated that five million children will have lost their parents to the disease Africans call "slim."

Nancy Reid, concerned that Ssenyonga might be infecting others, queried him about his sexual practices. He assured her, falsely, that he invariably wore a condom. He explained that in Africa he had gonorrhoea "several times" so he was always careful to protect himself during sexual intercourse. The doctor was satisfied that she was dealing with an ethical person. She recommended that Ssenyonga see London's eminent authority on AIDS, Dr. Iain Mackie, founder and director of the HIV/AIDS clinic at St. Joseph's Health Centre.

Ssenyonga's appointment with Mackie was on December 17, 1987. Mackie, a sturdy, quiet-spoken man then in his thirties, was an internist and an associate professor of medicine at the University of Western Ontario. In 1984, when AIDS surfaced in Canada, like many internists he was catapulted into the epidemic. That year he had one patient who died quickly of a fungus-like pneumonia typical of the disease. A few others followed, and then the deluge began.

That December afternoon in 1987 he examined Ssenyonga and confirmed that his symptoms could indicate the presence of the AIDS virus. He told Ssenyonga the infection might have some other origin, but, given his Ugandan background, he had to consider the likelihood of HIV.

Ssenyonga nodded agreement, his manner serious, dignified, and resigned. They talked about the disease, and Mackie was impressed by how much his patient knew. Ssenyonga was fully aware that the major transmitters of the virus are blood and semen. The two men discussed the risks of sharing needles or having unprotected sex.

"Based on the evidence at the time," Mackie testified at Ssenyonga's trial, "I could not say, 'You *must* have a test...'" Indeed, Mackie did not press Ssenyonga to be tested for HIV. Startling as this sounded in the courtroom, such advice was common in 1987 among Canadian physicians treating HIV. The period was one that Iain Mackie describes as "the space-suit era," when nurses and doctors wore masks and gloves and gowns to approach anyone with AIDS. In North America, hysteria over AIDS was at its ignominious worst. Hospital patients with AIDS could expect to have their food trays left outside their doors. A chaplain, called to the bed of a man dying of AIDS, came gowned, masked and gloved. In neighbourhoods, businesses, and schools, people suspected of having AIDS were abused and their homes defaced and smoke-bombed. Few infected people believed that health records would be safe from scrutiny by employers and insurance companies. Given the fears about confidentiality and the absence of effective treatment, many responsible and respected doctors in 1986, 1987, and even 1988 counselled patients not to be tested; doctors themselves avoided being tested.

Instead, doctors treated the symptoms as best they could and preached prevention. Dr. Cheryl Wagner says, "The message we hammered home to people was 'Safe sex, safe sex, *safe sex*'." Since almost all patients at the time were gay men, the warnings were intended to protect other men.

Dr. Mackie comments, "When I saw Ssenyonga in 1987 we were in a transition between a time when we had nothing for AIDS and the time when we started using AZT to prevent the pneumonia. Once we had a treatment, it made more sense to have people get tested."

Consistent with normal practice, Iain Mackie therefore didn't push Ssenyonga when his patient said he didn't want to be tested. Mackie, however, was unimpressed with the popular view that it was impossible for women to be infected. He spent almost two hours with his patient discussing safe sex practices and assuring himself that Ssenyonga was a decent, conscientious man who certainly would advise his sex partners that he might have HIV, and that Ssenyonga could be trusted to always wear a condom.

Ssenyonga, who at that time was having unprotected sex with at least three women and had informed none of them that he might be infected, assured the doctor that he had no girlfriend. In any case, he said, he always practised safe sex.

"Safe sex," sometimes called "safer sex" to emphasize that latex barriers may be fallible, refers to condom use. Iain Mackie says, "When used one hundred percent of the time, with no leaks or tears, a condom is one hundred percent effective. It does not permit passage of the virus. The problem is that people don't use them correctly. They use outdated condoms that have lubricants that dry and crack, and the condom may tear, or they use condoms that are too small, or they don't use proper lubricants. Or, as happens most of the time, they don't use them at all. Good studies show that people who say they use condoms all the time really don't. They find condoms are too inconvenient."

Mackie later said of Ssenyonga, ruefully, "He seemed very personable and honest, an articulate, charming man, a nice human being, the type you would be happy to talk with in a social setting and be friends with. He would impress anyone."

They scheduled a follow-up visit. When Ssenyonga failed to keep the appointment, Mackie dutifully checked with Dr. Nancy Reid, who said Ssenyonga was keeping appointments with her. Mackie put the man out of his mind; Ssenyonga's health was in good hands.

The next time Ssenyonga had sex with Jennifer Anderson, very soon after the discussion with Mackie, he wore no condom, nor did he suggest to her that he might be infected. Nonetheless, she was beginning to be uneasy. Newspaper accounts of the origin of HIV usually described the area around Ssenyonga's homeland as the source. She also had come to realize from hints dropped by her gay cousin that Ssenyonga was bisexual. That put him in two high-risk categories. She considered asking Ssenyonga to wear a condom but dropped the idea. If he was infected, it already was too late for her; they had been sleeping together without condoms for more than a year.

In any case, the relationship was cooling. She was finding his thoughtlessness intolerable. She was fed up with his phone calls at two in the morning and his indifference to punctuality. "I was beginning to question what I was doing," she explains with a wry smile. "When we were together, I was made to feel very special, but when we were apart I knew he had other girlfriends, many other girlfriends. What kept me going so long was that there was no one else in my life and we had developed a friendship. He was a very charming man, but I could see the relationship wasn't going anywhere."

She had lunch one day early in 1988 with Linda Booker, a friend of hers and of John Webster's. She knew John had introduced Linda to Ssenyonga and she wanted to get the other woman's opinion of him. When she mentioned Ssenyonga's name, Linda surprised her by saying, "I hope Charles told you, but I've slept with him too. It happened about a year ago. The affair didn't last very long, only a few weeks. It didn't end pleasantly. I found him very unreliable."

That was the final straw for Jennifer. Averse as she was to scenes, she simply stopped phoning Charles, and when she went to London, she stayed away from The African Store. Ssenyonga didn't seem to notice.

It was in early June of 1988 that a friend asked Jennifer to come with her to donate blood at a Red Cross clinic, with the fateful consequence that her blood was found to have an impurity. The Red Cross had been screening all blood donations since November, 1985. Out of every hundred thousand donations in Canada, 2.8 turn up positive on the screening test, and the Red Cross advises further testing. Jennifer Anderson was one of those found to have HIV antibodies.

The news came in a form letter from the Red Cross stating that her blood had been rejected for one of three reasons: exposure to HIV, syphilis, or hepatitis. She was advised to call the Red Cross at once and give the name of her family doctor.

The bureaucratic way of communicating such frightening news made her so angry that the shock did not sink in immediately. She called the official who signed the letter and demanded to know which infection she had. She was informed that the information would not be released to her, not even in person. It would be communicated only to her family doctor.

Jennifer was leaving on vacation in two days. She arranged hastily to see her doctor the next afternoon. The meeting with the physician was harrowing. The doctor opened the letter from the Red Cross, gasped, and said, "Oh, dear. I have bad news. You are HIV-positive. You better not have sex with anyone. You are a time bomb waiting to go off." Jennifer thinks she must have been the first patient with HIV that the doctor had ever seen. She cannot otherwise account for the insensitivity. "Such a lack of professionalism," she fumes. At the time she was rigid with indignation and grief; she waited until she was out of the office to cry.

She expected that she would die within weeks. From what she could glean from casual reading of newspaper articles, having the AIDS virus meant a quick and wretched death. Though she was numb with horror, she was obliged to go straight from the doctor's office to a business meeting where she valiantly presented a new advertising campaign to an important client.

The next day she left for a vacation that she believed would be her last. She was twenty-six years old, single, successful, a beloved daughter in a well-to-do family, and she tried to adjust to the knowledge that her life was over. Her employer had promised a raise and a promotion; she would never enjoy either. She would never find a mate and marry, she would never have a child, her death would bring unbearable grief to her parents. She decided to keep her dreadful secret to herself, except for one friend.

She was unaware that HIV infection and AIDS are not the same condition: HIV is the virus, AIDS the illness. Although almost everyone with HIV eventually will die of AIDS, people with HIV can look and feel perfectly healthy for ten years, or longer. A Toronto nurse infected by a blood transfusion in 1981 was still healthy and symptom-free in 1994. For reasons doctors cannot fathom, about five percent of people infected with HIV are perfectly well even fifteen years later. Maybe these fortunate ones will live a normal life span; only time will tell.

On Jennifer's return to Toronto, the friend had done some research. She gave Jennifer pamphlets supplied by the AIDS Committee of Toronto and told her that a second test to check the Red Cross finding could be done anonymously at a clinic called Hassle Free. Jennifer made an appointment at once.

The Hassle Free Clinic is located above some shops near the corner of Church and Wellesley streets in the heart of Toronto's large gay community. The clinic is a relic of the sixties, a medical service for street youth and later a trusted, non-judgemental resource for prostitutes, gays, illegal drug users, and homeless people. Early in the outbreak of AIDS it became a haven for people frightened of the new infection. Because the clinic has always operated slightly outside the medical establishment's rules, doctors there are willing to defy regulations that names of HIV-infected people have to be reported to public health authorities. At a time when AIDS carried a stigma of devastating proportions, Hassle Free provided and continues to provide anonymous testing. Anyone concerned about the infection can be tested without revealing any information about themselves except a birth date.

Jennifer had a difficult time persuading the counsellor at Hassle Free that she wanted to be tested for HIV. In the summer of 1988 almost no one knew of a North American woman being infected. Scientists were aware that AIDS was spread in Africa through heterosexual contact, but most of them believed that the AIDS virus prevalent in North America was so different from the African virus that it was almost impossible for it to be transmitted through vaginal sex.

The staff person at Hassle Free accordingly tried to convince Jennifer that she was wasting her time. Jennifer protested that she had been in a long relationship with a man from a high-risk area of Africa and the Red Cross had found HIV antibodies in her blood.

The staff person wasn't impressed. "I wouldn't worry about it," she said. "Those Red Cross tests can be wrong. And what would you do with a positive diagnosis anyway? There isn't much in the way of treatment. And a negative test would only give you a false sense of security. Believe me, you don't need to be tested."

When Jennifer refused to give up, the woman reluctantly yielded and blood was taken. When she was summoned back to Hassle Free, the same woman said contritely, "I'm sorry that I have bad news for you." The test was positive.

Jennifer was braced for that result, but it was a shocking blow nonetheless. She kept her composure and asked a practical question. "Can you recommend a doctor who knows about AIDS? Preferably a woman. I don't want to go back to my own doctor."

"I certainly can," responded the counsellor. "Cheryl Wagner." Jennifer says telling her about Cheryl was the one redeeming factor of her experience at Hassle Free.

Since she believed her situation was hopeless, Jennifer was in no hurry to see the doctor. She threw herself into her job, happy for the oblivion of distracting work. Her HIV-positive self was something separate from the woman who went to work every day and afterwards dined merrily with friends. The person with a fatal infection lived a silenced, mute existence, often weeping alone. Her only relief came from writing long letters describing her grief and terror to a distant friend.

She was raw to the insensitivity and ignorance about AIDS in the people she knew. Chatting one day with a fund-raiser for a health organization, they discussed a brewery that was donating to an AIDS group. The fund-raiser was annoyed. "Why doesn't the brewery help my organization?" she asked. "At least we didn't ask to have the disease." Jennifer felt a chill, but replied mildly, "I don't know that anyone asks for AIDS."

Her first act on receiving the confirmation of her HIV status from Hassle Free had been to warn Linda Booker that she might be infected too and then to notify Charles Ssenyonga. Jennifer called him at The African Store as soon as she was certain she could speak without crying. In a steady, even pleasant voice, she told him that she had tested positive for HIV and wanted to him to be tested too. "I think you must be infected," she said.

His tone was disconcertingly cool. "I am very sorry to hear that you are infected, Jennifer, but I don't think you got this infection from me. Let's talk about you. Are you really sure about your diagnosis?"

"Charles," she said patiently, "I have not had any other sexual partner but you. You *must* get tested, and you must not put any other women at risk."

"I tell you, I don't think I caused this infection," he insisted.

She told him she had notified Linda Booker that she too should be tested. Ssenyonga was annoyed. He could see no reason that she should do that.

Linda was as unconcerned about her own possible infection as Charles was. "I have no reason to be worried," she told Jennifer calmly. "Charles and I slept together only a few times, five at most. Only women in long-term relationships can get infected."

They parted civilly, but Jennifer was sure that Linda Booker, a careful woman, would reconsider and go for testing. Jennifer's parting shot was to tell her about the Hassle Free Clinic. Linda called Jennifer a short time later, her voice thin and ragged. She too had tested positive.

"Go to a doctor," Anderson told her. "Call Cheryl Wagner."

That reminded her that she had better see Cheryl Wagner herself. She made the appointment for late September, 1988. It was time to find out how much longer she had to live. One more spring would be nice.

2

LINDA BOOKER'S CONFIDENCE that she could not possibly
be infected with HIV, since she had slept with Charles
Ssenyonga only a few times, was not naive considering the
state of knowledge about AIDS in the fall of 1988. At that
time, most authorities in the field believed that women
were almost immune to HIV, except perhaps after multiple
exposure to infected semen. Vaginal walls are stronger than
delicate anal tissue, they reasoned, and less likely to tear
and admit the virus into the bloodstream — and therefore
vaginal sex was quite safe.

A study that received wide circulation in that period
found that more than eighty percent of the wives of men
infected through blood transfusions were not infected
themselves, even though marital sex had been unprotected
for a year or more. Some women had unprotected sex with
infected men over a five-year period before they became infected themselves. Women's magazines of the time carried
articles stating that women had no reason to fear AIDS.
Doctors and public health officials did not have their theory
challenged because none of them ever saw an infected
woman.

AIDS education, therefore, concentrated on the gay community, though, out of prissiness, it rarely was explicit about the kind of sexual behaviour it was intended to address. The impression grew that heterosexuals, especially "nice" ones, had nothing to fear from the AIDS virus. This was peculiar reasoning in light of the rapid spread of AIDS in Africa and Asia, where it is transmitted almost exclusively through heterosexual sex, but the difficulty Jennifer Anderson had in persuading Hassle Free Clinic to test her was evidence that the error was being perpetuated even by front-line AIDS experts.

AIDS support networks in the eighties were all-male, and the men almost without exception were homosexual or bisexual. A few women, in a panic at finding that a lover also had affairs with men, would come for information or testing but invariably their fears were groundless. Hundreds of women were infected at that time, as they were to discover eventually, but few of them knew it. Wives of infected bisexual men, for instance, were unaware of their own infections because they were not yet ill. Many ostensibly heterosexual men, unwilling to admit affairs with other men, simply kept their illness to themselves for as long as their symptoms could be explained away. North American women were informed by health educators that "everyone is at risk of AIDS" but public perception of the disease did not conform to the dire warnings: as far as anyone could tell, women didn't get it.

It was not until 1989 that doctors began to appreciate that HIV is a peculiar virus but almost everyone can get it. Some exceptions exist, notably a small group of women prostitutes in an African community who have a mysterious resistance to the infection. Despite active professional lives with customers who are infected, they show no sign of HIV themselves. Others, including the women with whom Charles Ssenyonga had intercourse, become infected readily, sometimes with only one exposure.

Another oddity of the virus is that some infected people remain perfectly healthy for years, while others sicken rapidly and die within a year of becoming infected. One of the women infected by Charles Ssenyonga developed full-blown AIDS in a few months; another, though infected with the same virus, had no AIDS symptoms eight years after her affair with him. Such disparities are believed to have something to do with how advanced the illness is in the infected person, a factor which interacts with the state of the immune system of the infected individual. Many believe that attitude contributes to immunity, but researchers have not yet unravelled that piece of the puzzle.

Linda Booker certainly didn't believe she could be infected. She is a confident, strong-minded person with sharp opinions she bases on close attention to what is going on around her. An attractive woman with short curly blond hair and a narrow, thoughtful face, she was a researcher with an electronics firm in Toronto when Ssenyonga crossed her path, and she was earning enough to buy her own home.

The introduction came through John Webster, whom she met in Geneva during the five years she spent working in Europe. Linda, the oldest of six children of a professional couple, was raised in a prosperous suburb of Toronto. All the young Bookers went to church regularly, did their homework, and upheld the family values of self-sufficiency and common sense. Linda graduated at the age of twenty-one from Queen's University in Kingston with an honours degree in science and decided on a life of adventure.

She lived in Paris a year, finding employment with a Canadian import company that enabled her to pay for side trips. On one of these jaunts she fell deeply in love with a Greek journalist. To be closer to him she moved to Athens and supported herself by working for a company with ties to Canada. While vacationing in Geneva one week she met John Webster at a party for visiting Canadians.

She was twenty-six when she returned to Toronto, parting from her lover reluctantly, with promises on both sides to maintain the relationship despite the distance. She was keeping in touch with John by mail, finding him a stimulating correspondent with a wry view of the world. Once when he was in Toronto he introduced her to his cousin, Jennifer Anderson.

One day in October, 1985, John called to say he was in town and wanted her to meet "a terrific guy," a man from Uganda named Charles Ssenyonga who was finishing a degree in political science at McMaster. Linda's first thought was that Ssenyonga must be homosexual, because John was gay and there appeared to be a strong bond between them. Later, when Ssenyonga turned the melting force of his attention on her, she decided she must be mistaken.

She found Ssenyonga fascinating company. When she asked him about the bloody regime of Idi Amin in his homeland, he told her the gripping story of the horror of growing up under a despot whose soldiers tortured and killed at random. He was at university, he said, just as Uganda was preparing to have an election that would result in a true democracy. Instead, the army once again launched a reign of terror, this time making students a target, and he had to flee to Kenya, penniless and without a passport, to save his life.

Linda was enthralled. After so many years of living abroad she found most Canadians of her age an uninteresting lot. By contrast the exotic Ssenyonga was mesmerizing on such subjects as African culture and philosophy.

He called her a few months later. He was coming to Toronto and wondered if she would like to take in a movie. They had another date, this time for dinner, and then returned to her house.

Contraception was important to Linda Booker. At university she took birth control pills but she didn't feel comfortable about that method after reading about side effects.

She switched to an IUD, but after a few years she read about the problems with it and had it removed. She purchased a supply of condoms, carefully checking the expiry date, and kept them in a drawer of her bedside table.

As she and Ssenyonga were removing their clothes in her bedroom, she said, "I need to be protected. I am not taking birth control pills but I have some condoms."

He said he hated condoms. "They are so unnatural." She wasn't to worry, he added. He would withdraw prior to ejaculation. The method was new to her, but she accepted his assurances. In the heat of passion, however, she couldn't be sure that Ssenyonga actually did withdraw in time to prevent his semen from entering her.

The next time they had intercourse, Ssenyonga told her that he had talked to a pharmacist about birth control. The pharmacist didn't think much of condoms either, Ssenyonga said. Instead he recommended a vaginal suppository, a capsule that would produce an anti-spermicidal foam, which Ssenyonga purchased.

Linda was willing to try it. She inserted the capsule and soon after felt a burning sensation. The foam was irritating the lining of her vagina. Ssenyonga promised to withdraw before ejaculation so she need not worry about the effectiveness of the foam. Again, she wasn't certain that he did.

A few days later Linda had a violent physical reaction. The upper part of her body and her face broke out in huge red welts. Yeast infections filled every orifice — her vagina, her throat, her ears, her nose. Even her eyes were seeping. She seemed to be having simultaneously a cold with a racking cough and the flu.

She called her doctor, who advised her to stay in bed. "You've got a weird kind of virus," he observed. "Keep to yourself for three days and then come and see me."

Linda has learned since that in more than eighty percent of new infections with HIV, people develop viral symptoms within a month that are severe enough to take them to a doctor. Doctors almost always treat what the symptoms appear to be: flu, herpes, a bad cold, maybe measles. With a gay man they may suggest a blood test for HIV, but with a woman this almost never happens, and certainly not in 1986.

When Linda mentioned her strange illness to Ssenyonga, he mused that it sounded like the one experienced by his former girlfriend at McMaster, a student who suddenly became so ill with a rash and diarrhoea that she had to be hospitalized. Maybe Linda had the same thing, he commented. In the case of his friend, doctors decided that it was a severe version of a children's illness like chicken pox or measles. "Or maybe you have an allergy," he suggested helpfully.

Linda did not think at the time that it was a curious coincidence that two women having sex with Ssenyonga would have almost identical acute infections. As ordered, she stayed in bed for three days and then went to see her doctor.

She asked him if she might have AIDS. "I've been sleeping with a man from Africa," she explained, "and I know the incidence of AIDS is very high there."

"Oh, come on," the doctor said with a patronizing smile. "People who have AIDS live in San Francisco. They are gay men who have a thousand sex partners a year. This is a disease that has not been detected anywhere else and only promiscuous people get it. So don't worry." He made an airy wave of his hand. "You can take the test, but can you live with the results? There is no treatment." Linda dismissed the idea.

Few doctors in 1986 were saying otherwise. The test to detect HIV antibodies in blood had become available only in November, 1985. Except for a handful of big-city doctors with caseloads of gay men, few physicians ever saw anyone with AIDS.

Linda dated Ssenyonga once or twice more. She cautioned him that her vaginal yeast infection was not responding to treatment. "I am very careful about my health," he told her severely. "I hope you haven't given me anything."

In April, 1986, Linda decided to end the affair. She is impatient with bad behaviour and Ssenyonga's lack of consideration irked her. Once he was two hours late for a dinner party she gave; on another occasion he was supposed to call on a Tuesday evening but didn't get in touch with her until Thursday. She told him she had no tolerance for such thoughtlessness.

More important, she saw the rascal beneath his charming exterior. She detected in Ssenyonga some disquieting characteristics: insatiable vanity coupled with insufficient ego, a supple way of altering his personality to suit the situation, and talent for deceit.

"That kind of man can't live up to his good first impression for very long," Linda comments dryly. "He came on strong at first, but there was no substance and I washed my hands of him. I told him his behaviour was completely unacceptable."

Also, she had changed her mind about his sexual orientation. From something John Webster told her, she was convinced that Ssenyonga was having affairs with men. She discussed her suspicions with Jennifer Anderson, who said she had come to the same conclusion. Neither women objected to Ssenyonga being bisexual, but they were annoyed that he had not been honest with them.

In March, 1986, Linda missed her period. At first she put it down to the lingering vaginitis, but as weeks passed she became alarmed. She hurried to a clinic for a pregnancy test. The next day, her period began.

"Stupid idiot," she scolded herself. "There was nothing to worry about."

The clinic doctor called later that day. "You're right," she said. "You are pregnant."

"That can't be, I'm having my period."

"If you are having a period, you are miscarrying," the doctor said. "Go directly to the hospital."

It was the long holiday weekend at the end of May. The hospital doctor confirmed that she was having a miscarriage and admitted her. Linda thought Ssenyonga should be advised. Since she didn't know where to find him, she called John Webster. John had some difficulty persuading Ssenyonga that he had a responsibility in the matter but finally, on the day Linda was discharged from hospital, he turned up at her home.

His behaviour was odd. He undressed to his underwear and lay beside her on the bed, caressing her. She could not be certain but she thought he might be expecting her to have intercourse with him. It made her uncomfortable and she was grateful when he left.

Over the next two years, Linda commuted every six months to Greece to see the journalist she adored. She always travelled with two diaphragms and many packages of condoms, but the couple, much in love, sometimes forgot about birth control. They often talked of marriage but neither was willing to change countries.

In the summer of 1988 she had a call from Jennifer Anderson to say she was infected with the AIDS virus, and that most certainly the infection came from Charles Ssenyonga. Linda's conversation with her doctor at the time of her "flu" had led her to believe that brief relationships posed no risk for women. Jennifer's infection, she decided, happened because her affair with Ssenyonga lasted a year. While Linda felt perfectly secure, she decided it would be prudent to be tested anyway. She made an appointment at the Hassle Free Clinic, as Jennifer had suggested.

Feeling confident when she went for the results, she was appalled to hear that the test was positive.

"You are going to die of this," the counsellor told her. "There is no treatment, and people last an average of eight months after diagnosis. You should get your affairs in order."

Linda descended the stairs from the clinic and stood on the sidewalk trying to breathe. She could not absorb the magnitude of her disaster. It must be someone else's life that was in ruins. It was not possible that she, a healthy, happy thirty-three-year-old, zooming along in her career, furnishing her own home, had just been asked to write a will and consult a funeral director.

A common experience among people who receive the news of a terminal illness is that everything around them becomes sharper. The leaves of trees stand out separately, so beautiful as they sway in the breeze that the eyes sting. Smells and sounds intensify; flowers are tiny heartbreaking miracles. The inner pain and terror are so great that it is difficult to believe that such strong emotions don't show on the face. It seems reasonable to expect that strangers will notice the distress and stop to offer comfort. People who hurry by without a glance therefore seem callous.

Linda's customary sense of appropriate conduct quickly asserted itself. She set her jaw and began to consider what to do next. Her first act would not be picking a grave: it was imperative that she warn the Greek man she loved. In an agony of despair for herself and for him, she composed the letter advising him to be tested. He did not reply. She never heard from him again.

She called Jennifer Anderson to say that she too was infected. They met to discuss what to do about Charles Ssenyonga, who was still insisting to Jennifer that there was no reason for him to be tested or for him to notify other sexual partners that they might be infected. Jennifer had heard from someone in London that Charles was telling people he had been tested and was negative. She didn't see how that was possible, and neither did Linda.

"He tells me that I should stop bothering him," Jennifer told Linda.

"He is a totally dishonest, promiscuous person," Linda replied fiercely. "I'll bet he is still infecting women."

"Surely not," Jennifer protested. "He wouldn't do that. No one would deliberately give someone else AIDS."

"*He* would," Linda insisted. "He doesn't give a damn for anyone but Charles Ssenyonga."

Linda had dinner most weekends with her parents, who were perplexed that she seemed distracted and inattentive. She kept insisting that nothing was the matter, but they knew her better. They demanded to know why she was so remote and finally she told them she had the AIDS virus. Her parents collapsed in tears.

Linda's appointment with Dr. Cheryl Wagner took place on September 26, 1988, five days after Jennifer Anderson's first visit. She told Cheryl that she was infected by the same unnamed man who had infected Jennifer. Cheryl's immediate response was to ask for the man's name and address so she could notify public health officials at once. Linda asked for a delay.

"So far we have no proof that Jennifer has been telling him to get tested," she explained. "If my hunch about Ssenyonga is right, nothing will stop him except to be arrested. We need to lay a paper trail so we will have some evidence to show police."

Cheryl agreed to hold off if Linda would move promptly to get the situation under control. On October 10, 1988, Linda wrote to Ssenyonga, with copies to Jennifer Anderson and Cheryl Wagner:

Dear Charles:

You will undoubtedly recall that both Jennifer and I have tested positive for HIV antibodies and, because of the high incidence of AIDS in Uganda and your promiscuous behaviour, that it is virtually 100 percent certain that you too are a carrier of the AIDS virus.

Allow me to get right to the point. Jennifer and I feel morally bound, not to mention legally obliged, to do our utmost to ensure that your past partners will be notified that they are at very high risk of having contracted the AIDS virus from you, and that your present and future partners should also be made aware of this risk. Yet we have no indication that you are making any attempt on your own at this time to notify the partners of the need for testing.

My doctor is urging me to report you to the public health authorities immediately. I have instead urged my doctor to give you a chance, in the hopes of winning your cooperation.

Here are the terms of the deal we have worked out. If you supply Jennifer or me with a list of the names of all the sexual partners you have had while in Canada, as well as the location of the affair, then we will ensure that those people will be contacted by a third party, where possible an anonymous testing service. If you do not cooperate within three weeks of the date of receipt of this (special delivery) letter, however, both your business partner (a mutual friend) and the public health authorities will be notified of the situation.

It is our sincere wish that you make our lives easier and comply with this request,

Sincerely,
Linda

Ssenyonga's reaction was rage. He complained to his partner, his current girlfriend, and his partner's girlfriend that he was being threatened heartlessly by "two women in Toronto." They were making wild accusations against him and he couldn't understand what was the matter with them.

Those who knew Ssenyonga at that time say he alternated between a state of indignation that people would abuse him so, and periods of deep, uncommunicative depression. In his moods of bravado he would tell near-strangers about his phenomenal good health. His doctors marvelled at him, he declared; he was one of the healthiest people they had ever seen.

Stories that Ssenyonga was HIV-positive had been circulating in the Ugandan community since 1985, when it was learned that an old girlfriend of his, Mildred, had died of AIDS in Uganda. Mildred, a prostitute who worked in the student bar at the university in Kampala, was a beautiful woman with whom Ssenyonga had an affair in 1982. Ssenyonga believed that he was the father of her daughter, and he was devoted to the baby. When he had to flee the university, he was depressed about leaving the child behind. Later, as a refugee in Nairobi, he was devastated by the news that the child had died.

The cause of the little girl's death was said to be a virus. Very likely the virus was HIV, as Mildred herself later died of AIDS. Ugandans who knew of Mildred's death beseeched Charles to be tested, but he scoffed at their fears. He was strong as a lion, he insisted. People with AIDS were sick, and he wasn't sick.

Sometimes he told a different story. He would say that he had been tested, and was negative. The subject of his excellent health became a fixation with him. Chris Karuhanga, his partner, and Chris's girlfriend, Constance Neill, heard about it every time Charles came to dinner at Connie's apartment with his steady date, Marian Clark. The two women, both nurses, urged him not to be tested. There was no treatment anyway, they said, and the stigma of a positive test would reflect not only on him but on the entire Ugandan community, with which both women had cordial relations.

Connie Neill, a tiny woman with huge brown eyes, a cloud of long soft light-brown hair, and a romantic nature, was awed by Ssenyonga despite her live-in relationship with Chris. Chris was a practical man, four years older than Charles and the more dependable of the two, but she was intrigued by what she saw as Ssenyonga's freer spirit. When the partners argued, as they often did, about Ssenyonga's failure to open the store on time, or his habit of giving away store merchandise to friends, or the traffic tickets he amassed with the store's van, or his unreliability about money, her sympathy often was with Ssenyonga. She felt the same pity for him over the behaviour of the "two women in Toronto." In her view they were persecuting a good person.

Connie Neill was to become a major figure in the life of Charles Ssenyonga. The youngest of three children raised in St. Thomas, a small city near London, she was drawn to nursing as a teenager because the man she planned to marry was a nurse. Nursing suited the person she wanted to be: nurturing and kind. She trained first as a medical secretary, worked a year, and at nineteen broke her engagement, travelled a bit, and then enrolled in a health care aide program in Chatham.

In 1987 Connie was working in a nursing home in London caring for seniors. Distressed by "the assembly-line approach" she quit and took a job nursing an elderly woman in Florida. She returned to London in March, 1988, and applied for nursing education at Fanshawe College. That summer she met Chris Karuhanga and Charles Ssenyonga hanging out in a coffee house. She liked them on sight; North American men bored her, she once explained.

Chris and Charles almost came to blows that summer of 1988, and they stopped sharing an apartment. The cause of the acrimony was Marian Clark, who originally was Chris's girlfriend. The relationship lasted about six weeks, with Chris much in love with her, but ended abruptly when Chris saw Charles emerging from Marian's car one morning. He concluded that Charles had seduced her. Marian and Chris parted bitterly, and Marian moved seamlessly into an affair with Charles. Chris, at loose ends, turned to Connie for comfort and they became lovers. Chris then moved in with Connie, who was renting a spacious apartment. Despite the bitterness between the men, the demands of their fragile business venture kept Chris and Charles together and after a time the friendship seemed to be restored. The two couples frequently spent evenings together.

Connie was the one most strongly opposed to Charles being tested. Her fear was that if word of his infection got out, he would be shunned. Working in hospitals, she often heard other nurses talking about AIDS patients in a contemptuous manner and complaining about having to provide them care. She didn't want Charles subjected to such disrespect. Marian Clark felt the same. What was the point? She shrugged. There was no treatment anyway.

All of them seemed to take for granted that Ssenyonga would test positive. Implicit in their concern that he should not be tested was acknowledgement that the result would be bad news best postponed. "He was a very old soul," Connie reflects. "I think he knew what was in store for him." Marian Clark, though at grave risk of being infected by him, seemed indifferent to her own danger. In fact, she had fallen tempestuously in love with Ssenyonga and was pressing him to marry her.

One warm night that summer she and Charles sat in a park until almost dawn, weeping together over the likelihood that both of them were infected. She decided, fatalistically, that she didn't care. It was too late for condoms anyway, and if they had to die together, that was fine with her.

By the fall of 1988 the fault lines in the Ssenyonga-Clark relationship began to appear. Both were possessive and jealous. Marian began to suspect him of being unfaithful, and, from time to time, she followed him.

She had reason to be suspicious. Ssenyonga was courting Leslie-Anne Jenkins, a tall, elegant, disabled woman, one of the few black women he ever dated in Canada. They met on June 14, 1988, when Ssenyonga was working with a small social agency that found jobs for unemployed youth and people on social assistance by placing them in homes for elderly and disabled people. It was his function to check the placements, so he called on Leslie-Anne, who at that time was bed-ridden with an infection. Eleven years earlier a car accident had left her so broken in body that she was obliged to use a wheelchair.

Ssenyonga told Leslie-Anne that it was his thirty-first birthday and he had no one to celebrate it with him. She was touched by his loneliness. He gave her his card from The African Store and wrote on it his home phone number. The friendship developed quickly that summer, although Ssenyonga ostensibly was fully occupied with Marian Clark and, more furtively, with Katie Newman, a psychology major from Brantford who was paying for hotel rooms where they had lusty sex. As well, he had date-raped a co-worker at the agency, Danielle Fitzgerald, and was pursuing her for another encounter.

Leslie-Anne is a deeply religious woman, and Ssenyonga presented himself as a man engrossed in matters of faith and spiritual values. She was impressed to hear about his years in a Roman Catholic seminary in Uganda. He said he once wanted to become a priest. He went to church when he first came to Canada, he told her, but he was disturbed by the liturgy that differed from the Catholicism he had known in Africa. That pleased her. He was the kind of serious, god-respecting man she could care about.

One day he said to her, in a formal way, "May I have the pleasure of being your boyfriend?" Equally grave, she said yes.

"He was very sweet," she reflects.

They began to date, and Jenkins fell in love.

Jenkins comes from a distinguished Canadian family. Her mother, Gwen Jenkins, was the first black woman in Canada to graduate as a registered nurse and the first black nurse in London's Victoria Hospital. There she became head nurse, another first for a black woman. Leslie-Anne's father was a well-to-do businessman in London. Her grandfather was the first black judge in London, though the prejudice of the time restricted him to trying only cases involving black youths.

Ssenyonga was dazzled by the family's upward mobility, proof to him that blacks could make it in Canada. He became a dedicated suitor. Leslie-Anne gave serious consideration to marrying Ssenyonga. She hesitated only because of a miraculous change in her life. One morning in October, 1988, when she was worshipping in the United Pentecostal church, she discovered that she could leave her wheelchair and walk. While she yearned to marry Ssenyonga, another part of her felt she owed her mobility to Jesus Christ and should serve the church instead.

She made plans to move to California and enrol in a Bible college there, but she was irresolute. Though the call to a religious life was compelling, she was convinced that Ssenyonga was the mate for her. She knew of his many women, but it seemed to her that they were predators and he was helpless to resist. She thought his attraction to white women had something to do with the novelty of it: in Uganda blacks and whites never mixed.

With Jenkins, Ssenyonga was a gallant courtier. "He treated me the way he wanted men to treat his three sisters in Uganda," she says now. She told him she didn't believe in sex before marriage and he told her he admired her for it.

Ssenyonga seemed to brood about his promiscuity. Often he asked Leslie-Anne if she thought he was sinning by sleeping with other women. She always replied emphatically that she did indeed think so. "Obviously it was something he really struggled with, or why else would he need to talk about it with me?" she asks.

The Charles Ssenyonga she knew was an honourable, courteous, considerate man. "Respect and trust were always important to Charles," she says. "He was always so sensitive, so nice."

She is an astute woman, observant and thoughtful. She concedes that there is overwhelming evidence that Ssenyonga was a consummate liar, but it mystifies her. When she considers the puzzle of Ssenyonga, she speculates that with her he enjoyed being his best self and was bolstered by her belief in him. "With me he could be the ideal man that he wanted to be," she comments with a sigh.

That summer the collapse of The African Store appeared imminent. The location in a dismal, unfashionable mews was wrong for an upscale boutique catering to the well-to-do. When Galleria London, a sparkling, airy mall with marble floors and tall trees under atrium ceilings, opened across the street, The African Store was doomed. With irate creditors closing in on them, the partners were destitute. Ssenyonga took a weekend job in the post office and Karuhanga, saving what he could to go to university in the fall to take a teacher's course, worked in a service station pumping gas.

Ssenyonga's fights that autumn with the hot-headed Marian Clark, who was keen on marriage, were spectacular. Ssenyonga grew so harried and despondent that he talked of leaving town.

Long after midnight one night in October, 1988, Charles Ssenyonga called an acquaintance, Martha Allen, a retired high school history and English teacher in her seventies who took a motherly interest in him. He gave her the phone number of his brother John in Kenya, a law professor.

"Why do you want me to have that number?" she asked.

"Because I don't know what will happen," he replied.

When she hung up the phone, she was desolated. It seemed to her that Ssenyonga was considering suicide.

Martha Allen, a stately, cultivated woman, met Charles Ssenyonga in The African Store and was charmed by him. She was involved in a weekly cable television program, "Calling All Seniors", and once gave space to Charles Ssenyonga and Chris Karuhanga to talk about African culture. "The boys," she said, "were very good." On another occasion Ssenyonga, she says, lectured an adult education course on African studies and was a big hit.

Whatever Ssenyonga's inclinations that autumn towards suicide, they were not improved by the wild telephone calls he was receiving from Jane Campbell. Along with all the other complications of his life, Jane, his former girlfriend at McMaster, had a habit of phoning him in the middle of the night threatening to kill herself if he didn't marry her.

His relationship with Jane, a tumultuous woman, began soon after he arrived in Canada in 1983 and continued for almost two years while both were students. Jane, a black woman raised in St. Lucia, is the person who had a mysterious disease, diagnosed as possibly chicken pox, which put her in hospital for a while. She and Ssenyonga lived together in a small apartment in Hamilton in a fierce, sometimes violent relationship that was the talk of their friends. Charles, deeply in love, was embarrassed by Jane's excessive personality. Each was wildly jealous of the other. Charles believed that Jane was having affairs and she accused him of sleeping with John Webster and other men.

The couple broke up many times but always drew together again, fascinated by one other. Once he said something odd to her. "You don't know me," he told her. "You don't know the man I really am." She believed he was referring to his secret homosexual life. He spoke to her several times of sex with men while he was in university in Kenya. In a moment of deep confidence, he told her that his distress at being attracted to men once drove him to attempt suicide.

Jane decided that a therapist might help her control her behaviour, but didn't know where to turn since she was mistrustful of authority and had an especially low opinion of psychiatrists. In the spring of 1988 she was directed to a family physician in Toronto who was conducting a psychotherapy practice under the mentorship of a psychiatrist. The doctor's non-threatening qualifications included a sympathetic and supportive attitude with patients and a feminist perspective. Her name was Cheryl Wagner.

"I had this patient that summer who kept talking about an African man named Charles from Hamilton, and these two patients talking about a Ugandan named Ssenyonga from London," Wagner says. "I didn't put them together. But when Jane became pregnant I thought it advisable for her to be tested for HIV. I said her friend Charles was in a high-risk group."

Jane accused her doctor of racism. Just because Charles was an African didn't mean that he was infected with the AIDS virus. She flounced from the office and Wagner lost touch with Jane Campbell for a year and a half.

3

WITH SO MUCH ON HIS MIND, Ssenyonga found it intolerable that Linda Booker would send him the ultimatum of October 10, 1988, that he be tested for HIV. For days he seemed a broken man. Finally, a week after receiving the letter, he rallied and placed a call to Jennifer Anderson. He could depend on Jennifer to be considerate of his feelings, while he knew all too well the sting of Linda's contempt.

Ssenyonga's telephone call to Jennifer shook her stubbornly held confidence in his credibility. His tone rang with insincerity as he told her blithely that he had been too busy to be tested for HIV. He gave her assurances, however, that he was notifying all his sex partners to get themselves tested.

She didn't believe a word of it. She discussed her concern with Linda Booker, who suggested written verification of the phone call. The next day, October 19, 1988, Linda Booker sent the second instalment of her "paper trail."

Dear Charles:

I am encouraged to hear that on 18 October 1988, upon receipt of my recent letter, a telephone call was made to Jennifer to discuss our requests. We were both relieved to hear that you are now informing your partners that you are very likely a carrier of the AIDS virus, although I personally was disturbed to hear that you have so far not taken the HIV test or any subsequent blood tests. These might be able to gauge to what degree the virus is active in your system or what treatment may be worthwhile.

I ask now that you forward a written statement to me declaring what preventive measures you have taken to date and what efforts you have made to notify previous partners (partners during your time in Canada) of their very high risk of having been exposed. This statement will be forwarded to Dr. C. Wagner as testimony of your responsible behaviour and willingness to cooperate.

Please note that without a concrete account of your response to this life-threatening situation, and without a decision to be tested for HIV, the doctor's only rational conclusion might well be that you are locked in a pattern of avoidance behaviour that creates a moral dilemma for all witnesses. And without your written testimony it will be up to Jennifer and I to vouch for your responsible behaviour based on our personal experience of same. I think it is time for you to take some sort of stand.

Sincerely,
Linda

There was no response. Booker called The African Shop and spoke to Chris Karuhanga, who said he didn't know where Charles was. His tone was odd. Linda remembered John Webster, a gossipy man, telling her that Charles had slept with Chris's girlfriend, Marian Clark, while Clark was still involved with Karuhanga. She groped for some way to negotiate the awkward situation, but not until the end of the conversation was she able to mention HIV. She told Karuhanga that she was infected and Jennifer was too.

"Possibly," she said tactfully, avoiding any direct reference to Marian Clark, "you are also at risk."

A furious Ssenyonga telephoned her the next night. "How dare you cause trouble by talking to my partner," he stormed. "You have no business making these accusations."

Booker was unmoved. "If you don't take the appropriate steps, I'm going to tell Chris to advise Marian Clark that she's at risk. In fact, so is Chris."

"I'll sue you," Ssenyonga shouted. "I won't stand for this harassment."

Linda Booker and Jennifer Anderson talked it over with Cheryl Wagner, who insisted it was time to notify the authorities. In January, 1989, Wagner informed the City of Toronto public health department that a man in London, Charles Ssenyonga, very possibly was infected with HIV and likely had infected two women in Toronto. To comply with rules of medical confidentiality, she designated Linda Booker Patient X and Jennifer Anderson Patient Y.

Normally, such notification is done by telephone to an intake nurse, but Wagner wanted to speed up the process. She called a physician in the Toronto public health office, Dr. Joel DeKoven, and told him of Patient X and Patient Y and the suspected contact, Ssenyonga. DeKoven, as regulations require, promptly advised Ontario's chief medical officer, Dr. Richard Schabas, and passed along the information to the Middlesex-London health unit.

"After that it was out of my hands," comments Wagner, with a grimace. She has little admiration for the Middlesex-London health unit.

Like all Ontario's forty-two public health units, the Middlesex-London health unit operates with a startling degree of autonomy. In the absence of uniform, province-wide directives, each health unit is allowed to treat AIDS as it pleases, some reacting vigorously and others behaving as if the disease scarcely exists. Middlesex-London was widely regarded at the time as one of the stuffiest in the province. The London medical officer of health was Dr. Douglas Pudden, who rarely was available to reporters. His assistant, Dr. Nancy Tuttle, also rejected inquiries from the media, especially requests for information about Ssenyonga. All that can be gleaned directly about the response of Middlesex-London's health office in January and February of 1989, therefore, comes from the testimony at Ssenyonga's preliminary hearing and trial and at tribunal hearings.

It appears that the Middlesex-London health unit was in no particular hurry to respond to the alarm. On February 21, 1989, a month after Wagner's call to public health, Tuttle dispatched a nurse, Marylin McConnell, to find Ssenyonga. McConnell, a veteran of twenty years in the unit's infectious disease program, is a no-nonsense, firm-bodied woman with short hair and a blunt manner.

She located Ssenyonga at The African Store, identified herself, and said that two people with HIV had named him as their sexual contact. She told Ssenyonga to see a doctor at once for testing.

"He was somewhat startled when I said I was from the public health department," McConnell later said in the witness stand. "He certainly seemed even more surprised when I told him he was named as the contact in two HIV-positive cases."

This was new ground for McConnell. AIDS had only begun to surface in London and seemed to be confined to gay men. As elsewhere in the country, cooperation in London between the gay community and public health officials was imperfect. Most of the counselling of infected people was being done by the AIDS Committee of London, one of the grassroots organizations that sprang up in most large

Canadian communities in the mid-eighties to provide education and support for people infected and affected by AIDS.
Ssenyonga was the first ostensibly heterosexual man with a
possible HIV infection that McConnell had encountered.

Though Ssenyonga continued to show astonishment that
anyone would think him infected with HIV, the public health
nurse was pleased to find him a cooperative, serious young
man. He told her he wasn't involved sexually with anyone,
so no one was at risk. (At the time, of course, he was having
very active affairs with Marian Clark and several others.)
When the nurse advised him to be tested, he was pleasant
and agreeable. He said he would get tested "shortly" by his
family physician.

Ssenyonga was playing a tangled game. Only four days
earlier, he had been tested and he was awaiting the results.

On the afternoon of Friday, February 17, 1989, Ssenyonga
kept an appointment with Dr. Henry Bendheim, who shared
offices on Oxford Street with Ssenyonga's regular physician,
Dr. Nancy Reid. Reid was away and Bendheim was seeing
her patients.

Dr. Bendheim, stocky, composed, middle-aged, and
speaking with a trace of South African accent, testified at
Ssenyonga's trial years later that Ssenyonga asked him for an
AIDS test.

Bendheim had had few patients who wanted to be tested
for HIV. He asked why Ssenyonga was concerned. Ssenyonga
explained that he was from Uganda and AIDS was prevalent
in that country.

"Are you sexually active?" the doctor asked, his immediate concern the spread of infection. By 1989 doctors were
changing their minds: women *could* be infected with HIV
through unprotected sex, especially if sex tears the vagina
and damages the cervix, or if the woman is menstruating, or
if she has a venereal disease or genital sore, or if the vaginal
walls are thin because of youth or old age. The casual view

that women were at little risk from infection had been replaced by rising alarm.

"No," Ssenyonga lied, as he always did when anyone in
authority asked about his sex life, since an admission of his
promiscuity would invite disapproval.

Though Bendheim was fairly new to AIDS, he was aware
that being HIV-positive meant dramatic changes in the life
of the infected person. He cautioned Ssenyonga of the implications of a positive result, such as difficulty in buying
insurance and the impact on sexual activities. Ssenyonga
replied sombrely that he appreciated the consequences of
being HIV-positive.

Five cc of blood were drawn from a vein inside Ssenyonga's
elbow. Bendheim wrote Ssenyonga's name on a label he
affixed to the test tube, along with a laboratory number,
A10784, which he obtained from the sequenced form required for HIV testing.

The office nurse placed Ssenyonga's blood sample in a
styrofoam cooler, which was left on the front porch to be
collected by a courier from the London Biochemical Reference Laboratory. There it was subjected to the HIV test
known as ELISA, an acronym for enzyme-linked immuno-
sorbent assay. It tested definitely positive for the presence of
HIV antibodies.

A positive ELISA test is distressing but not conclusive;
false ELISA positives have occurred. A second, more elaborate, expensive and reliable test, Western Blot, is always
conducted following a positive ELISA. This confirmatory
test is done in the provincial lab in Toronto. To avoid the
possibility of damage to a liquid specimen during winter
transit from London to Toronto, Ssenyonga's blood was
separated by centrifuge. The more vulnerable red liquid
blood fell away, leaving the stable yellowish serum, or
plasma. Some of this serum was retained in the London lab,
as procedure requires, and the rest forwarded to Toronto.

When Ssenyonga told McConnell that he would be tested "shortly," the sample already was in the Toronto lab. McConnell's visit took him by surprise. Instinctively, protectively, Ssenyonga fell into a pose of innocence, pretending to be astonished that "two women in Toronto" were claiming to be infected by him. That left him with no logical explanation for being tested for HIV, so he had to feign that the test had not already occurred.

Once launched on a path of injured virtue, Ssenyonga was stuck with the role. During the almost two years of what became a warm friendship with Marylin McConnell, he continued to behave as a rather simple, decent, bewildered, and abused man. He wanted McConnell to like him; his life would be easier if she did.

McConnell is no fool. An experienced nurse and a sensible woman, she is embarrassed that she was taken in by Ssenyonga, but, as she notes dryly, "he successfully deceived many people."

In order to carry out his promise to be tested, Ssenyonga was obliged to go through the motions of seeing a doctor. That same day he made an appointment with Dr. Joanne Fox. He failed to keep the appointment and called to schedule another on February 27, which he subsequently postponed a day. When he appeared on February 28, 1989, he told Fox he was worried about AIDS. She obtained a medical history from him and made a physical examination, during which she found large lymph glands in both his armpits and his groin. She told him these indicated the presence of an infection which could be HIV. She wanted to test his blood for HIV but he told her he would have it done some other time.

On March 2, 1989, the Middlesex-London health unit had the result of the Western Blot test from the Toronto lab. Charles Ssenyonga was very strongly infected with HIV. Dr. Henry Bendheim was notified and he had his secretary call

Ssenyonga to come at once for an appointment. Ssenyonga met with the doctor on March 6, 1989, and Bendheim gave him the terrible news. At the trial Bendheim commented, "To my best recollection, he took it rather stoically. He did not become hysterical or angry or upset."

Bendheim again asked Ssenyonga, "Why were you concerned about AIDS?"

Ssenyonga replied smoothly, "A woman I knew in Uganda had a boyfriend who died of AIDS. I thought I had better be tested." The lie slipped out easily. He couldn't tell Bendheim that he was the boyfriend of a woman who died in 1985 of AIDS because the doctor would wonder why it had taken Ssenyonga four years to come for testing, when clearly he might be infected as well. Neither did Ssenyonga burden Bendheim with the information that public health had requested him to be tested.

Bendheim repeated his question about Ssenyonga's sexual activities. Ssenyonga replied that he had no girlfriend; he was celibate.

For half an hour, Bendheim went over the ramifications of HIV infection. Ssenyonga was subdued but showed himself to be exceedingly well informed about the transmission of HIV. Bendheim was impressed by him: few heterosexual men at that time bothered to know so much about the AIDS virus. The doctor ascertained that Ssenyonga was fully aware that he must wear a latex condom in all sexual relationships.

Bendheim said, "You cannot *ever* have unprotected intercourse." Ssenyonga assured the doctor that he fully appreciated the risk he offered to a future sexual partner, should there ever be a woman in his life. Bendheim was satisfied the man could be trusted. He advised Ssenyonga to see Dr. Iain Mackie of St. Joseph's Health Centre, whom he described as an AIDS specialist. Ssenyonga gave no indication that he knew Dr. Mackie as Bendheim made an appointment for him for March 15. He did not keep the appointment; it would have been an awkward encounter.

Upon receipt of the result of the Western Blot test, the Middlesex-London health unit dispatched Marylin McConnell to do what public health officials do in such circumstances: warn the infected person to protect sexual partners and, at the same time, obtain names of previous partners who should go for testing.

She visited Ssenyonga in The African Store. When McConnell broached the subject, he seemed to find his infection beyond comprehension. "He was obviously upset, nervous, fidgety," she later testified. She asked about his recent sexual contacts. He told her there were only two, Linda Booker and Jennifer Anderson in Toronto. McConnell surmised they were Patient X and Patient Y in the report from Dr. Cheryl Wagner, but said nothing. She told him that all his sexual contacts should be informed that they were at risk for HIV.

They talked about condoms, with Ssenyonga vigorously agreeing that his future sex partners must be protected. McConnell said it would be better if he did not have any sex partners at all. Ssenyonga seemed to accept the wisdom of that. When she left, he looked depressed.

"I think Charles understood what I was talking about from square one," McConnell said at his trial. "I felt he had a great deal of intelligence."

A few days later he telephoned McConnell. He had remembered two more names, he said, both of them in London. McConnell followed up on both but neither woman could be found at the addresses he gave and she gave up trying to find them.

That tidied up the situation: two women infected, two women who couldn't be traced, and Charles Ssenyonga a chaste and chastened man.

Ssenyonga's affair with Marian Clark came to a crashing end that autumn on a night when Ssenyonga uncharacteristically had too much to drink. Prodded by Marian, he bragged about the men and women he had taken to bed. She decided to get even for his infidelities. One day while he was at the store, she broke into the miserable room he rented. Clark ransacked his possessions, finding some family pictures and letters she knew he prized, which she took. Though she denies this, she is suspected of having sent letters denouncing Ssenyonga to the Middlesex-London health unit, the Ugandan ambassador to Canada, and the London police department, asking that he be jailed or deported, or both. She augmented these activities with vituperative telephone calls to Ssenyonga to tell him she was going to be revenged.

Marian Clark's explanation for these anonymous accusations is that they must have come from the Ugandan community, which was aroused by Ssenyonga's behaviour and the disgrace by association that he could bring down on them all. "At least I hope that's what they were doing, trying to stop him," she says. "It wasn't me."

The Ugandan community, however, was in disarray. It simply didn't know what to make of a man who seemed so charming on the surface but was deceitful at heart. One of those who attempted to get in touch with him was Ocan P'Oculi. Like many others, he wanted to offer comfort, but there was no answer at the telephone numbers he was given. "I guess Charles was in hiding," he says. (Ocan P'Oculi is not the man's real name. Though he sought the interview because he wanted to establish for the record that Charles had many sterling qualities, he later asked not to be identified. After months of consulting other Ugandans, he concluded that he might be seen as colluding in a book that could discredit them along with Charles Ssenyonga.)

Ocan, a slight, studious-looking man in his mid-thirties, is a writer living in Toronto. He knew Charles Ssenyonga from May, 1980, to June, 1981, the time of the student uprising in Kampala. He describes a man very different from the sly, lying womanizer others saw.

Ocan, like Ssenyonga, became a refugee when the democracy movement at Makerere University failed. Though they were colleagues in the uprising they were never close; the two men saw one another only once in Canada. Ocan's knowledge of Ssenyonga's background is sketchy, since Ocan is one of the Acholi people from northern Uganda, mortal enemies of the southern Muganda people. The two men were separated by the gulf of Uganda's bitter tribalism, which made it more remarkable that, at Ssenyonga's insistence, they became colleagues. Ocan does not speak or understand Runyankole, the Bantu language that Ssenyonga speaks. He speaks Luo, which is relatively rare. The only language they had in common was English.

Makerere University is handsomely situated on a hill overlooking Kampala. It represents the pinnacle of learning for young Ugandans and is the route to political and economic success. Ambitious families sacrifice to send their sons, and sometimes their daughters, to Kampala for higher education. Ocan and Ssenyonga were among the cream of Uganda's youth.

Ocan went to Makerere in August, 1979, to study political science. The despot Idi Amin had fled the country a few months earlier and the university was only beginning to recover from his bloody rule. Like all Ugandans, Ocan grew up with the terror of soldiers randomly shooting unarmed civilians. "Nobody wanted anything more to do with the army," he says. "People were tired of the killing, regardless of who was doing it. The mood was to get rid of the army."

Students at the university, representing as they did the country's future elite, committed themselves to the birth of democracy in their newly liberated country. To their dismay, warring factions once again arose and a struggle for domination began. The focus was Makerere University where each side sought the support of the influential students.

At the insistence of Ssenyonga, Ocan P'Oculi ran in the Student Guild election in opposition to candidates believed to be sympathetic to the army. "Charles was in law school and he was very eloquent," Ocan comments. "He was very firm." Ssenyonga was a big man on campus, rallying students to work together to achieve democracy in the face of the resurgence of the army led by Milton Obote, who later seized power of the country.

"Charles came into my room and he said, 'There is nobody else who can run,'" Ocan recalls. "I told him I don't talk in public, but he wouldn't hear that. I told him students from the south wouldn't vote for a northerner, and the south was the majority, but he kept saying I should do it. So I did."

Ocan, then twenty-two like Ssenyonga, was a retiring, peace-loving man by nature, but Ssenyonga's zeal was contagious. "The election was life and death," Ocan says. "The army wanted a student organization it could control." Milton Obote, preparing himself for the power vacuum left by Amin's departure, poured money into supporting his candidates. Though soldiers surrounded the campus that August of 1980 and the mood of intimidation was intense, Ocan was elected.

"Charles was in the middle of it," Ocan says. "Charles was my close adviser. We went from house to house and room to room. I admired his clear-mindedness. He really had a very lucid argument for what we should do. He was a moral, very principled person. He never gave me the impression he was untruthful. He was always very forthcoming. I came to be very close to him."

Ssenyonga was taking great risks. Every indication was that Obote would succeed in rigging the national election scheduled for December, 1980. Though Ssenyonga was making himself a target for fearful reprisals, he didn't waver. "He said we had to stand firm regardless of what the consequences would be," Ocan remembers, "or else Uganda would fall." He and Ssenyonga went into the country to persuade Ugandans to vote for the Democratic Party and against the Uganda People's Congress led by Obote.

The end came after the election. Obote announced that he would not publish the result of the vote. Commonwealth observers, including a Canadian, Barney Danson, a former Liberal cabinet minister, protested in vain. Obote then announced himself the winner. In February, 1981, the student government at Makerere University was under attack. For four days the young rebels did not dare sleep in their own rooms. Ocan hid in the women's residence, where he heard on the evening of February 23, 1981, that the Student Guild had been dissolved. Army terrorists squads were hunting for the most prominent student leaders, among them Ocan P'Oculi, Charles Ssenyonga, and Ssenyonga's closest colleague, John Kakooza.

"You will be dead by morning," some students assured Ocan.

"In my mind I am thinking, 'Let's get out of here,'" Ocan says, "but in Charles's mind and in Kakooza's they are thinking, 'We must demonstrate. We must fight.' They were adamant. They said, 'You must lead the fight. Whatever it takes, even if it means we are killed, you must lead it.'"

Ocan P'Oculi could see no point to continuing to resist. He asked for a few minutes to go to his room on the second floor. He and another student jumped out of the window and ran.

Charles Ssenyonga remained behind in that dangerous situation and help to rally five thousand students to demonstrate all night against Obote's rule, despite a ring of men-acing soldiers. The following morning the patience of the army was exhausted. As arrests of demonstrators began, Ssenyonga escaped. Ocan, also on the run, disguised himself as a garbage collector and slipped through the army cordon around the university. He later fled to safety in Kenya. With the prompt assistance of the Canadian Embassy in Nairobi and the World University Service of Canada, Ocan was at the University of Toronto only months later.

"We were probably the fastest group to get landed im-migrant status in Canada's history," he says. The applica-tion was made in April and by June 8 Ocan was in a lecture room in Toronto.

He lost track of Ssenyonga's whereabouts, though he was aware that Ssenyonga attended university in Nairobi for a while and then, two years later, also immigrated to Canada by the same World University Service of Canada route. Ocan, anxious to put the terrifying events in Kampala behind him, had no urge to seek out his former colleague.

They met by accident one summer day in 1986, when Ocan spotted Ssenyonga on a street near the Rideau Canal in Ottawa.

They talked a short time but found little common ground. Ocan P'Oculi's general impression was that Charles had not pulled himself together very successfully in Canada. "I had a distinct feeling that he never really overcame the depression of having suddenly been thrown out of Uganda and then suddenly finding himself in Canada. He was no longer the same Charles with a clear vision of what he had to do."

The Ugandan university students who came to Canada so abruptly after that February uprising have adjusted well. One became a close adviser to Bob Rae when he was elected premier of Ontario. Another, George Seremba, is an actor-playwright of distinction. Many are teachers; two are doctors. None, however, made the transition with ease. The universities that accepted the refugees were ill-prepared to offer social and emotional support. Ocan found Toronto inhospitable for a homesick youth from Africa. Without the kindness of a professor and his wife, who took him into their family, he doesn't know how he could have borne the loneliness.

"I am not sure that Charles had that kind of help," he says. "I think the one who suffered most was sent to university in Saskatoon. He was a third-year medical student in Uganda and he was told in Saskatoon that he should return to high school. For a while he did manual labour in a factory. Eventually McMaster medical school accepted him, but the experience had devastating effects on him for a while. He was shattered."

Ocan was not surprised, talking to Ssenyonga in Ottawa, that Charles had a job as a night watchman. "We all had to do things like that," he says tersely. Ocan, with two postgraduate degrees acquired in Canada, once worked as a window cleaner.

For years Ocan thought that his misery was a temporary state and that one day it would be safe for him to return to Uganda. Now he knows he has changed too much; he would not be at home in Uganda either.

"I don't know how much of that feeling Charles had too," he reflects. "I think he must have been suffering terrible psychological damage. If you know you are HIV-positive and actually go ahead and infect someone, your psychological makeup needs to be examined."

George Bwanika Seremba, Ugandan-born actor and playwright, is not an admirer of Ssenyonga. "I think he knew exactly what he was doing. He was a very intelligent and witty man, but I find it very hard to sympathize."

Seremba has vivid memories of Ssenyonga and Ocan in the flaming days of the uprising at Makerere, though Seremba occupied the less popular and more dangerous middle ground. Seremba escaped to Kenya to finish his education but slipped back into Uganda at the time of the student election. He was captured by the military, tortured for three hours, and then taken into the forest and shot six times through his body. Left for dead, he managed to crawl to a road and was found there the next morning by villagers who got medical care for him. He wrote about that nightmare and performs it in a one-man award-winning show, *Come Good Rain,* which has been seen all over North America.

Seremba, an elegant man in his mid-thirties with close-cropped hair and a short goatee, often reflects on the mystery of Charles Ssenyonga's unconscionable behaviour. "He had a lot of loyal friends," he says. "At university Charles was liked by a lot of people across ethnic lines. His friends in Canada loved him dearly but condemned his actions. But this later man he became is very frightening. It must have been buried in him, the later thing that he became. He was a killer. That's the bottom line."

Soon after the breakup of the relationship between Marian Clark and Charles Ssenyonga, the Middlesex-London health unit received an anonymous letter signed "Huron," probably from Marian Clark, which declared that Ssenyonga was sleeping with a new sexual partner, a woman who worked in a hotel. Nurse McConnell was dispatched to discuss this with Ssenyonga. He admitted he had spent a weekend with the woman and they had sex three times. He said he wore a condom, as he always did with his sex partners; in fact, he wore two. Unfortunately the condoms were not reliable. Once, one of them broke. "Bad luck," he said, shaking his head.

McConnell checked with the woman in question, who corroborated Ssenyonga's story. She was tested for HIV and found negative.

And then, in December, 1989, a third patient infected by Ssenyonga showed up in Dr. Cheryl Wagner's office, another woman from Toronto, and only recently infected.

"It took me quite a while to straighten out all the places Ssenyonga lived," Cheryl Wagner comments. "He was in Hamilton at McMaster from 1983, when he arrived in Canada, until 1986, when he graduated. Then he lived in Ottawa about a year, then he was in Montreal for a while before going back to Ottawa. In 1988 he went to London. What worried me was that I kept seeing all these women in Toronto who had been infected by him, and he never lived here. I figured they were just the tip of the iceberg. I wondered how many more were out there."

All parties agree that the legal case against Ssenyonga would never have unfolded as it did, or perhaps might never have come to public attention at all, except for the fierce and stubborn efforts of Dr. Cheryl Wagner. She calls it a fluke of timing that Ssenyonga's victims wound up on her caseload one after another, which might not have occurred had she not then been one of the few women doctors with experience in AIDS.

As women infected by Ssenyonga in the London area began turning up, Wagner was asked to find them a sympathetic doctor there. She directed them to Dr. Janet Gilmour, who had gained experience with AIDS in a Toronto clinic. Gilmour then was working with Dr. Iain Mackie in the HIV/AIDS clinic of St. Joseph's Health Centre in London.

After seeing a second Ssenyonga-infected patient, Janet asked Iain if he had ever treated a black Ugandan man with HIV.

Mackie, startled, replied, "Yes, I think so. I'll look it up. Why?"

"I have two patients who identify him as their contact," she told him.

Cheryl and Janet kept in touch as each of them acquired more Ssenyonga-infected patients. As the number grew, so did their horror and frustration.

"That coincidence couldn't happen in the United States," Wagner comments. "Canada is such a small country that people working with AIDS keep running into one another, and it doesn't take long to put the pieces together."

4

WHEN SHE IS IN HER DOCTOR MODE, Cheryl Wagner is a
thorough professional, gentle, up-to-date in her knowledge,
sensitive to her patients' feelings, and forthcoming with information. All this takes time and stretches out her appointment schedule. Her modest lifestyle is testament to a
bare-bones income, far below the average for physicians.

Cheryl is a respected member of the Toronto HIV Primary
Care Physicians Group, a loose organization of some thirty
doctors, mostly men, founded by Dr. Philip Berger, which
meets in Casey House Hospice, a Toronto mini-hospital that
provides palliative care to people in the terminal stages of
AIDS. Half the meetings deal with such business matters as
government directives and access to new medications, the
other half are devoted to speakers on such topics as AIDS and
nutrition or AIDS and the gastric tract.

When Cheryl Wagner is out of her office, her exquisite
face, her frail figure, her mild manner, the wild cloud of
dark hair, and a light voice that one must strain to hear
make her seem fragile, even vulnerable. Her gossamer manner has misled experts. A veteran court official, encounter-
ing Wagner just before she testified at Ssenyonga's trial,

decided she would be a washout in the stand. After she gave her evidence, precisely and clearly, he pronounced her "a wonderful witness, a rock."

Police investigators and Crown lawyers praise Wagner's dedication, her sense of fairness, her compassion for the infected women, and her toughness and tenacity in pushing authorities to do something about Charles Ssenyonga. Without her, it is likely that Ssenyonga would have infected many more women.

The advocate in her comes from Cheryl's background. Unlike most doctors, whose training is a continuum from kindergarten to examining room, there is a gap of about ten years in Cheryl's life when she was active in the peace movement. She applied for medical school as a mature student when she was almost thirty and was already imbued with a healthy scepticism of people in power.

Cheryl was born on September 24, 1950, and raised with three brothers in the midwestern United States by parents with doughty principles based on the trinity of correct deportment, the Roman Catholic Church, and the Republican Party. Just as she finished high school, her father, manager of a paper mill in Wisconsin, was transferred to Butler, Alabama. It was 1968, the hottest time of the civil rights movement in the South. Soon after the family arrived in Butler, a young black woman was killed, run down by a motorist who drove his car into a peaceful demonstration in the town square. The Wagners showed exemplary courage. Unhesitantly, they put themselves on the side of school desegregation. While the rest of Butler's leading white citizens indignantly pulled their children out of the public schools, the young Wagners continued to attend.

Science came naturally to the Wagner brood. Cheryl's three brothers have engineering degrees. Dissatisfied with that, one became a dentist and another a doctor. Cheryl herself once won a state science competition for a physics project. She went to university at Spring Hill, Alabama, where she took pre-med courses because they corresponded with her interest in science, and then transferred in 1970 to the University of Dayton, where she graduated in one year instead of the regulation two.

No American college student of that era could avoid being drawn into the moral issues presented by the Vietnam war. The year Cheryl went north to Dayton was the year the National Guard fired on protesting students at Kent State College and killed four. In her college classes were young men sweating exams because low marks meant they were eligible for the draft.

One day in mid-term of her year at Dayton, Cheryl spotted a flyer on a bulletin board advertising a one-month summer program in peace research on an island called Grindstone somewhere in Canada. Two months later, in the midst of an organic chemistry class, the memory of it flashed in her mind. She waited impatiently for the class to end and rushed to find, to her relief, that the flyer was still there. On an impulse that she still doesn't entirely understand, she applied for the peace program. When summer came, off she went. "It must have been a bad day in organic chemistry," she mused twenty years later.

At the idealistic age of twenty, she embraced the peace movement with all her heart. Grindstone Island, in lake country between Ottawa and Kingston, was then a legendary centre run by the Quakers and a magnet for disarmament conferences and non-violence training sessions to which academics, activists, and the remnants of the sixties flower children flocked. When the course ended, Cheryl accepted a job organizing similar peace programs for Norman Alcock's Canadian Peace Research Institute, which had its modest office in Dundas, near Hamilton, Ontario.

Her parents were appalled. The Wagners supported the war in Vietnam and regarded peace demonstrators as traitors.

"It was difficult for them," Cheryl comments sympathetically.

By the age of twenty-four she was running everything that happened at Grindstone Island in the summer, from the kitchen clean-up to a conference of diplomats. In 1974, with Grindstone Island about to be sold, she was one of a handful of people who raised the money to buy it on behalf of a co-op of user groups, with Cheryl as administrator.

When autumn came after the first summer of the ownership change, Cheryl found herself too drained to return to the Canadian Peace Research Institute. Instead, she stayed on Grindstone Island by herself all winter, skiing two and a half miles over the frozen lake to pick up groceries and mail. She prepared for the retreat with boxes of books she intended to read but spent the time instead in such survival tasks as splitting wood for her stove and such pleasures as skiing in the woods. The hermitage silence and loveliness of the winter-bound island restored her spirits and made her a gift of the discovery that she was self-sufficient. She spent another four summers setting up Grindstone Island programs and then called it quits. She was twenty-eight years old, single — if you didn't count the boyfriend — and she needed a change. She began to consider medicine. Her Toronto doctor was a woman, so that helped put the idea in her head, but she realized that medicine had been at the back of her mind for a long time.

In 1979 she began her medical education at McMaster and she was thirty-four when she finished her residency in family medicine, a field she chose in part because it required the least specialization training and therefore was the quickest way to start working. She had delayed her medical career long enough. She parted from the boyfriend, who was moving to the States, and she became a Canadian citizen.

Her first job was a posting to Sioux Lookout in Ontario's northland, where she was one of the "flying doctors" who patrol isolated communities. In the spring of 1986 she was in the clinic in Moose Factory when she got a phone call from a medical school colleague and friend, Evan Collins.

"Cheryl," he said. "I've got a job for you." Greg Fraser, a Toronto family physician, had a vacancy in his practice. A partner had died of AIDS, and Fraser, whose caseload consisted in good part of people with AIDS, was desperate to replace him. Fraser and Wagner talked on the phone and she agreed to fill in for four months.

Cheryl Wagner first heard of AIDS in 1983, when it made the cover of *Time*. During her residency she had only a brief brush with the disease, when she and Evan Collins were asked to prepare a workshop on medicine for homosexual men. They both read the scant literature on AIDS, a disease so new that no one was certain even of how it was transmitted. One theory, prevalent in the gay community, was that a commonly used sex-enhancing drug called "poppers" was responsible. Since AIDS seemed to be infecting only gay men, it had to be something in their lifestyle. As one gay man observed at the time, "It can't be that we all have great apartments."

A lesson Cheryl learned at McMaster was that medicine is not a static science. Professors in that medical school, regarded as one of the most progressive in Canada, used to say, "Don't expect us to teach you medicine because medicine is always changing. We'll teach you how to think." Attending a class reunion ten years later, Cheryl reflected on that wisdom. She had become a specialist in a field of medicine that didn't exist when she graduated.

When she joined Greg Fraser in the medical suite at the corner of Sherbourne and Bloor, Cheryl knew almost nothing about AIDS but she knew how to find out. She was shocked to learn that there was no known effective treatment. The function of AIDS doctors then was simply to monitor patients' health and do what they could to relieve such symptoms as peculiar skin cancers, thrush, and digestive complaints.

Wagner launched her medical career in Toronto with an office full of frightened gay men. At first, they didn't know what to make of her.

When she said, "Take off your clothes. I need to examine you," they responded, *Whaaaat?*

One said indignantly, "No woman has ever seen me naked, except my mother."

"Just think of me as your mother," Wagner responded pleasantly, "and we'll be fine."

They came to love her. Some took a proprietary interest in her clothes, deploring Wagner's indifference to fashion, and several expressed a wish to tame her luxuriant hair. When she announced in May, 1989, that she was about to be married to John Schaffter, a City of Toronto specialist in training and development, they were delighted for her.

She loved their affectionate attention, but the good times vanished in 1987 when her first patients started dying.

The death of the young is always an intolerable affront to the natural order, but it is especially poignant for AIDS physicians, who tend to be of the same generation as the population they serve. The relationships, despite the tradition of professional detachment, become intensely personal because patients bring to their doctors such painful matters as whether parents should be informed that they are gay and dying.

Treatment of bisexual men with AIDS is equally fraught with difficulties. Most are married and are obliged to tell their wives of the infection and at the same time admit to homosexual affairs. Some marriages come abruptly to a crashing, bitter end, but Wagner is impressed with how many wives stay with dying husbands out of graciousness and love.

HIV/AIDS physicians witness the descent from good health and a flourishing career through to, in many cases, poverty, isolation, despair, and, invariably, death. Doctors live with grief. While family practitioners have maybe one unexpected death in a year, HIV primary care physicians, working in the eye of a disaster, see thirty or more.

In the latter years of the practice she shared with Greg Fraser, Cheryl Wagner never knew a month without the death of at least one of her patients; in one harrowing week, three died. Her friend Dr. Philip Berger, the best known of all Canadian doctors treating AIDS, once had two patients die on the same morning.

When the tenth international conference on AIDS ended in August, 1994, in Yokohama, Japan, scientists who attended were despondent. They confessed they still didn't know when or if there will be a cure; they didn't think a vaccine is likely to be available in this century; they didn't even know why the AIDS virus is so unpredictable.

"What is fascinating and frightening about Ssenyonga," Cheryl Wagner says, "is that he managed to infect every woman with whom he had unprotected sex. *Every one of them,* including a woman who slept with him only once. Either his virus was shedding, multiplying like crazy, or his strain of the virus was especially contagious."

Dr. Iain Mackie speculates that the reason Ssenyonga infected women so readily was that intercourse lasted so long. Ssenyonga was able to sustain an erection for hours. Also, Ssenyonga's penis was larger than average. Did this result in fatal rips to vaginas? Several women infected by him say no, they suffered no trauma to their vaginas. One woman, torn in a date-rape, says yes.

On December 4, 1989, Cheryl Wagner had a first appointment with a new patient, Francine Dalton, a social worker in her early thirties, a tall blonde with huge blue eyes and large spectacles that slip down her nose. Francine told the doctor that she was infected with HIV and was desperately worried that she might have infected a recent sex partner, a man she loved passionately. She had been racking her brains to think where she might have acquired the infection, going back over the men in her life in recent years, but none of them seemed a likely candidate.

"This is terrible enough for me," the patient said, beginning to cry, "but I can't bear the thought that I have infected this wonderful man in my life. We met only a few months ago and I'm crazy about him."

Francine brought with her the results of two HIV tests, the first one doubtful but the second positive. Cheryl glanced at them side by side on her desk and was struck with an idea. She had never seen such a thing before, but it looked to her as though Francine Dalton's infection was a new one, in the early stage of development. *She is in the process of seroconverting,* the doctor thought. Seroconversion is a medical term referring to blood that is changing its state, in this case from HIV-negative to HIV-positive.

"Wait a minute," she said to Francine. "I think you just got this infection. Tell me about this new relationship."

Francine was startled. "He's from London, Ontario," she said. "His name is Ssenyonga."

Doctors are required to maintain patient confidentiality, so Cheryl had to control her shock. She could not suggest in any way that the name meant anything to her. She blinked, but she kept professional composure.

"In all likelihood," she said carefully, "I think this new man is the source of your infection. When did this affair begin?"

Francine poured out the story, speaking in a soft rush of words, her hands flying about distractedly. She met Charles Ssenyonga that summer, she said, August 13 to be exact, when she went with a girlfriend to a music festival in Toronto. Ssenyonga approached her to chat and she felt instantly at home with him, something she later described as a sense of "spiritual affinity."

Her tremulous manner made her seem emotionally fragile, and indeed she was. Some months earlier a man broke into her apartment while she was sleeping and tried to rape her. Her screams wakened a neighbour and the man fled, but not before inflicting severe injuries in his attempt to choke her. Since then she had been unable to work; the ordeal turned her into a nervous, weepy woman, dependent on antidepressants and in the care of a psychiatrist.

Ssenyonga's reaction to her story could not have been more sympathetic and kind. He said she could trust him, she could be sure he would never hurt her.

She comments, twisting her hands, "I was very vulnerable at the time. Ssenyonga seems drawn to vulnerable people."

They danced and she was charmed. He asked her to lunch with him on the following day, and she accepted. When he didn't turn up, she called him at The African Store in London. He apologized and explained that he had lost her telephone number. He invited her to come to London. They arranged to meet at the Elephant & Castle on August 26, 1989, after which he took her to the store. Dalton is knowledgeable about African art and was impressed with the collection that Ssenyonga and Chris Karuhanga had assembled. Ssenyonga's stories about the history of the artifacts enthralled her, and she was touched by his pride in his heritage.

She decided it was too late to drive back to Toronto. Instead she checked into a modestly priced hotel. Ssenyonga accompanied her into the room and kissed her. He asked if he could spend the night with her. When she refused, he left without protest. The next day, they had a picnic lunch together at a beach and then she returned to Toronto, totally smitten with the man.

The next date was in Hamilton on September 8 or 9. Ssenyonga said it would save her the long drive to London, and besides, he wanted to show her around the city he knew so well from his years at McMaster. To her surprise, their first stop was a gay bar, where Ssenyonga seemed to be completely at home. They danced — Ssenyonga was a wonderful partner on the dance floor, she says — and became aroused. They decided to find a motel room.

She told him she believed in safe sex and always insisted that her sex partners wear condoms. He said that was fine: he had a condom with him. She undressed in the bathroom and when she emerged he was lying on the bed in his underwear. After ardent foreplay, Ssenyonga opened the condom package and started to put the condom on. He seemed to have difficulty. At the moment he was about to enter her, he pulled off the condom and threw it aside, saying, "I only have one anyway."

As she was to testify at his trial, she had no time to stop him from having unprotected sex with her. He was a strong man and his penis was in her before she could resist. They slept after the sex and in the morning had sex again, again without a condom.

The incident merits consideration. When Charles Ssenyonga pulled off the condom, he knew he was infected with HIV and knew at least two women had been infected by him. It was seven months since his assurances to nurse Marylin McConnell that he never had sex without a condom. In the expectation that he and Francine would have intercourse, he had purchased one condom, somewhat of a token for such a virile male but at least an indication that the man who hated condoms intended to behave responsibly.

Why, then, did he pull it off and expel his lethal semen into her body? It could not have been that he thought Francine would escape infection. He was well informed about AIDS, so up-to-date in his knowledge that he impressed doctors, so he certainly was aware that the old theory about vaginas being almost invulnerable to HIV had been exploded. Perhaps he cared nothing for her life because she was a woman, a white woman. This guesswork is on shaky ground. Ssenyonga never displayed any contempt for women: indeed, many of the women in his life were strong feminists who would not have cared for him if his attitude had been patronizing or domineering. Nor is it possible that he had a genocidal view of whites as dispensable objects. His upbringing had instilled in him admiration for white society and he seemed a man who longed to fit in and be accepted by whites.

More likely, something immature and nasty was at work, an infantile, egocentric view that the world revolved around Charles Ssenyonga. An indulged son, much pampered for his charm and place in the family, he was not accustomed to being held accountable for bad behaviour. His carelessness about financial responsibilities, his habit of lying to avoid criticism, his vanity and preening ways all suggest a man whose emotions had not developed beyond an elementary stage of narcissistic self-gratification. And when he clearly was behaving badly, he had a talent for rising above self-blame.

Added to this was Ssenyonga's driven need to imagine himself healthy and invincible. A master at deceiving others, he seemed able to deceive himself so that unpleasant reality, such as being HIV-positive, could almost vanish from his mind. This escape into utopian fantasies resembles that of an HIV-infected bisexual man in a 1994 award-winning French film, *Savage Nights,* who has sex with a woman he loves without wearing a condom. When someone asks him about his behaviour he replies, "It was like a dream, like I'd forgotten the virus was part of me."

The day after Ssenyonga and Francine Dalton had intercourse in the motel, Ssenyonga followed her in his car to

Toronto and spent the night in her apartment. They had un-protected sex again. Francine is a health-conscious woman, and the absence of a condom concerned her. She told him she was worried about venereal disease. Ssenyonga assured her she had nothing to fear from him because he too was very particular. He had just been checked by excellent doc-tors and he was free of infection.

Francine told this story at Ssenyonga's trial three and a half years later. "I was very enamoured of him," she said steadily, glancing occasionally to where Ssenyonga, slumped in his chair, stared fixedly at the opposite wall. "He was ex-tremely charming, intelligent, fun to be with. He conveyed a sense of trust. He said that I could trust him. It seemed he was looking for a stable relationship as much as I was. I was in a very vulnerable state."

Their next meeting was in London. She was stunned when she saw his apartment on Elm Street. "It was on the main floor of a house and it was completely bare. There wasn't even a chair. His mattress was on the floor of the bedroom and there was a chest of drawers and a full-length mirror leaning against the wall. That was all." In that sad place, they had sex twice.

A few days later, on September 22, 1989, Francine Dalton was hit with a severe case of what she thought must be flu. The symptoms included such strange manifestations as a fine rash on her torso and an intense itchy feeling every-where except her face. Her doctor was baffled and sent her to an internist. The specialist was also puzzled. He pre-scribed antibiotics, and on October 31, a month later, when her symptoms were unchanged, he ordered a full range of blood tests for a possible virus, including HIV. Doctors — careful doctors, that is — were no longer assuming that women could not get AIDS.

Ssenyonga came for a visit on November 3. Francine told him about her strange illness. He did not tell her that many of his sex partners had succumbed to strange rashes and severe flu soon after having sex with him. They had sex without a condom; as Ssenyonga knew perfectly well, it now was too late for safe sex.

On November 15 her doctor informed Francine that the blood test was weakly positive for HIV. She was aghast. The internist hastened to add that the results were so ambiguous she should not be too concerned. It could well be a false positive, he said, perhaps from a thyroid disorder. He would repeat the test, but, meanwhile, she should not have sex without condoms.

She went to London three or four days later, distraught that she might have infected Ssenyonga with HIV. Though she was appalled to consider that she might have an infection that would soon kill her, it horrified her more to think she might have inflicted the same fate on someone else. She told Ssenyonga they would have to use the condoms she had purchased because he would need to be protected from her. He made no comment on the irony of her concern for him. She stayed a few days, grateful for the comfort he offered her agitated state. They had sex once; he wore the condom she provided.

Francine's second HIV test was more clearly positive. The internist recommended that she see an AIDS specialist and gave her a name: Cheryl Wagner.

On the afternoon of December 4, 1989, when Francine was confronting the possibility that Ssenyonga had infected her, Cheryl Wagner asked tactfully if Francine possibly was seeing someone else. Maybe Ssenyonga was not to blame.

Francine shook her head, her eyes full of tears. No, she assured her doctor, Ssenyonga was her only lover. Cheryl told her gently that the infection most certainly must have come from him. Francine fell apart. At one sweep she had to face her own imminent death and the fact that the man she loved was responsible. Her first thought, a strange one in view of the fatal calamity that had befallen her, was that her sex life was ended. Ssenyonga was her last lover; she could never have intercourse with anyone else because she would never put another person at risk. Besides, who would want to have sex with an HIV-infected woman?

Cheryl drew blood for a third, confirmatory HIV test, and Francine, experiencing what she described as "the most upsetting time of my whole life," drove home. Ssenyonga was in her kitchen having a cup of coffee. She was furious at him and weeping with rage and grief, but when she said she was recently infected, he appeared curiously unmoved.

"Have you been tested?" she screamed at him.

"No," he replied stiffly. Lying was his only recourse. Telling the truth at that point would have involved acknowledging that when he pulled off the condom that night in Hamilton he knew he was infected. He could not admit to being the kind of man who knowingly would expose another human being to a deadly virus.

"Are you HIV-positive?" she yelled. He stuck to his story. He insisted stonily that he was not infected.

She didn't know what to make of his denial, or of his curious lack of concern for her. "I think you should be tested," she told him, struggling for control.

"It isn't necessary," he insisted. "I've got many doctors and they tell me I am in perfect health."

She collapsed, weeping uncontrollably, in a chair. He didn't move to touch her. She thought it strange behaviour from a man who had always shown her compassion.

"You have *got* to be tested," she told him.

"All right," he conceded. "When I have time."

Cheryl Wagner meanwhile was on the telephone to the Toronto public health department to demand action. She had Patient X infected by Ssenyonga, and Patient Y infected by Ssenyonga, and now Patient Z, who was *right now* having an affair with Ssenyonga.

Francine's third blood test came back very strongly positive. Wagner called Dr. Rick Galli, head of the province's HIV testing lab in Toronto. Galli is a slender, easy-going man in his forties with owlish glasses, tightly curled hair springing ecstatically from a high forehead, and a thick black moustache. As a child in Windsor, he collected snakes and bugs; his mother stopped checking his pockets before doing the laundry. That interest took him in the direction of science. In 1973 he obtained a degree in biology from the University of Windsor and went to work in the Ministry of Health laboratory in Toronto, testing blood for parasitical bacteria.

Two years later he was the senior technologist responsible for confirmatory testing for such sexually transmitted diseases as syphilis. A bright and conscientious scientist, he was chief technologist in the serology section in 1985 when HIV testing began, which made him one of the pioneers in the field. He became head of the province's HIV lab, which in 1989 was receiving between two and three hundred samples a day. In the nineties, this escalated to a thousand tests a day.

The Ontario government has satellite HIV-testing labs in London, Kingston, and Ottawa, but these handle only the ELISA test, which acts as a screen. The central Toronto lab performs ELISA tests for the rest of the province, as well as for Newfoundland, which has no such facility, and does all Western Blot confirmatory tests for both provinces.

Galli is largely responsible for the sanctity of the testing process, relying for this on procedures that are double-checked at every stage and on a small, dedicated staff who never forget that what they do has life-or-death meaning for some anguished human being. Galli, a engaging man, is proud of the brilliant state-of-the-art technology in his lab.

The Western Blot test, he explains, is known in HIV labs as "the gold standard" because of its reliability. "It is exquisitely sensitive and specific," he says admiringly. Western

Blot involves breaking down the component proteins of the virus into a kind of soup, then separating these components according to their molecular weight. Further along, the rainbow band of proteins is transferred, or blotted, to a strip of nitro-cellulose paper where the elements can be read. And there, plain for the knowledgeable to see, is a snapshot of HIV.

Cheryl Wagner told Galli that she was in the midst of an unusual situation. Would he pull Francine Dalton's three Western Blot test results and tell her if he thought this was a new infection? He was excited by what he found: a textbook example of the phenomenon of seroconversion, progressing in two months from the earliest, barely discernible stage of HIV infection to the irrefutably positive.

Rick told Cheryl that she was right. "This is consistent with a very new infection," he said.

Christmas came and went and Cheryl had no response from her complaint to public health about Patients X, Y, and now Z. She found the silence intolerable. Another doctor might have folded, having done her best, but this doctor had been a political activist for ten years. Determined to force the issue, Cheryl put together a dossier on her three cases that no one would be able to ignore. During the next checkup visits with Jennifer Anderson and Linda Booker, she asked them to tell her more about the dates of their contacts with Ssenyonga. Each woman guessed the reason for her interest.

"You're asking these questions because you've got another Ssenyonga victim, haven't you?" Jennifer asked.

She couldn't lie. "Yes, I have," Cheryl confessed.

On February 1, 1990, when she had her facts in order, Cheryl composed a letter to Dr. David McKeown, the acting medical officer of health for the City of Toronto, with copies to Dr. Richard Schabas, chief medical officer for the province, and to Dr. Nancy Tuttle of the Middlesex-London health unit. In a tone of barely concealed wrath she gave a clinical report of Patients X, Y, and Z. Then she added:

> Clearly with Patient Z, C.S. [Ssenyonga] knew of his risk status as he was informed by the two previous partners and, one hopes, was contacted by the London public health department. What action did public health take to counsel and test C.S. when informed of the fact that he likely infected X and Y? Whatever action, this was inadequate to prevent other women from becoming infected.
>
> Does public health plan to take any action against C.S. for knowingly infecting patient Z?
>
> What action will public health take to prevent further women from becoming infected by C.S.? Both X and Z have a clinical picture compatible with a primary HIV infection after their first or second sexual contact with C.S. One can surmise that C.S. is highly infectious. Furthermore, if I have three Toronto women infected by C.S. when he has never lived in Toronto, there are likely numerous infected women in Ottawa, Montreal, London and Hamilton. These women must be informed of their risk to others and offered counselling and treatment if appropriate.

To emphasize the urgency of the situation, Cheryl added that both Patients X and Z already were showing heavy damage to their immune systems. One of them (this was Francine) was taking AZT, a recently-introduced drug that was believed to help prevent the pneumonia associated with the onset of AIDS.

Cheryl ended the letter with an icy, "Thank you for your attention in this matter."

The letter came as a shock to the Middlesex-London health unit, which was being assured by nurse Marylin McConnell that her meetings with Ssenyonga were going splendidly. She reported that he had no sex partners; the man was celibate.

"I am not interested in sex," he told McConnell piously. "I don't even want to get into a relationship. I'm trying to save enough money to go home to Uganda and see my mother."

In the despair that must have settled over the Middlesex-London health unit that February of 1990, the only weapon at its disposal was Section 22 of the Health Protection and Promotion Act of 1983 referring to communicable diseases. Public health legislation covers three levels of such diseases. One is reportable diseases, which include such contagious but fairly harmless diseases as chicken pox. Doctors, school nurses and others are required to notify public health of these cases so that epidemiologists can track patterns, but the name of the infected person usually is not taken.

A second tier of reportable diseases lists those that may have a more serious impact on community health, and the name of the carrier may be taken. This category, which includes AIDS and hepatitis B, permits the medical officer of health the authority to issue a restraining order.

Most restraining orders are effective because enforcement is within the power of authorities. A child with measles can be kept out of school; a typhoid carrier can be forbidden to work in food services. Enforcement in the case of AIDS, however, is problematic: the HIV-infected person is asked to make a behaviour change at an intimate level where surveillance is impossible.

The third category is the smallest, containing only twelve reportable diseases — among them leprosy, gonorrhoea, syphilis, bubonic plague, and tuberculosis. These are labelled "virulent," which in the Ontario health legislation is not so much a medical term, since AIDS is also a virus, as a legal one. It includes only diseases that public health has some confidence it can contain by enforcing treatment and a stay of up to four months in hospital or jail.

Although AIDS also is virulent and is running amok worldwide, the legislation deliberately excludes HIV from the category of virulent diseases for a practical reason. People with HIV cannot be cured, and most are already undergoing whatever treatment they can get. Locking them up for four months would change nothing, but would invite lawsuits citing violations of personal freedom and due process provisions in the Charter of Rights and Freedoms. Drafters of the public health legislation came to the logical conclusion that it would be unwise and unproductive to lock up an HIV-infected person.

Public health consequently is left with few tools. The first is to warn and counsel the person to protect others. If that doesn't seem to work, the person can be issued an order to be celibate, though this has dubious weight. A public health nurse is sent to advise the person not to have unsafe sex and to notify sexual partners. Infected people, indeed, already get this message from all sides. Almost everyone with an HIV infection keeps regular contact with doctors, and all HIV primary care physicians offer the same counsel. Infected people are encouraged to seek out community support groups, which also perform the invaluable service of informing infected people of their responsibilities. In fact, these non-profit grassroots HIV/AIDS organizations, which are found in every major centre in Canada, are primary dispensers of education about HIV and safe sex.

The matter of finding previous sex partners and suggesting that they should be tested is a delicate one. Many infected people are reluctant to do it, and doctors rarely have the time or resources for the task. Public health officials, trained and experienced in contact-tracking, are the most effective but are called into action only when it appears that someone is showing brutal disregard for sexual partners. The real gate-keepers in the chain are the front-line doctors who make a judgement call about their patients' credibility.

In the case of Charles Ssenyonga, his family physician, Dr. Nancy Reid, believed he was a responsible person; London's leading AIDS specialist, Dr. Iain Mackie, believed he was a responsible person; Dr. Henry Bendheim, who conducted the blood test, believed he was a responsible person, and nurse Marylin McConnell, who saw Ssenyonga seven or eight times in a year, believed he was a responsible person. The gate-keepers, everyone of them, were duped.

On February 12, 1990, Dr. Douglas Pudden, Middlesex-London medical officer of health, decided it was necessary to get tougher with Charles Ssenyonga. He issued an order under Section 22 of the Health Protection and Promotion Act forbidding Charles Ssenyonga to have sex. The order formally stated that there were "reasonable and probable grounds" to believe that Ssenyonga had "continued to engage in sexual activity since becoming infected." The order to Ssenyonga declared that he was "not to engage in sexual acts that involve any penile penetration into [his] mouth or anus, or into the mouth, anus or vagina of another person." Failure to comply, the order stated, would result in a fine of up to $5,000 a day.

The threat was empty: Ssenyonga was penniless and without property.

Dr. Richard Schabas, Ontario's chief medical officer of health and technically Pudden's boss, has praise for Pudden. "He showed a great deal of fortitude in issuing the order. Orders like that are highly controversial. There have been very few public health authorities in North America that have had the courage to issue a restraining order."

In some jurisdictions in Canada, notably Ottawa, Section 22-type restraining orders are issued quite frequently. Their advocate in that community, Dr. Ian Gemmill, associate medical officer of health for the Ottawa-Carleton health unit, had issued eighteen orders for HIV-infected people to come for counselling and to reveal the names of their sex partners. More rarely, the order also requires the recipient to refrain from penetrative sex. Gemmill insists to sceptics that in about half those cases sexual behaviour is altered by the counselling and the shock of being under official scrutiny.

Other medical officers of health are less certain. The *Canadian Medical Association Journal* ran an article by Cameron Johnston in which the Vancouver medical officer of health, Dr. John Blatherwick, was quoted as saying, "It's ludicrous for public health officers to think they could enforce a sex ban, and it's ludicrous for us to think we could prove that somebody was breaking the ban."

The problems of detection are insurmountable: how is anyone to know if someone under a restraining order is having sex? As Charles Ssenyonga amply demonstrated, a reckless or desperate person is not restrained by a piece of paper.

Richard Schabas is one of those with little confidence in the efficacy of restraining orders. Schabas is a big, affable man with guileless eyes behind wire-rimmed spectacles. An internist who has spent most of his career in public health, he exudes an air of competence and pragmatism. "No one has ever pretended that these restraining orders are a panacea for preventing the spread of HIV infection," he observes. "But it is one tool we can try."

Nurse Marylin McConnell was given the assignment of serving this uncertain document on Ssenyonga. She was stunned by Cheryl Wagner's report that Charles Ssenyonga recently had infected someone else. The possibility that Ssenyonga had been devious with her was mortifying. Like so many people who knew Ssenyonga, she trusted and liked him. She had fallen into the habit of dropping by The

African Store every few weeks, each visit lasting longer than the last. While such regular visits were part of her official responsibility, she also simply enjoyed talking to him. A friendship had developed, with the nurse in the role of mother-confidante.

In court, McConnell had difficulty remembering what they discussed, but she did recall that Ssenyonga often mentioned his outstandingly good health. He was seeing a doctor regularly, he said, and he was extremely fit. That seemed very important to him.

The other topic that obsessed him was what he described as harassment. Some women (this would be Marian Clark and, less frequently, Linda Booker) made abusive telephone calls, he complained. Ssenyonga did not provide Marylin McConnell with details but he said women were accusing him of having sexual intercourse without wearing a condom. He appeared baffled and hurt. He assured the nurse that he wasn't sleeping with anyone. If he did, he certainly would wear a condom.

McConnell found him wholly creditable. In a hearing in Toronto three years later, she observed bleakly, "I wanted to believe Charles, but every time I talked to him I always came away with a thread of doubt that he was honest with me. Not a nagging doubt, just a thread."

She explained, "Charles reminded me of a used car salesman. You always hope that what he tells you is the truth."

"You bought the used car?" asked the hearing commissioner in a sardonic tone.

McConnell nodded stiffly. "I bought the used car. I had no alternative. I couldn't follow him around twenty-four hours a day."

5

WHEN MARYLIN MCCONNELL was instructed in February, 1990, to serve the Section 22 restraint order on Charles Ssenyonga, she realized that she had lost touch with him in recent months. When she went around to the Mews, she was alarmed to find that The African Store had closed and there was no forwarding address. Repeated telephone calls were met with a recorded message that the number was not in service. She had a home address for Ssenyonga, but when she drove there she learned he had moved. No one knew where he had gone.

After several days she tried the store telephone number again. Suddenly it worked; it had been reconnected to a new location. To her vast relief, Charles Ssenyonga answered. She made an appointment to see him at the store on February 14. He wasn't there. Though she waited an hour, he didn't appear. When she telephoned the next day, there was no answer. On February 16, Ssenyonga finally kept an appointment with her, forty-five minutes late.

Marylin McConnell had never served a Section 22 on anyone before. Indeed, it was a first for the Middlesex-London health unit. She had no wish to embarrass her friend, so she waited for Chris Karuhanga to leave before presenting Ssenyonga with the restraining order. She asked him to read it carefully and watched him do it. His reaction was not what she expected. He assumed an air of relief.

"I want to thank you," he told her warmly. "This will help me. Now I have something to prove to people that I am not as bad as they say. Maybe this will put a stop to all the ugly rumours that have been going around about me, and the unpleasant phone calls, and people saying I have sex without condoms."

McConnell was bewildered. She never imagined anyone being pleased to be ordered to be celibate.

"Do you understand it?" she asked incredulously.

"Certainly," Ssenyonga replied. "Yes, this will help me. The false accusations against me will end."

She couldn't follow the logic. The only explanation that she could imagine for his odd response was that he would show the Section 22 order to his accusers as proof that he was celibate because he was bound by an order of the department of health. It was convoluted thinking, but Charles seemed such a decent, troubled man that she was glad that he found some comfort in Section 22.

Two weeks after McConnell delivered the restraining order, she received a telephone call from Ssenyonga. He said he needed to see her, could they have a cup of coffee? Sometime early in March, 1990, they sat in a restaurant for almost two hours. Ssenyonga was no longer happy about the restraining order. She reminded him of an option set out in Section 22, that he had the right to appeal the restraint to the Health Protection Appeal Board if he acted within fifteen days of the service of the order. He still had time, but just barely. Maybe he should consult a lawyer. If he failed with the appeal board, he might want to apply to a high court judge to cancel the restraint.

Ssenyonga could not decide. He had a lot on his mind, he said. The business was going poorly: the new location was no better than the old one. He had no money, even for rent. He had moved in with a friend and her child but the estranged husband was making threats. He longed to return to Uganda. On the subject of his sex life, he said he was not sleeping with anyone.

He changed the subject to return to a familiar complaint about tormenting phone calls and letters, which were still continuing. Maybe, he said, there was a leak of information in the Middlesex-London health unit. Was someone there stirring up trouble for him? One person in particular, he told McConnell, seemed to know everything about him. She must be following him. She phoned all the time and she always knew what he had been doing.

"There was always this dark figure in his life," McConnell testified. "Someone who knew everything."

Whoever that person was — and most people close to the situation say it was Marian Clark — the campaign was beginning to show results. Police interest was stirring, if only in the impressive pile of traffic violations for parking, speeding, and failing to observe stop signs that Ssenyonga was amassing. Rumours of a man in London who was infecting a lot of women with HIV reached even to the Toronto headquarters of the Ontario attorney-general, where lawyers speculated about the role the law could play in containing such a person. Not much, they decided.

The case of Charles Ssenyonga stuck in the mind of Richard Schabas, chief of Ontario's public health department. If something couldn't be done to stop Ssenyonga, then the system would never work. Ssenyonga was not the first irresponsible HIV-infected person to come to the attention of the authorities, but his was the best-documented case, thanks to Cheryl Wagner's cluster of patients. Most infected people are conscientious. They either remain celibate or else notify sexual partners and take precautions by insisting on at least one condom, usually two. Renegades are few, but they exist. The gay community has tales of men far gone in rage and despair who don't care what happens to lovers and brag about how many men they have infected. Like public health officials everywhere, Schabas had pondered what to do to contain such aberrant behaviour.

"Public health is flying blind so far as to know what to do in these circumstances," Schabas says bluntly. "There are people who say that this is a public health issue and should be handled that way, but that view is controversial. Some people don't think public health should try to deal with it at all. They think that it is a matter that should be handed over to the criminal courts."

London's leading AIDS specialist, Dr. Iain Mackie, has some sympathy for public health in the impasse that developed around Ssenyonga. "Public health officials should not be chastised or castigated for this," he says. "They are caught in the dilemma of a disease for which there are no good answers."

Schabas doubted that Ssenyonga would be stopped with a Section 22, judging by what he could gather about the man. What was needed, he decided, was authority to hold Ssenyonga long enough to talk sense into him. He came up with an idea. He wrote to Evelyn Gigantes, then Ontario Minister of Health, recommending that HIV infections be moved into the category of virulent diseases so that infected people could be confined in a hospital or jail for up to four months. Perhaps counselling over that length of time would alter behaviour like Ssenyonga's; in any case, for four months a callous HIV-carrier would not be infecting anyone.

When word of the recommendation hit the media, AIDS organizations across the province rose in fury. Schabas received death threats and a police guard had to be posted to protect him. In a Toronto protest demonstration, an effigy of Schabas was set afire to the cheers of a crowd. The opposition, however alarming, could have been predicted. With gay men doing most of the dying from AIDS, the concept of jailing people for being sick appeared, on the surface, to be blatantly homophobic. Civil libertarians were similarly incensed that the medical officer of health was asking for power to imprison people without a trial.

The uproar caused Evelyn Gigantes to back off. A statement was issued denying that there was ever serious consideration of the Schabas recommendation. Schabas, smarting from a thousand cuts, quietly returned to running his department.

As Schabas gloomily had suspected, Ssenyonga was undeterred by the restraining order not to have sex at all, protected or not. He continued to have sex with Francine Dalton, using the condoms she provided. Astonishingly, her love for him was unshaken. A clinging woman, she felt helpless to manage without him. "Here I was with someone who accepted me even though I was HIV-positive," she explained at Ssenyonga's trial three years later. "I didn't think I would have another chance. And I was getting emotional support from him."

Also, Ssenyonga was in the habit of borrowing money from her, money that she, on a disability allowance, could little afford. Sometimes it was only a few dollars for cigarettes, sometimes it was $100 for a car repair, once it was $400 for a shipment of African art caught in customs. By early 1990, he owed Francine $1,400, a total that didn't include such gifts from her as a $200 leather jacket. Francine reasoned she would never see her money if she kicked him out.

Meanwhile, it became a major issue between them that he refused to be tested. After months of argument, during which he maintained the fiction that he didn't need to be tested because his doctors said he was healthy, he yielded for the sake of peace. Early in March, 1990, at about the same time he had the long conversation with Nurse McConnell,

Ssenyonga gave in to Francine's plea that he go to the Hassle Free Clinic to submit to the farce of a second HIV test. She drove him there and stood by while he gave his name as Jonathan and his address as Woodstock.

As Francine waited in the corridor while he received counselling about the gravity of a decision to be tested, she discovered she could hear the interview through the closed door. The counsellor asked Ssenyonga if he believed himself to be in a high-risk group.

He replied in a deep, resonant voice that carried easily, "My girlfriend is HIV-positive."

Francine Dalton was shocked. They had discussed this very point during the drive to the clinic, when Ssenyonga promised that he would not implicate her.

When he emerged from the office, she asked, "Did you tell about me?"

Ssenyonga said, "No, I didn't."

She realized, for the first time, that Ssenyonga was a liar.

It was almost two months before Ssenyonga returned to Hassle Free for his test results. Francine thought his indifference was strange; she wondered why he wasn't anxious to know his status.

This time she waited in the car. When he came out he got into the passenger seat and stared straight ahead.

"What is it?" she asked.

"I'm positive," he replied, not looking at her.

She put her hand on his. "I'll always be there for you," she told him tenderly. "Don't worry."

He pulled his hand away sharply without speaking.

She went to London a month later, in June, 1990, and registered at a hotel. He watched her as she prepared to change her clothes. When she was partly undressed he put his arms around her, lifted her to a table, and entered her. She was appalled because he didn't put on a condom. When she protested, he grinned like an embarrassed child.

"It all happened so fast," he apologized, shrugging.

The relationship was in trouble. During that summer of 1990 Ssenyonga's sexual interest in Francine Dalton appeared to be waning. Many times he spent the night with her without wanting intercourse. She was convinced that he had another girlfriend. When she accused him of it, he was offended.

"How could I be having sexual relations with anyone else when I am HIV-positive?" he asked indignantly. "If I told anyone that I'm infected, she would run away."

Once when they were at her family cottage, sitting across a fire from one another, she commented sympathetically that he must feel terrible guilt for infecting her. He responded in a contemplative tone, "I'll have to think about that. I think you infected me."

That summer Leslie-Anne Jenkins returned from her first year at the Bible college in California and dropped in a few times at The African Store to see Ssenyonga. He would embrace her warmly and they had long, affectionate conversations, but he didn't seem interested in reopening the courtship.

She has some explanations for that. "What we were able to share was very special, and it was good to look back on it," Jenkins says in a soft, troubled voice. "But he knew I still had three more years of Bible college so there was no point in talking about marriage."

Ssenyonga did not confide in his friend that he was HIV-positive. Her impression of his situation was that he was a troubled man pursued by sex-crazed women he was obliged to accommodate to spare them embarrassment. "In Canadian society," she explains, "you are supposed to have sex when you are attracted to someone. Charles was so sensitive that he wouldn't want to hurt women's feelings by saying that this wasn't what he wanted."

She adds, "He kept saying it was important to him that, no matter what happened, the way I felt about him wouldn't change." Jenkins has a charitable theory that Ssenyonga truly believed, at least some of the time, that he wasn't HIV-positive. "The mind protects us from horrible things," she comments. "It blots them out."

Cheryl Wagner had a feeling she was missing something. One day, out of the blue, she remembered Jane Campbell, the patient who had come to her for psychotherapy but flounced out when Cheryl suggested that she should be tested for HIV because her boyfriend, Charles, was from Africa. Wagner suddenly put it together. Charles was Ssenyonga.

It took her some time to track Campbell to her new address in Montreal. After an exchange of pleasantries on the telephone, Wagner said gently, "I think you had better get tested for HIV."

Jane instantly replied, "Is this about Charles?"

"I can't say," Wagner told her. "Just, *please*, be tested. And your baby too."

Campbell and her eight-month-old baby were both HIV-positive. (Happily, the child later was found to be free of the virus: the mother had passed on her antibodies, which the test detected, but not the virus itself. About three-quarters of babies born to infected mothers do not have the virus — and the odds improve impressively if the pregnant woman is taking AZT.)

Wagner now had knowledge of Patient X, Patient Y, and Patient Z. She had come to the bottom of the alphabet with no place to go for Jane Campbell, so she reassigned her code names. Jennifer Anderson became Patient A, Linda Booker was Patient B, Jane Campbell Patient C, and Francine Dalton Patient D.

Cheryl Wagner was sickened by the time span indicated by Campbell's infection. Since Campbell's relationship with Ssenyonga dated from 1983, the man had been infecting women for almost seven years. How many more were out there?

The doctor was not long in hearing of another. One day Ssenyonga carelessly left his address book on a coffee table in Francine Dalton's apartment. She leafed through it and found about twenty-five names, most of them women, with accompanying phone numbers. She copied them all and put the book back. Her plan was to notify the women in the book that they should be tested for HIV if they had sex with Ssenyonga.

Her first calls were answered by women who said they were friends of Ssenyonga's but not sexual partners. Francine's nerve failed. She asked a friend to make the next call.

The friend called Joan Estrada in Hamilton. Estrada was then twenty-two years old, a dark-haired, strongly-built woman, a fitness buff with a wholesome girl-next-door look about her. Her university degree was in kinesiology, and she was newly employed in the Hamilton school system as a phys-ed instructor.

The call about Ssenyonga brought back unpleasant memories. Joan's affair with him occurred in the summer of 1989 in London, six months after Ssenyonga had been advised that he was HIV-positive and at a time when Marilyn McConnell was making regular visits and swallowing Ssenyonga's story that he was celibate.

When her tragedy began, Joan was a twenty-one-year-old student at the University of Western Ontario. She was shopping in the mews one morning in July, 1989, a few weeks after breaking up with a boyfriend, and was drawn to the display in The African Store. Ssenyonga was working that day and they "got talking," as she testified at his trial. He opened up the African world to her, conducting her on a tour of the artifacts in the shop and telling her fascinating stories of their origin. The man's sophistication and intelligence overwhelmed her.

Joan Estrada was the middle of three children raised in a small town in the Ottawa valley by her mother. An alcoholic father deserted when she was small and her mother married a much older man, a construction worker. The household was a chaotic one, and Joan was miserable as a child. Because money was short, she could stay in high school only by working in fast-food outlets nights and weekends. A star athlete, she decided on a career as a fitness instructor and enrolled at Western, assisted by a scholarship the first year and then student loans and after-hours jobs.

It was a life that was long on hard work and self-denial and short on glamour. Joan dreamed of travel to exotic places. Charles Ssenyonga was the next best thing. He invited her to meet him after work for a drink. She rode her bicycle to the store and they went to the piano lounge of the Radisson Hotel a few blocks away. She drank water while he had two beers. His eloquence and animation impressed her strongly. He told her of his eight years of university education. He was still hoping to go back to university and get a law degree, he told her. He put her bicycle in the back of his car and drove her home, but made no sexual overtures.

"It progressed slowly," she says.

They went to drive-in movies, to the beach, and then, several dates later, to his dismal apartment with the mattress on the floor. He told her how beautiful she was, how he couldn't resist her. He put his hands on her breasts, but she nervously pushed him off. She tried to distract him, speaking rapidly out of shyness, but he persisted.

"Don't worry," he said. "You don't have to be afraid of me."

He also said he didn't have any other girlfriends; in fact, he rarely dated. She was something special in his life. He would wear a condom, he said.

"I trusted him. All my life I have trusted people. I still do it to this day," Joan says. After all, Ssenyonga had attended a Roman Catholic seminary in Uganda and considered becoming a priest. Such a man would be honourable.

She had sex with him three times that night on the mattress on the floor. She saw no sign of any condom but it didn't matter: she was on the pill.

A week later Estrada had a painful vaginal infection. A doctor gave her medication, but the infection worsened. Another doctor diagnosed it as herpes, but nothing he gave her helped. By that time Joan had a rash all over her body and was in severe pain. From the healthy athlete she had been, she lost fifteen pounds and couldn't summon the energy to get out of bed.

Ssenyonga continued to have sex with her, despite the herpes. Though she was horrified, he didn't seem to be put off by her condition. They compromised by her giving him oral sex. She was grateful that he was supportive, even accompanying her on some of her many trips to the doctor. Once she suggested that her herpes must have come from him. He denied it: it was impossible, he was a very healthy man. After that she worried that she might infect him.

In truth, Ssenyonga arrived in Canada in 1983 with active symptoms of herpes, according to health records secured by police.

Joan's information about AIDS was hazy. One day she idly mentioned to Ssenyonga the theory, one of several about the source of AIDS, that HIV was an infection that began with green monkeys in Africa and spread to humans because some African people eat monkey meat. She had never seen Ssenyonga so angry. He said the stories were preposterous lies invented by white racists. He charged her with trying to demean and humiliate him.

For the most part, however, his manner with her was ardent and loving. He pressed her "at least ten times" to marry him and go with him to Africa, where he said his father was a kind of king. But she was changing her mind about him. She caught him in petty lies. When they first met, he told her he was thirty-one, which she thought was too old for her, and then, apparently forgetting what age he had claimed, admitted he was thirty-three. He asked her to celebrate his birthday with him, and she paid for the dinner, later learning that it wasn't his birthday at all. When she commented on the discrepancy, he said something about his birth records getting mixed up.

One day she was visiting Charles in the store when a handsome young man entered, saw her, and wheeled out. Ssenyonga's reaction was strange. He flew into a rage about "that faggot" who was always bothering him. She was amazed by his homophobia, so out of keeping with his liberal views on other matters. After that, he frequently made derogatory remarks to her about homosexuals.

Gradually, her interest in him waned. She was back at university and fully preoccupied with her studies. Although she continued to see Ssenyonga at The African Store whenever she was in the neighbourhood, she resisted his entreaties that they resume their affair.

One beautiful summer day in 1990, months after he had been served the restraint order, Ssenyonga turned up unexpectedly to invite her to go to the beach with him. She accepted and they slept together, for what turned out to be the last time.

To her surprise, Ssenyonga put on a condom, something new in her experience with him. "We need to do the adult thing," he explained. Seconds after the intercourse began, however, he withdrew and ripped the condom off, saying, "This thing is bugging me." He resumed without it.

That Christmas he left a gift at her door, a sweatshirt from The African Store, and a card with a note saying he was leaving soon for Uganda.

Two weeks later, on January 11, 1991, she received the shocking telephone call from a woman who said Charles Ssenyonga had AIDS. Joan's mind flashed to the scene the previous summer when Ssenyonga had pulled off the condom. The caller said that if Joan had slept with Charles Ssenyonga, she had better get tested at once.

Joan Estrada went to her doctor the next day. A roommate went along to be tested as well. They had shared lipsticks, she explained to Joan, so she had grounds to be worried too. Joan thought the woman was neurotic and self-centred, but she was suffering enough without picking a fight.

Three days later the roommate had her results which showed her blood non-reactive for HIV. Joan, however, heard nothing about her test. She waited impatiently, calling the doctor repeatedly without reaching him. A few days later, January 18, when finally he took her call, he said the first test done in London had shown her blood to be positive. The sample had been sent to Toronto for a second, confirmatory test.

"Why didn't you tell me?" she cried.

The roommate departed for the weekend, leaving Joan in a suicidal state of mind. Her only thought was to die at once to avoid the shame of people learning of her condition. She could not face the loneliness and slow, ugly death from AIDS that lay ahead of her. She hunted frantically through the medicine cabinet for pills that might end her life but could find nothing strong enough. She ran over the other possibilities. She flinched from using a knife; perhaps she could get her hands on a gun. She could not stop crying; her body ached from sobbing.

What saved her life, she says, was a call from Dr. Cheryl Wagner. Francine Dalton's friend had telephoned Joan to inquire about her well-being and was alarmed by the woman's hysterical state. She notified Wagner that Joan was alone and terrified; the doctor made a call at once.

"There is a doctor in London you could see," Wagner told her. "Her name is Janet Gilmour and you'll find her in the HIV clinic in St. Joseph's Health Centre."

Joan says, "Cheryl is probably the reason I'm here now, because I was very suicidal. She's been a life-saver for all of us."

Cheryl's support got Joan through the nightmare weekend of shakes and cold sweats. She saw Janet Gilmour and gave blood for another test.

On January 22, 1991, Cheryl Wagner was at home on maternity leave, her baby expected in about two weeks. She couldn't get Joan Estrada out of her mind. Francine Dalton had called to give her more information about her. Cheryl was stricken to hear that Joan was young, barely in her twenties, and was infected by Ssenyonga well after he knew he was HIV-positive.

Wagner made a desperate call to her colleague and friend Dr. Philip Berger to ask what she should do. Berger was the perfect person to consult. Few people in Canada know the politics of AIDS better, and his reputation for probity is outstanding. One Toronto medical officer of health has described Berger as "one of the most ethical doctors I know."

A thin, pale, prematurely hunched man with an intent, scholarly face behind round glasses, Berger is beloved by people living with HIV and AIDS for his kindness and his fearless advocacy on their behalf. Nominated to several government advisory committees, Berger has become familiar in the media because he is one of the most articulate and informed authorities on AIDS in Canada.

Wagner gave Berger the newest development in the Ssenyonga mess, telling him that now there were at least two women knowingly infected by him since the warning from public health. She was furious, but Berger pointed out that public health really didn't have the tools to deal with a Ssenyonga. Perhaps it was time to have the man arrested and jailed. Cheryl agreed; she said that when people act like criminals, they should be treated like criminals.

These were controversial waters, as the inflamed reaction to Schabas's recommendation to impose hospitalization on HIV-infected people had demonstrated. She and Berger decided on a compromise. Wagner would make one more attempt to blast public health out of its complacency. If that didn't stop Ssenyonga, the criminal law might have to be invoked.

Cheryl went to bed after the phone call but couldn't sleep. She rose well after midnight and sat in front of her computer. What emerged an hour or so later was a letter to Dr. Richard Schabas, which she sent to him by courier as soon as morning broke:

Dear Dr. Schabas:

I am writing to convey my deep concern about a failure in the public health system to protect women from HIV infection and the need to act quickly to remedy this situation.

In the fall of 1988 I counselled two HIV-positive women who named the same male, X, as the source of their infection. This information was passed on to the appropriate public health authorities in January 1989 and I presume action was taken by them to counsel and test this individual.

In the fall of 1989, a third woman came to me with a primary HIV infection, indicating recent exposure to the AIDS virus. Her only recent sexual partner, September 1989, was the same male, X. This would have been at least eight months after I initially informed public health. After the third case I again informed public health authorities and asked that stronger measures be taken to stop this man.

In November 1990 a fourth patient of mine tested positive along with her eight-month-old child. Her husband, the father of the child, remains negative.

Once more she named X as the only high-risk contact. The time frame of her exposure is unclear. She has moved from Toronto and I have been unable to have a follow-up visit with her to clarify this.

Two weeks ago a fifth woman contacted me concerned about HIV infection. She had unprotected sexual contact with X in the summer of 1989 and the summer of 1990. Her HIV test returned positive today.

This man did not inform any of these five women of his HIV status, nor use condoms. All of these women have indicated that they know other women that X has had sexual contact with and continues to have sexual contact with. There are surely a number of other women infected by this man and continuing to be infected.

The first two women asked me to intercede with public health in the fall of 1988 when their own efforts to discuss the matter with X convinced them that he was unwilling to change his behaviour. They were not vindictive but acted out of a concern that other women avoid their fate. Unfortunately we have failed in this.

It is difficult as a physician and as a woman to watch these women struggle with their HIV infections and the vast implications it has for their lives. It is even more difficult to know that at least two of these women and potentially others may have been spared this fate.

Clearly current public health practices have failed these women and likely other women. This man has displayed anti-social behaviour, with no willingness to change. He remains a menace to women and needs to be stopped. I believe this is a case where stronger action is warranted.

One presumes a Section 22 order was issued after the third woman became infected. If so he would have been in breach of this order when he had unprotected sex with patient number five in the summer of 1990. If it is not possible to take stronger action under the Health Protection and Promotion Act then criminal charges should be brought to bear. Indeed it is likely the only thing that will stop this man's behaviour and protect more women from being infected.

There is particular urgency to act swiftly because indicators are that X is planning to leave the town he's in. He has closed his business and has given notice on his apartment for January 31.

I hope that my concerns will be acted on swiftly before I have to counsel yet another HIV-positive female contact of X...I would appreciate being informed of what action you plan to take. I await your reply.

Sincerely,
Cheryl Wagner, M.D., CCFP
Copies to the Toronto MOH and the Ontario Minister of Health

With that, everyone got off the sofa. Two hours after Schabas received her letter, Wagner had a reply by courier. Schabas wanted to talk. He was arranging a meeting and he wanted Cheryl to attend. Cheryl said, most regretfully, she couldn't; her doctor, pointing out she was due to deliver a baby in a matter of days, had grounded her.

Over the telephone she told him bluntly that she didn't think the Middlesex-London health unit had pushed hard enough to counsel Ssenyonga and stop his behaviour. Maybe it wasn't the fault of public health, she conceded, but there was no excuse for what had happened.

Her low opinion of the health unit, indeed, was recipro-
cated. By the grapevine, Cheryl had heard that the Middlesex-
London health unit thought her an interfering busybody
from Toronto. Though Schabas describes Wagner as "absolutely pivotal in bringing the matter to public health attention," even he had reached the point of wincing every time
he saw her signature on a letter.

He promised Cheryl that he would take every possible
action, and she went back to awaiting labour pains.

Schabas's strategy meeting two weeks later was impressive, a tribute to the high-level frustration Charles Ssenyonga
was creating. Dr. Douglas Pudden and Dr. Nancy Tuttle
came from the Middlesex-London public health office, and
Dr. Perry Kendall and Dr. David McKeown from the
Toronto one. Dr. Evelyn Wallace, an epidemiologist from
Schabas's office, was there with Gilbert Sharp, a lawyer with
a reputation for knowing health legislation inside out, and
others with assorted, relevant skills.

Wagner, in hospital with her newborn daughter Claire,
was the only significant figure missing.

The option the meeting decided upon — indeed, the only
option available to public health — was to apply to the
courts to invoke Section 101 of the public health act. This
essentially is Section 22 but brings in the power of a court
to enforce it. The relevant paragraph of Section 101 states:
"Where any provision of this Act [i.e., Section 22 of the
public health act] or the regulations is contravened...the
Minister [of Health] may apply to a judge of the Supreme
Court for an order prohibiting the continuation or repeti-
tion of the contravention or the carrying on of any activities
specified in the order...and it may be enforced in the same
manner as any other order or judgment of the Supreme
Court."

Lawyers discovered Section 101 under layers of archival
dust; no one could find any evidence that it had ever been

used. Until Charles Ssenyonga, public health authorities never had compelling evidence that someone was defying a Section 22 restraining order. Section 101 allows health officials to force a suspected violator to appear before a judge to face charges of failing to obey a court order. Disobeying a Section 22 order wasn't a criminal offence, but failure to heed a court order was. Section 101 was a roundabout way to jail Ssenyonga for failing to protect sexual partners.

A major advantage of an application for a Section 101 court order would be that Ssenyonga's name would become public. Rules of medical confidentiality had prevented public health from releasing his name as a warning to his previous sex partners to be tested. With Section 101, the media would accomplish that useful service.

Section 101, however, is meant to come into play in a timely fashion, within six months of issuance of Section 22. It was more than a year since Marylin McConnell had served Ssenyonga with the restraining order, which posed a procedural problem. Another problem was that the only way to prove that Ssenyonga had violated Section 22 was to have the women he infected testify before a judge.

Cheryl Wagner was consulted to ascertain if the women would cooperate. She replied that Francine Dalton had a real sense of mission about stopping Ssenyonga but would not come forward publicly; her parents didn't know she was infected. Cheryl inquired if criminal charges were being considered. Schabas told her he had asked the attorney-general's department to look into it.

Brian Trafford, head of criminal prosecutions in the department, was indeed studying the matter. He didn't see how a criminal charge could be laid because, officially at least, the department was not supposed to know Ssenyonga's identity. Until the Section 101 application brought Ssenyonga's name out in the open, Trafford had to abide by the rules of medical confidentiality. To facilitate the 101 application, he lent to public health one of his best lawyers, Tom Wickett, deputy director of the civil law branch of the Ontario Crown, a silver-haired man with a sharp, pointed face and the courteous manners of a diplomat.

Trafford, later appointed judge in the General Division of the Ontario Court, presented the Ssenyonga case to his staff to consider on the theoretical level: assuming that Ssenyonga was identified in a Section 101 application, what criminal charges could be laid against him? Nothing in the Criminal Code forbids anyone from knowingly transmitting HIV, but was there something that could be bent to fit the Ssenyonga situation?

Criminal lawyers love this kind of exercise. It demands recall of precedents and obscure rulings, ability to anticipate what an opposing lawyer will do and what the judge will think, and a degree of spry creativity. After a few sessions of these gymnastics, Trafford reported to Cheryl that the charge least likely to succeed, in the opinion of his staff, was sexual assault. The women, after all, had consented to have sex with Ssenyonga. A charge of criminal negligence causing bodily harm had a fifty-fifty chance of being accepted as appropriate by the courts. A charge of committing a common nuisance, while it didn't sound like much, was the easiest one for the prosecution because it wouldn't be necessary to produce evidence to show that the infections came from Ssenyonga: the Crown would need to prove only that Ssenyonga had unprotected sex while aware that he was infected. In the other charges, the prosecution would have to find some way to prove without doubt that Ssenyonga, and only Ssenyonga, caused the women's infections.

It seemed to Cheryl that the attorney-general's lawyers were hoping the Ssenyonga problem would go away. With no assurance that witnesses would cooperate, there was no case. She began to hear evasions: no point in going ahead with criminal charges, she was told, until Tom Wickett had a crack at getting a Section 101 application. And Wickett was not too confident himself, since the application was late and the women were unlikely to testify. To encourage them to come forward, Wickett speculated that maybe the women could testify anonymously by way of affidavits.

Even so, Cheryl wouldn't tell Wickett their names. Public health knew first of Patients X, Y, and Z, and then that the women were re-identified as Patients A, B, C, D, and so on, but to protect confidentiality, Cheryl could not reveal who they were. Success with Section 101 hinged on the availability of witnesses.

"If the women aren't willing to come forward," Trafford told Cheryl, "there really isn't anything we can do."

Cheryl Wagner conveyed this to Francine Dalton.

"Ssenyonga has to be stopped," Francine said bravely. "I'll do it. I'll testify. But I have to be sure my name won't get out."

Cheryl Wagner was uneasy with the direction events were taking. Tom Wickett was assuring her that the identities of the women could be kept secret, but she needed to be sure her patients knew their legal position. She made some inquiries and then directed Jennifer Anderson, Linda Booker, and Francine Dalton to the Parkdale Community Legal Services, an outreach law clinic of the Osgoode Hall Law School where a celebrated criminal lawyer, Diane Martin, was the director. Martin, who teaches at the law school, has a long history of social activism.

Cheryl then called Dr. Janet Gilmour in London and suggested that she give the same advice to Ssenyonga victims there. Cheryl also sought guidance from workers at the Barbra Schlifer Clinic in Toronto, which specializes in counselling victims of sexual assault. She wanted to know from them how much protection her patients might expect in the courts. She was told, and Diane Martin confirmed this, that they could be sure a judge would protect their identities only if Ssenyonga was charged with sexual assault; otherwise, no one could be certain what a judge would do.

Following a meeting with a lawyer in London, Joan Estrada nervously said she would sign an affidavit if she could use an alias, "Jane Doe." Francine Dalton was wavering. She was alarmed to learn from Diane Martin that if the police knew her name and address, they could issue a subpoena and haul her into court against her will. She changed her mind about participating. She decided that one Jane Doe would have to be enough.

6

BRUCE LONG, the regional Crown attorney for southwestern Ontario, was in his early fifties, a tough, craggy-faced, restless, hard-working man with neatly combed brown hair and stony brown eyes. He has a reputation for being abrupt, gained from a nature that is decisive, organized, and impatient. He began working for the Crown while still a law student, astounding his professors who would see him one day in their classrooms and the next day opposing them in court. Sometimes he worked so late in law libraries that the staff arriving in the morning would find him asleep, his head pillowed on a book.

When he was called to the bar in 1975 he immediately went to work in the office of the Ontario attorney-general. "Let's just say that I have problems with the other side," Long explains tersely. He considers a moment and decides the statement needs amplification. "I have difficulties with the situation where you would defend someone knowing they are guilty," he continues, "and because of your skills as an advocate, they might be acquitted. It's an ethical problem." He says he is not critical of lawyers who defend guilty clients if they do so honourably and ethically, but "I can't do defence work myself."

His moral indignation at criminal behaviour is a reflection of his strict Baptist upbringing. Born in Windsor in 1942, he majored in religion but decided to be a teacher and spent nine years in classrooms before entering law school.

In March, 1991, Long was attending a legal gathering in Niagara Falls when he heard gossip about a man in London who had infected several women with the AIDS virus. He was told that the attorney-general's office in Toronto was looking into the matter but nothing was happening.

Bruce called the attorney-general's office in Toronto and was referred to Brian Trafford, head of criminal prosecutions. He asked what was going on, pointing out that London was in his jurisdiction. To his dismay he learned that the trials, if they happened at all, would be scattered all over Ontario in whatever city the women happened to live. He protested that this was lunacy. Worse, he gained the distinct impression that some people in the department were lukewarm about proceeding at all: the case was seen to be an abyss into which a million dollars in costs could disappear without a trace.

That week he wrote in his journal an indignant comment, "I'm not being informed!"

Trafford invited Long to come to a meeting in Toronto.

When Bruce Long learned more about Charles Ssenyonga, he was offended that such a man could escape justice. He decided to take command. He told Trafford that the prosecution should be consolidated in one location, London being the most appropriate, and he personally would get the ball rolling. At Long's urging, Trafford called the Ontario Provincial Police criminal investigative branch and asked that an officer be assigned.

The choice of the Ontario Provincial Police rather than the London city police was inescapable. Ssenyonga lived in London, where Bruce Long had his headquarters, but the women infected by him appeared to be all over the province.

An investigation entrusted to city police departments in London, Toronto, Hamilton, Ottawa and who knew where else would be encumbered by sibling rivalry.

Someone walking by the office door of the OPP criminal investigative branch superintendent that day heard the superintendent say, "Let's give it to Hall."

The OPP's legendary Terry Levi Hall was a forty-five-year-old inspector at the time. He received the assignment on his car phone late in the afternoon of March 25, 1991. His instructions were blunt: Trafford in the AG's department wants an investigation. It seemed a medical doctor in Toronto knew of seven women infected with AIDS by the same man. A civil action (this would be the Section 101 application) had just been launched but might not go anywhere, so it had been decided that criminal charges should be instigated as well. Hall was instructed to be in Toronto the next morning for a meeting with Brian Trafford.

Hall's awesome reputation was gained, in part, from the years he spent working undercover in biker gangs. People who knew his rugged history were surprised that he was assigned to the Ssenyonga case, where finesse and sensitivity were necessary to secure the trust of the women.

He shrugs. "Bikers mistreat women, so I was used to working with the women they had victimized. Ssenyonga is a biker, a different type of biker. He just doesn't have a bike."

At eleven in the morning Terry Hall presented himself in Trafford's office. He learned that there was not much to go on. Trafford didn't know the names of the women Ssenyonga had infected, and what Ssenyonga was doing was not a crime in the Criminal Code. Hall, a veteran of bureaucratic idiocy, saw nothing unusual in the situation.

"You begin at the beginning," he explains of his investigative technique. That meant starting with Dr. Cheryl Wagner, the only person who knew the two women infected by Ssenyonga after the Section 22 order was issued. The women infected by him earlier were significant to build the case, but Ssenyonga's incriminating behaviour was failing to protect sex partners *after* he officially knew he had HIV.

Cheryl had been talking to Francine Dalton, who was reconsidering her decision to stay out of it. Cheryl was uncomfortable that Joan Estrada, the youngest and most devastated of all Ssenyonga's infected partners, was the only one coming forward. Francine told Cheryl that she would give the police a statement as long as it was on an anonymous basis.

Cheryl Wagner advised Terry Hall that Patient D would talk to him but only at the doctor's home and only if he didn't ask her last name or address. The inspector was invited to Cheryl's house at seven o'clock on the night of March 28, where Wagner would go over the conditions. If all went well, Patient D would arrive at eight.

Hall received directions to Wagner's house on a street of neat, narrow houses near Toronto's High Park. When the doctor saw the policeman, she was taken aback. This huge man, she thought privately, would scare her patients to death.

Hall is the son of tobacco farmers, descendants of Virginians, all of them big men and some of them sheriffs and police officers. He was raised on a tobacco farm near Tillsonburg in southwestern Ontario, and when he started high school in Aylmer at the age of thirteen, he weighed 220 pounds and was six foot three — and still growing. In 1963, when he was seventeen, he joined the Toronto police force as a cadet at a salary of $2,900 a year. He was so green that once he got lost going to work and, in full uniform, had to ask directions. Hall trained on motorcycles and was put to work on traffic patrol, issuing parking tickets and chasing speeders. In 1967, yearning to be out of Toronto, he transferred to the Ontario Provincial Police, squeaking in with the connivance of the recruiting officer even though he was bigger than OPP regulations of the day allowed.

He worked motorcycle patrol in Oak Ridge, north of Toronto. Hall is a natural on a motorcycle; he made the police crack Golden Helmets precision team, which is not unlike flying with the Blue Angels. For him motorcycles represent freedom, and the raw roar of a Harley-Davidson is music. "You can get rid of your frustrations," he explains.

His duties in Oak Ridge included traffic enforcement of motorcycle speeders, which is where he first became familiar with such feared bike gangs as Hell's Angels and Satan's Choice. When the OPP vice squad invited him to go undercover, he accepted. He grew his crinkly hair until it covered his shoulders. With a rich beard that concealed most of his face, a leather vest on his bare torso, and a beer belly, he blended right in.

Beginning in 1973 Hall worked undercover for two years, off and on, with Satan's Choice and other gangs; bikers not only accepted him but made him a leader. Hall is dismissive of the mortal dangers he faced if discovered. "Killing a policeman could give them a problem," he observes offhandedly.

After that Terry joined in joint ventures with drug squads all over North America. Mostly he was out in the open in a suit, but occasionally he donned his black leather disguise for some short-term undercover work.

After eleven years in the OPP bikers' squad, and promoted to sergeant, Terry Hall headed the OPP's investigation branch out of Barrie. In the fall of 1986 he was made detective-inspector and transferred to London.

Terry is a giant, but his normal demeanour is not intimidating. The passing parade of a police officer's life amuses him and he is gifted with common sense and a wry, self-deprecating humour. The women infected by Ssenyonga came to love him as a protective brother. When he gave them his personal promise that they would not be compelled to testify, none hesitated to believe him.

When Terry met Cheryl Wagner on March 28, 1991, he brought with him a burly, white-haired OPP veteran, Detective Sergeant Albert Ciampini. Terry picked Ciampini as a sidekick because Al had worked with Ministry of Health people during a long investigation of the Church of Scientology. Terry figured he would need someone who knew how to get along with the ministry. With two actions, one criminal and one civil, proceeding against Ssenyonga at the same time, Terry was resigned to the inevitability of jurisdictional screwups.

Cheryl gave the policemen a copy of her first letter to public health describing Patients X, Y, and Z. Y, she said earnestly, was now A, and X was now B . . . The attorney-general's office also used codes, lettering them differently from either of Wagner's systems. The introduction of the use of the alias, Jane Doe, only added to the confusion. It was some time before the police sorted out that A and Y were both Jennifer Anderson, and she was not a Jane Doe.

At an appropriate moment early in the discussion with Cheryl, Terry put on a nonchalant air and said, "I was wondering about AIDS. When we go to arrest Ssenyonga, do I have to gag him or something?"

She grinned, guessing that he had the fear common to people inexperienced about AIDS and rife among small-town police even years later, that HIV can be spread by casual contact. "You can't get AIDS from arresting him," she assured him. "Not even if he bites you." (While HIV can be detected in saliva or even the tears of an infected person, the concentration is so low that, as one doctor put it, "you would need a bucket of spit" to approach even the possibility of transmitting the disease that way.)

Francine Dalton arrived at eight. She was introduced by her first name only and nervously took a chair. Hall held his eyes levelly on her and made a promise. "If ever you want to back out of this, if ever you change your mind about testifying, I will honour your decision. I am going to ask you a lot of questions, but what you say will remain confidential, if that's what you want, and no use will be made of it. We won't include you in the application without your permission."

She looked at him warily for a long moment. Terry's steady gaze reassured her; she nodded. Ciampini got out his notebook and the questioning began.

Wagner left the room to tend to her baby as Terry slowly reviewed with Francine her long relationship with Ssenyonga, paying particular attention to dates. Hall explains, "It's not that simple when you open an investigation. You don't know what you are looking for, so you ask about everything, every little thing." Hall was seeking an element of coercion or force that would support a charge of sexual assault, but it was not there. Dalton admitted she had been in love with Ssenyonga for more than a year.

Dredging up memories made her weep. After five hours, the statement was only half complete. They called it quits at one in the morning and arranged to meet again a few days later, Easter Monday, April 1, at OPP headquarters on Toronto's lakefront, which would be deserted for the holiday.

Francine Dalton was prompt. Her initial tremulousness had changed to a cheerful relish for the task of convicting Ssenyonga, so she brought with her notebooks that proved invaluable to the investigation. Dalton, a methodical, compulsively organized person, had begun writing a chronological account of her long affair with Ssenyonga with a view to turning it into a book. Already one of the sickest of the women infected by Ssenyonga, with her immune system almost at the vanishing point, she could think of no other way to make sense of the catastrophe that had befallen her. On days when she was not racked by weakness, she spent hours at a computer working on her manuscript or making telephone calls all over the province to track down other women Ssenyonga might have infected. Hall, the expert, credits her with having "an investigative mind."

She turned over the fruits of a year's work: names and numbers from the book she had taken from Ssenyonga, including the phone number for Joan Estrada. She had records of the vendetta being waged by Marian Clark, the names of Ssenyonga's partners and backers in The African Store, and Ssenyonga's present address in London at the home of a Ugandan woman, Margaret Nansamba. The material was a police officer's dream.

Francine offered to make copies of all her material. Terry gave her access to the OPP photocopying machine and left her to it.

Terry Hall's notes of March 25, 1991, the day he was assigned to the Ssenyonga case, indicated that the number of women infected by Ssenyonga had grown to seven. Just after Cheryl Wagner's stormy letter to Dr. Richard Schabas in January and while lawyers were engaged in debate about whether to act and how to act, she learned from Dr. Janet Gilmour in London that a sixth woman, Patient F, a rape victim, had turned up in London and that Ssenyonga probably had infected another, Patient G, whose status was still indeterminate.

The latter was Nancy Gauthier, a thirty-four-year-old single mother living on welfare in London with her lively five-year-old daughter. Ssenyonga had infected her only weeks before; Gauthier's HIV status indeed was so new that her tests still were inconclusive.

Nancy's possible infection surfaced quickly because of a slip Ssenyonga made: he used her telephone to call Francine Dalton in Toronto. Early in March of that year, Gauthier opened her telephone bill and found on it a Toronto long-distance charge to an unfamiliar number. Gauthier called the number and got an answering machine. She said to the machine, "Excuse me, but you're on my telephone bill. Do you mind telling me who you are?"

Francine Dalton played the message later that day and put it together at once.

She returned the call and asked quietly, "Do you know a man named Charles Ssenyonga?"

Nancy said, "Well, yes. Did he call you on my phone?"

"Have you been sleeping with him?"

"What is this about?"

"If you have been sleeping with him," Francine said evenly, "get tested for AIDS. He is infected and he infected me."

Nancy said weakly, "I have a little girl. This just can't be happening. I just slept with him a few times. Mostly we used condoms because I practise safe sex. But there were maybe three times without one."

"When was that?" asked Francine.

"Last month," said Nancy.

"Last month! My god."

Nancy Gauthier is a spunky, small, and dark-haired. She makes an immediate impression on all she meets with her disconcerting candour and shrewd insights. The turmoil of her upbringing, which was sometimes vicious, resulted in an adult who is generous-hearted but wary and sceptical; she trusts very few people.

Nancy was married once, as a teenager, and the relationship was brief. She took up residence in London, where she later met the father of her child, and held a variety of office jobs. For a few months in 1984 when she was unemployed she took a whirl at being a prostitute, working the lobbies of London hotels, reeling in middle-aged business travellers. She is open about the prostitution, often bringing it up on the first meeting with someone she expects to know for a while. She likes to get her cards on the table, face up; it makes her feel safer.

Nancy speaks with rushes and pauses, fearful that her weakness in grammar will embarrass her. Her conversation, however, is riveting: she has unexpected ways of expressing herself and her perspective is unfettered by convention.

Still, Ssenyonga completely fooled this street-smart woman. Two years after he tested positive for HIV, and while under the Section 22 order to be celibate, Charles Ssenyonga had unprotected sex with Nancy Gauthier.

"I run on instinct. That's how I rule my life, and I'm usually pretty good," Nancy says ruefully. "With Ssenyonga it was a combination of that smile and the way he has of focusing on a woman. And he was very polite. He always waited to see what I wanted to do. He put a value on me."

Ssenyonga caught Nancy at a vulnerable time. She had moved with her daughter to a shabby apartment house occupied mostly by people who spoke little English. Her dark-skinned daughter was shunned by the neighbours (the child's father was black), and Gauthier herself, broke and living on welfare, was friendless. She spent Christmas and New Year's of 1990 alone. A week later, on January 7, 1991, she encountered Ssenyonga in the laundry room of the apartment house. He was putting dirty clothes into a machine, carelessly tossing in white fabrics with dark ones.

She said to him with a friendly smile, "I don't think you should be doing that."

He was amused and grateful as she showed him how to separate the wash by colours. The attraction was mutual. She was drawn to him at once because he was black and because of his warmth and humour. She still talks of how handsome he was. "He had a wonderful smile and long curling eyelashes," she says, dreamy as an adolescent. "He told me he was moving back to Africa. If he had asked me, I would have gone with him. I would have done anything for Ssenyonga."

Over the next few days she saw him around the apartment house and her fascination grew. Ssenyonga lived with a woman friend in the building but hated the squalor. He spent his nights instead at the Chester Street home of Margaret Nansamba and her child. He said the woman was "just a friend" who was being kind to him and who needed protection against the husband from whom she recently had separated.

To Gauthier's delight, Ssenyonga showed affection for her lonely daughter, who responded gratefully. Gauthier's life revolved around Sarah, but most of the men she knew ignored the little girl.

One day Gauthier invited Ssenyonga into her apartment and they talked; his erudition impressed her. She fell in love. "That doesn't happen to me very often," she confesses.

When he dropped by a few days later, she seated him in the living room, went into the bedroom, and emerged with a condom daintily held between fingers and thumb. Gauthier says that Ssenyonga was the most extraordinary lover of her experience. "He was very skilled, very controlled," she says. "He could go for hours and hours without coming. He would watch my collection of soft-core porn videos and he wouldn't get an erection unless he wanted to. He was really amazing."

He spent the night. In the morning he wakened her by entering her from behind without a condom. "I was like a new, clean woman, he just couldn't get enough," she comments. "He was so crazy for oral sex that he would follow me around the kitchen while I was cooking, trying to get under my dress. He was a powerhouse; he was too much."

Nancy thought it odd that he behaved so furtively. As soon as Charles came into her apartment, he would close the blinds. "He was like a scared animal trying to hide," she says. "I asked him if he owed money."

She could understand that. He was closing down The African Store at the time, trying to sell off the stock that remained. It necessitated trips to Toronto that lasted a day or two. He explained that he was waiting for some woman there to make a large purchase of the goods.

The woman was Francine Dalton, who had hit upon a ruse to get back the $1,400 Ssenyonga owed her. Dalton sought the help of a friend who was an expert on African curios, and in early February they invited Ssenyonga to bring a selection of his stock to her apartment. There the friend helped Francine choose some carvings, candlesticks, and cloth to the value of $1,400. Francine wrote a cheque for that amount and she and Ssenyonga parted, both feeling triumphant. As soon as he was out the door Francine called her bank to cancel the cheque.

Later, when Ssenyonga telephoned to ask for a receipt for the goods he had left with her, saying he needed it for the store's records, she told him coldly that she wouldn't give it to him. He owed her money and now they were quits. He called again and left a tirade on her answering machine, threatening to get back his property. She didn't return the call. That was the last contact Francine had with Charles Ssenyonga until she saw him in court a year later.

On February 10 Ssenyonga dropped by with a gift for Nancy, a shirt from the store. He said he was leaving for Africa very soon and wanted to say goodbye. She felt her heart breaking. They had sex and he didn't wear a condom, but since he usually didn't climax she was not concerned. She could count the times he had ejaculated in her without a condom: three.

Then, in early March, Gauthier's February telephone bill arrived with a long-distance call to Francine Dalton's number. After the shock of hearing that Ssenyonga was infected, Gauthier went to her family doctor for an HIV test. She was told to wait three weeks for the result. She dutifully obeyed, though she was in an agony of suspense. She called exactly three weeks later. She was informed that the test results had not arrived; call again in a week.

Nancy couldn't bear it. She called the next day and a different receptionist told her she should be more responsible for her health. She should have called sooner.

Nancy slammed down the receiver and strode to the doctor's office in a fury. In a room filled with patients waiting to see the doctor she yelled at the receptionist, "What the fuck do you mean, I should be more responsible for my health?"

She grins, recalling the moment. "They never liked me after that."

She telephoned Francine Dalton for help. Francine in turn appealed to Cheryl Wagner. Nancy was in danger of going out of control, she said. The Toronto doctor called Gauthier at once and suggested that she go to the HIV/AIDS clinic at St. Joseph's Health Centre and ask for Dr. Janet Gilmour. When she did, Gilmour said she would do her best to hurry the testing process. Noting Gauthier's distraught state, Gilmour put her in touch with a social worker at the clinic, Marlene Rees-Newton.

Cheryl Wagner also advised Nancy to notify the Middlesex-London public health unit. The next morning Nancy placed calls to Dr. Nancy Tuttle. "It took me quite some time to reach her," Gauthier says bitterly. "They kept telling me she was in meetings."

Nancy informed Tuttle that she might be infected with HIV by Charles Ssenyonga. As Nancy recalls the conversation, Tuttle told her she should have been protecting herself. Nancy replied that she did use condoms. Her quick temper flaring, she charged the health unit with not doing its job. "There's some kind of cover-up going on," she yelled.

Nancy Gauthier waited in unbearable pain for the results of the next test. To spare her daughter the sight and sound of her distress, she would lock herself in the bathroom and scream silently. She was so distracted that she put chocolate milk in her coffee; she put the sugar bowl in the refrigerator. She developed a terror of darkness, which she equated with her death: she could not sleep unless all the lights were on.

It was not until March 20, 1991, that Gilmour obtained the results from the provincial lab. The report was ambiguous. Gauthier's blood reacted positive on the ELISA test, but when the sample was forwarded to Toronto for the more exhaustive confirmatory Western Blot test, the result was indeterminate. The report came to Gilmour stamped, "HIV status inconclusive. Suggest repeat testing."

Nancy was trapped between hope and despair. Janet Gilmour tried to console her with the information that indeterminate tests sometimes are followed by good news. One of her patients had an indeterminate Western Blot test for a year but eventually she was in the clear; something in her blood had tricked the system. Nancy perked up immediately. "I decided I was going to be one of the people to beat a positive ELISA," she says. "I just had to believe it."

Gilmour drew several samples of Gauthier's blood on March 21, and sent them to the London lab. By this time the Ssenyonga case was foremost in the minds of health department authorities and the samples received special treatment. Instead of doing the ELISA themselves, people at the London lab sent the samples directly to Dr. Rick Galli, the biologist who heads the provincial lab in Toronto where all Western Blot tests are done. The result again was maddeningly inconclusive: a reactive ELISA and an indeterminate Western Blot.

Gilmour received the new report towards the middle of April, 1991. She called Nancy, who didn't know whether to weep or cheer. Gilmour herself was racked by the strain. She was thirty-four years old and relatively new to the field of AIDS. A pretty woman with short fluffy hair and large blue eyes, she trained as an internist in Toronto, where she "got hooked," as she puts it, working with HIV infection. The disease fascinated her, and she liked the patients, who primarily were young gay men. When her husband, Dan Gregson, a doctor trained in microbiology, internal medicine and infectious diseases, obtained a placement in London, she followed him there and joined Iain Mackie in the HIV/AIDS clinic at St. Joe's.

When Cheryl Wagner referred Joan Estrada and Nancy Gauthier to her, Gilmour was appalled to realize that Ssenyonga remained unchecked. The HIV/AIDS clinic at St. Joseph's Health Centre cares for some four hundred HIV-infected people at any one time, but she had almost never known such a situation. Gilmour says, "Most HIV patients are very moral people. The majority would no more pass on the virus than they would go out and murder someone."

Still, she knows another man who infected several women with HIV. "He died of AIDS very young, at about twenty-four," she says. "He didn't infect as many women as Ssenyonga but there were a few. He was out for a good time and didn't care what happened to anyone else. That's my view of Ssenyonga too. He was an arrogant, self-centred man who didn't give a hoot about anyone else."

Like her colleague Cheryl Wagner, Gilmour found the Middlesex-London health unit unhelpful when she reported to them the Ssenyonga-infected women she was treating. "My impression was that there was nothing they could do," she says. "Basically, I ran into a stone wall."

It wasn't the first time. Once when she was working in the HIV/AIDS clinic in Toronto she encountered a man who boasted that he was going to infect as many people as he could before he died. Gilmour, horrified, notified the public health department and the police. The response from both was the same: we can't stop him unless we are in the bedroom when he has unprotected sex.

Cheryl Wagner notified lawyers in the attorney-general's department that another woman was very probably infected by Ssenyonga, and they passed the information to Bruce Long and Terry Hall. Cheryl was in no mood to tolerate more delay. Terry made a note of the name, which Cheryl gave him with Nancy's consent, and plodded on with the investigation. Francine Dalton's testimony alone might have been sufficient to convict Ssenyonga, but the thought of stopping with her never entered Hall's head. "You want all the corroboration you can get."

Cheryl's initial apprehensions about Terry Hall because of his intimidating size gave way to respect for his integrity. She gives him credit for the fact that in the end so many of the women infected by Ssenyonga agreed to testify. "I don't know how the women could have come forward at all if Terry Hall had not been so sensitive and supportive," she says. "In time he absolutely endeared himself to them."

That spring of 1991, Joan Estrada talked with lawyers from public health a dozen times to prepare her Jane Doe affidavit. She was assured that her involvement would end with giving the information, that the affidavit would be seen only by the judge hearing the Section 101 application, and that afterwards it would be sealed forever. Her name would never be revealed and she would not need to attend the hearing; once the Section 101 order was obtained, she would never be bothered again.

That was an essential consideration for her. Her parents didn't know she was infected. Joan's mother was fighting lung cancer and had enough troubles of her own; her stepfather was not someone she cared about. Joan couldn't tell her brother either; they never did get along. The baby of the family, a twelve-year-old brother she deeply loved, was too young to be burdened with such grief. Not even her close friends knew she had the AIDS virus. She feared her job as a phys-ed teacher in the Hamilton school system would be jeopardized if word leaked out.

She shared her worry about being exposed with Francine Dalton, who felt exactly the same. Francine was the adored only child of elderly parents, both with heart conditions, and she shrank from giving them a shock that might kill them. She knew they would be appalled to learn that the man who infected her was black; neither would even shake hands with a black person.

7

EARLY IN THE INVESTIGATION, Terry Hall learned that Ssenyonga, a Canadian citizen since 1987, had applied for and received a passport valid for one year and was planning to return to Uganda. Alarmed, Hall alerted airport police and put a surveillance team on the Chester Street house in London where Margaret Nansamba lived.

"We had everybody going in every direction that Easter weekend to make sure he didn't leave," Hall comments, grinning at the memory of the uproar.

Ssenyonga was indeed planning to travel. Ever since The African Store folded shortly after Christmas, he had been at loose ends. Margaret Nansamba, who was providing him with a place to sleep, was thinking of driving to Vancouver to escape her husband. Nansamba's sister had died in London of AIDS, which severed her last tie to the community. She was anxious to leave but she was concerned for Ssenyonga, who was in a pitiable frame of mind, depressed and withdrawn. He had counted on the cheque from Francine Dalton and it shocked him when she cancelled it before he could get the money. When Nansamba invited him to join her on the trip to Vancouver, he accepted. There was nothing in London to keep him, he said.

At that time Chris Karuhanga was planning a buying trip to western Africa. It seemed unlikely the business could be revived, but he wanted to look around. When he was in a homesick mood for Africa, he often talked wistfully of moving back. He and Connie Neill discussed buying some property there and someday building a house. Chris had finished a teacher's course at the University of Western Ontario and the board of education in a nearby city already had hired him, his job to begin in the fall. He and Connie, after more than two years of living together, were looking at houses and apartments in that city.

Connie was distressed by Ssenyonga's sadness and poverty, which aroused her nurturing instincts. Over the years of knowing him, seeing him almost daily at the store when she visited Chris, she always found Ssenyonga attractive. In contrast to Chris's pragmatism, Charles was a more vulnerable and interesting man. She suggested more than once to Chris that they should invite Ssenyonga to move in with them, pointing out that there was plenty of room in her three-bedroom apartment, but the arrangement never came about.

Ssenyonga was confiding in a big, pleasant woman, Lois Swift, who ran a small business in London. Lois first met Chris Karuhanga on a day in 1987 after she returned from living a year in Kenya. She was still in a daze of delight with African culture and went straight to the newly opened African Store to see what it had to offer. From that day on she enjoyed a casual friendship with Karuhanga, whom she describes as a decent, upright man, but it was erudite, fascinating Ssenyonga who became a close friend.

"To understand Ssenyonga," Lois says, "you have to know that he was not really part of the African culture he so passionately admired. He didn't grow up as an African man. He told me his parents talked constantly about the need for him to be 'civilized'. So he lost his culture. He didn't really belong anywhere. Wherever he went, he was an outsider."

Hers is a valuable insight into the complexities of Charles Ssenyonga. She spent many hours with Charles and he poured out to her the story of his childhood, which she deduced had estranged him from his African heritage. To her disappointment at the time, he made no sexual advances, not even when they spent a night camping together. She speaks about him almost exactly as does Leslie-Anne Jenkins, the theology student who also didn't sleep with him. Swift says, "He treated me like one of his sisters. He was a polite, kind gentleman."

One afternoon in the autumn of 1990 Charles had a curiously bleak conversation with Lois. They were sitting under an apple tree when he unburdened himself of some deep inner grief. "I'm no good," he told her. "No one should get involved with me. I'm a failure."

"Are you talking about affairs with women?" she asked.

"No," he said. "I'm celibate." She knew that wasn't true; she wondered what he was getting at, but he said no more.

On Tuesday, April 2, 1991, Nancy Gauthier called Terry Hall on his pager, having obtained the number from Francine Dalton. She had just remembered that Ssenyonga told her in March that he had an airplane ticket to Uganda, valid for two months. She was alarmed to think that Ssenyonga would get away. Terry checked with the surveillance team watching the house on Chester Street. Ssenyonga was still there.

Meanwhile, Terry was trying to gather medical evidence, most especially medical records to establish in court that the women were infected with HIV. He hoped for the cooperation of the Middlesex-London health unit, but when he approached that body he encountered an obdurate Dr. Douglas Pudden, London's medical officer of health. Pudden advised Hall, correctly, that medical records are protected by rules of confidentiality. If the police wanted to see Ssenyonga's records or those of any of the women, they should talk to Ontario's chief medical officer of health in Toronto. Hall called Dr. Richard Schabas, who said the decision was up to the London unit.

"I was expecting quite a bit of cooperation from public health, since the Ministry of Health started this whole investigation," Hall says with the resignation of a man who is never surprised at anything bureaucrats do, "but they didn't give it." He adds, "Everyone was afraid of the legalities, whatever, covering themselves. It was confusing and very frustrating."

Tom Wickett, the attorney-general's lawyer on loan to the Ministry of Health, in the meantime had finished work on the application for a judicial order under Section 101 of the Ontario Health Protection and Promotion Act, which would compel Ssenyonga to respect the restraining order or go to jail. The hearing was scheduled for March 21, 1991, in one of Toronto's most magnificent buildings, Osgoode Hall, before a judge of the Ontario Court, General Division. The application, issued in the name of Dr. Richard Schabas, included affidavits from Dr. Douglas Pudden and Marylin McConnell. There also was a sealed affidavit from one of the women infected by Ssenyonga, together with a motion to keep the affidavit sealed. On the cover of the affidavit the woman was identified only as Jane Doe. Jane Doe was Joan Estrada. Court documents alluding to the Jane Doe affidavit described in general terms what it contained: that Jane Doe had been infected by Ssenyonga after a Section 22 restraint order was served on him.

Justice Eugene Ewaschuk, one of the court's most able and fair-minded judges, noted that the Ministry of Health had been somewhat impetuous. Charles Ssenyonga had not yet been served with notice of the motion and presumably was not even aware of it. Ewaschuk ordered an adjournment until that nicety could be completed.

The immediate effect of the hearing was that the story of Charles Ssenyonga was out. Tracey Tyler, an astute legal affairs reporter for the *Toronto Star*, had wind of it from the court docket. She didn't name Ssenyonga but she pursued leads as best she could. Tom Wickett would tell her little of how the unprecedented order came to be requested so she turned to other sources. Steve Manning, a former priest who headed the AIDS Committee of Toronto, gave a foretaste of the controversy to come when he said the government's application was "irrational and insane." Tyler quoted Manning, who was under the impression that Jane Doe knew her lover was infected, as saying, "If a person wants to have sex with an HIV-infected person and knows about the condition, it's not the state's business to prevent them."

Jennifer Anderson read the paper with mixed feelings. She was glad that the Ssenyonga case was beginning to roll, but she was terrified that it might expose her. She was now an account executive: her career would be ruined. When HIV-positive people encounter severe stress, the reaction often is a flare-up of infection. In Jennifer's case, the emergence of the Ssenyonga case in the media caused a severe case of shingles that manifested itself as gruesome, weeping blisters on her torso and down one arm.

Linda Booker read the same report with great satisfaction. Almost three years had elapsed since she and Jennifer Anderson discovered that Ssenyonga had infected them. The waiting was over; the creaky system was beginning to move.

A few days later, on April 2, 1991, the *London Free Press* carried the four-column headline "Sex Ban Sought In AIDS Case" on a story under the double byline of Meg Milne and Joe Ruscitti.

Though the two journalists were resourceful, they were as stymied as Tracey Tyler had been. Douglas Pudden said stiffly, "I can't comment on the case." Dr. Iain Mackie, director of the St. Joseph's Health Centre's HIV/AIDS clinic who had seen Ssenyonga three years earlier, said he knew about the matter but couldn't violate confidentiality. He conceded, "The law is not in some respects strong enough for people who are knowingly spreading infection."

An AIDS activist, Peter Quick, was quoted as cautiously approving the government's application "provided the order is being used in a responsible way...I don't know how they are going to enforce it." Clarence Crossman, a thoughtful man who is education coordinator of the AIDS Committee of London, agreed that public health officials have "a clear responsibility" to try to limit the spread of disease.

Stephen Manning changed his position on Ssenyonga in the light of dawning awareness in the AIDS community that Ssenyonga had not informed his partners that he was HIV-positive. In the *Globe and Mail*, Manning described that behaviour as "unconscionable."

Charles Ssenyonga appeared in the Toronto courtroom on April 2, before Judge Robert Sutherland. He said in a humble manner that he had no lawyer. Sutherland adjourned the case until April 16 to allow Ssenyonga time to obtain a legal aid certificate and retain a lawyer. That appearance put his identity on public record: the media could name him. The next day, the *London Free Press* did. (Significantly, the media never commented on Ssenyonga's colour. Over the two years and four months that he was in the public eye, no mention was made of the fact that he was black and most of the people he infected were white.)

The provincial Minister of Health, Evelyn Gigantes, was besieged with calls from the media. Her response was the same to all: the situation indeed was "unusual, very extraordinary," but the action was warranted. Richard Burzynski, head of the Canadian AIDS Society, an umbrella organization for AIDS groups across the country, declared sombrely, "These are the kinds of situations that we're always afraid of."

Ssenyonga inquired of a Toronto lawyer where he might find a good lawyer in London. He was directed to Fletcher Dawson. With thirteen years of courtroom experience behind him when he started the Ssenyonga case, Dawson is rated one of the finest criminal lawyers in western Ontario. His strength lies in his resourcefulness, sharp intelligence, and bulldog determination not to overlook anything that might help his client. His work habits are awesome. When he is in the midst of a trial, it is not uncommon for him to be in his office until eleven at night. Taking one day off on the weekend represents for him real indolence.

Dawson is man of sturdy build with a shock of sandy hair, a thick moustache to match, pale eyes that glitter behind gold-rimmed glasses, and quiet intensity when he speaks in a low, gravelly voice. Eloquence doesn't come as easily to him as it does to such celebrated Toronto criminal lawyers as Clayton Ruby, Morris Manning, and Eddie Greenspan. In his youth Fletcher suffered anxiety attacks when he had to speak in public. He thought for a time that he should choose a career as a corporate lawyer, but in his first year at law school at Queen's University in Kingston he took a criminal law course and loved it. In his second year, when he discovered that criminal lawyers have to be fluent and persuasive, he was dismayed. He enrolled in a class on public speaking and then won the law school's advocacy prize.

After articling with a London firm, Fletcher settled in that city and rapidly rose to partnership in Cohen, Highley, Vogel and Dawson, a firm of some twenty lawyers able to afford splendid offices in London's tallest and newest office tower, a blue glass obelisk that dominates the city's skyline.

When Dawson agreed to defend Ssenyonga against the Ministry of Health's application for a Section 101, he had little experience in civil or administrative law and knew nothing about defending a client who was facing a public health restraint order. In fact, there wasn't a lawyer in London who had ever known a client banned from having sex under Section 22, let alone one who faced an application for a Section 101.

Fletcher Dawson was aware that the public would find the actions of his new client repellent, but that only fuelled his interest in the case. He holds a principled belief that everyone, however unpopular the person or odious the crime, is entitled to the best defence possible. "We work in an adversarial system and it is part of the function of that system that both sides have representation," he says. It is his view that the Crown must be pushed to prove every aspect of its case. In the absence of a vigorous defence, he points out, the prosecutorial arm of the law would grow flabby.

Dawson's view of his responsibility as a defence lawyer resembles that of a celebrated English barrister, Henry Brougham, who in 1820 said, "An advocate, by the sacred duty which he owes his client, knows, in the discharge of that office, but one person in the world, that client and none other. To save that client by all expedient means — to protect that client at all hazards and costs to all others, and among others to himself, — is the highest and most unquestioned of his duties; he must not regard the alarm, the suffering, the torment, the destruction which he may bring upon any other."

Besides, Dawson was fascinated with the case. "It was new and interesting and odd," he says. "With the involvement of HIV and AIDS, it's a nineties kind of case." Dawson is known to be attracted to cases that have a human rights component, and Ssenyonga's situation had all the markings. On one side was a penniless black man, sick with a fatal disease; on the other was the panoply of the state's unlimited resources with the strong wind of public opinion at its back.

Though he refuses to confirm it, it is clear that Dawson conducted the case on a legal aid certificate, the fee pegged well below the hourly rate he can command. Nonetheless, estimates of what Ssenyonga cost legal aid start in the high six figures.

On Tuesday, April 2, the day that Ssenyonga appeared in court in Toronto, Terry Hall called Nancy Gauthier and Joan Estrada in London to make appointments to see them. Initially, Nancy was less than agreeable. When he identified himself on the telephone, she snapped, "I don't like cops."

"Probably a lot of people don't," he responded affably.

Nevertheless, Nancy agreed to give a statement the following day, and Joan, though occupied with exams at the university, said she would see the officers the next evening.

Terry Hall and Al Ciampini arrived at Nancy's apartment at two in the afternoon, and the statement was completed seven and a half hours later.

Since Hall had conducted the questioning of Francine Dalton, it was Ciampini's turn. "Was I ever glad he had to do it," Hall says. What he meant was that Nancy was difficult to keep on track. In conversation she has a scattered approach that tends to propel her along a tangent at considerable velocity. Obtaining a coherent statement presented a problem to Ciampini and a greater one to Terry, whose responsibility it was to take notes. Nonetheless, both officers soon warmed to Nancy. "She's so open," Hall says. But when they asked for her previous sexual contacts dating back a year, she was evasive. "My tests were still indeterminate," she later explained, "and I wasn't going to give up the names unless I had to."

When the two officers kept their appointment with Joan Estrada in her basement apartment, they found a woman so angry and upset she could scarcely speak. Only the day before, Joan had learned from Dr. Janet Gilmour that further HIV tests of her blood were incontrovertibly positive. The stress of waiting for verification of the test had taken a frightful toll on the twenty-two-year-old. Sleepless, racked by crying spells, often suicidal, and yet still attending classes regularly and doggedly completing her essays on time, she was haggard and near collapse from the strain.

It didn't help that the police officers who knocked on the door were both male and one of them appeared in her confined space to be eight feet tall. She hated the specific questions they asked about her sexual relations with Ssenyonga. "I felt dirty, I felt like a slut," she says, eyes filling with tears. "I'm the type of person who has had very few boyfriends in my life and the subject of sex for me was something uncomfortable, something not to talk about. I was forced to do it, but I really hated it. I kept telling them their questions were ridiculous." She pauses, tears running down her cheeks, and then brightens, "But it turned out Terry Hall is just the greatest guy. I really like him."

Terry's terse notes on the interview are compassionate. "During taking of statement," he wrote, "experienced mood changes, nervous, emotional, anger. At times trying to talk about the contacts she would start crying and have to leave the room."

He comments, "It was a very upsetting experience for Joan. Very embarrassing."

Joan produced for Hall and Ciampini the Christmas card that Ssenyonga had given her. Hall set it aside on a table to take for evidence but at one point he had to dive across the room to rescue it. Joan, inflamed by grief and humiliation, suddenly seized the card and started to tear it to pieces.

The four-hour session went so poorly that the two officers decided the statement would have to be taken again. This time the interview was smooth: Hall was accompanied by a woman officer, Beth Pimm, a calm, tactful person with experience as a counsellor of rape victims.

"We didn't have to get hit with a shovel to figure it out," Hall observed. "We realized we should have brought a policewoman in the first place."

Joan says, "In the future, they ought to think about that. Here was I, scared to death, and they send *two men*." (Joan Estrada shows a sunny, sweet disposition to the world but her frightened eyes reveal her youthful uncertainty and vulnerability. People associated with the Ssenyonga case came to have strong protective feelings about her that went far beyond their professional responsibilities. Some months later, for instance, when Joan made up her mind to confront the doctor who had been so insensitive about her HIV test, two OPP policewomen volunteered to go along. As she gave the doctor a piece of her mind, Joan had officer Beth Pimm, a six-footer, on one side of her and Pat Vooy, a motherly officer from the neighbouring Tillsonburg division, on the other.)

Two nights after taking Joan's second statement, Terry Hall received a midnight telephone call. The woman on the line spoke in a strangled voice he couldn't recognize. He asked who she was and she sobbed, "Joan."

"What's the matter?" he asked, alarmed.

She replied, "Charles," and hung up.

Ssenyonga had called to ask how she was feeling. He said he was concerned about her health, but it is not unreasonable to suspect that the call, which she quickly terminated, was intended to ask her not to talk to the police.

The following day, April 7, Joan had a call from Margaret Nansamba. Nansamba hoped she was in time to ask Joan not to cooperate with the police. What was happening to Ssenyonga was unfair, she told Joan. That same day Nansamba made several other calls in an effort to dissuade former girlfriends from helping the police. She did this at Ssenyonga's urging but she, like many in the Ugandan community, may have had other concerns. Ssenyonga's growing notoriety was alarming Ugandans everywhere. They feared that the publicity he was receiving would stir up prejudice against them. The feeling was growing that Ugandans had better keep a low profile until the Ssenyonga mess ended, and the sooner the better.

Charles Ssenyonga had his first meeting with Fletcher Dawson on April 3. The substance of this discussion later was revealed in his testimony. He told Fletcher about his miserable treatment since his picture had appeared in newspapers and on television. The photograph, taken from some promotion material prepared for The African Store, had made his face well known around London. Employers would not accept job applications from him, he said, and strangers telephoned with threats. Even walking the streets was a humiliating experience because people stared.

Fletcher asked about the Health Ministry's charge that Ssenyonga had sexual relations after the Section 22 restraint order was served on him. Ssenyonga told Fletcher that he was being unjustly accused. He was, in fact, celibate, and had been celibate for more than two years. He had not had sex since learning of his HIV status in 1989.

Fletcher looked at him sharply and said, "I should warn you it is important that you tell me the truth. If you are not telling me the truth, you're making a mistake."

Ssenyonga nodded.

"Are you sure?" Fletcher persisted. "This will come back to haunt you if you're not telling me the truth. I urge you to think very carefully about this."

Ssenyonga assured his lawyer that he was telling the truth. "I am celibate," he repeated. "I did not have relations with any women since I found I was infected."

Fletcher comments that he had no personal stake in Ssenyonga's sincerity. "It wasn't from the point of view of convincing me," he explains. "It was from the point of view that he would be making a seriously wrong decision to maintain that position if it wasn't true. Having made that completely clear to him, I then sought his instructions about what he wanted me to do about it. And he wanted me to fight back. So we made public statements."

Like all criminal lawyers, Dawson is trained to expect a level of untruth in initial interviews with clients. People facing criminal charges have a natural tendency to want their lawyers to like them. They tell their lawyers what they wish had happened. They may not tell complete falsehoods, as Ssenyonga did, but they hold back the incriminating bits and errors of judgement.

Though Fletcher is well aware of this proclivity, he believed Ssenyonga. He saw his client as an innocent man who was being persecuted by the government. He shrugs off the error. "I'm no better than any other human being at judging who is telling the truth and who isn't."

The next day, following Ssenyonga's instruction, Dawson issued a denial of the accusation. Lynn Marchildon of the *London Free Press*, under a six-column headline "Man With HIV Virus Denies He Ignored Sex Ban," quoted Dawson that Ssenyonga "absolutely denies that he has had sexual intercourse since he's been diagnosed as suffering from HIV." On behalf of his client, who was not made available to the media, Dawson declared, "He feels he is being placed in a position where he is unable to defend himself against untruthful allegations, while at the same time suffering greatly from the publicity that has portrayed him as an individual who has recklessly spread the AIDS virus."

Fletcher also expressed his own dismay that Ssenyonga's name was out in the streets while his accuser was being sheltered behind an alias. He announced that Ssenyonga had instructed him to call for an investigation into whether his constitutional rights were violated by the attorney-general's refusal to unseal the Jane Doe affidavit.

On April 9, Terry Hall got some much-needed help from Schabas. He learned where health records of HIV-positive people were kept and what he could expect to find if he executed search warrants on doctors' files and public health offices. His partner Al Ciampini's long experience with the Ministry of Health paid off. With the help of Casey Hill, a lawyer in the attorney-general's office, the search warrants were prepared for public health offices, doctors, and HIV-screening labs in the cities where Ssenyonga had lived, as well as Rick Galli's Western Blot testing lab in Toronto.

On the morning of Monday, April 15, a justice of the peace in the London courthouse signed the warrants. Soon after, Terry Hall was in the office of Dr. Douglas Pudden, who had been told what the police were seeking. Pudden handed over a file containing original documents, already photocopied, of everything the unit had pertaining to Ssenyonga and his known sexual contacts.

The next stop was the HIV/AIDS clinic at St. Joseph's Health Centre, where advance notice was not given. Dr. Iain Mackie says that "five OPP officers, all in grey suits, looking very imposing" turned up and asked for his file on Ssenyonga. The situation was unprecedented in Mackie's experience. He wondered if doctor–patient relations were protected from such raids. He called the Canadian Medical Protective Association and said, "What do I do? They want my records." And the association official replied evenly, "What you do is, you give them your records." Mackie promptly turned over a file containing only two pages.

With stories about Ssenyonga in the media almost daily, the AIDS Committee of London faced a decision: if Ssenyonga came to them for emotional support or financial help, would they give it? The simple answer was yes. They reasoned that their mandate was to assist people with HIV and AIDS. Ssenyonga had HIV and maybe AIDS. Therefore, it would be unethical to refuse him. "If you don't offer support to all infected people," asks Michael Sauer, a staff member, "then where do you draw the nice line?"

The senior staff of the agency consisted of Executive Director Betty Anne Thomas, Michael Sauer, Education Coordinator Clarence Crossman, and Tom Donovan. That agency, housed in handsome, high-ceilinged offices in a walk-up in London's downtown core, is unusual among AIDS organizations in Canada because it is headed by a heterosexual woman. Betty Anne Thomas is a salty, sensible, compassionate person with a coxcomb of bright red hair and clear blue eyes. Her interest in the issue came when her beloved brother, Michael Bidner, an artist, was diagnosed with AIDS in 1985. He died four years later.

"AIDS is one of the places in society where one person can make a difference," she says simply. "I won't say I'm not real angry, and I won't say I'm not real sad, but you can use that anger and sadness to do something positive."

Despite occasional upheaval, the London AIDS Committee has a reputation for cohesiveness, something not all AIDS organizations enjoy. The founders say they made an early decision to be inclusive, and the policy has worked. When the four senior staff people met to discuss Ssenyonga, they agreed to respond to all media inquiries with the same position: they would not condemn Ssenyonga. "We didn't know what kind of counselling he had," Betty Anne explains. "He was from a different culture, so we didn't want to make assumptions about his behaviour on the basis of newspaper stories. There was too much we didn't know."

On the other hand, the staff agreed it was cowardly to hide behind "no comment." Betty Anne talked every day with Steve Manning, Executive Director of the AIDS Committee of Toronto, about the approach their flagship organizations should take. In the end, London AIDS issued statements that the courts were not appropriate places to solve the kind of problem Sseenyonga posed, that some intervention such as serious counselling should have been done much sooner, and that people have a responsibility to protect themselves from being infected.

People close to AIDS organizations were being asked what they thought should be done to stop people like Ssenyonga. The first response, that the government should back off, was crumbling. Dr. Iain Mackie in London told reporters Rod Mickleburgh and Paul Taylor of the *Globe and Mail* that in cases where people can't be educated not to pose a public health threat, "society may have no option but to look at long-term confinement or incarceration." At the same time he was telling the *London Free Press* that he doubted that fines or a jail sentence would change sexual behaviour; education programs should be used to persuade an infected person to practise safer sex. "I don't think it's good enough for the health unit to serve this man with a piece of paper saying 'don't have sex any more' if they have not educated him about safer sex practices," Mackie told reporters Lynn Marchildon and Meg Milne.

Betty Anne Thomas suggested psychiatric counselling. She was one of the first to point out that AIDS education stresses individual responsibility; since it seemed Ssenyonga's victims had not insisted on being protected, obviously the message was not getting out that everyone, even a woman, is at risk from unprotected sex.

Dr. Perry Kendall, medical officer of health for Toronto, called for the power to order "some kind of coercive confinement, combined with education and rehabilitative counselling." Kendall made it clear that he was not advocating jail. What he had in mind was something like a supervised halfway house. "A public health approach is still much better than a criminal approach," he observed.

Iain Mackie agreed. In an unpublished paper on the subject he came down strongly in favour of educational campaigns targeted at people who don't believe they are at risk: heterosexuals, especially women. He wrote, "It is virtually impossible to deal legally with the rare case whereby someone *knowingly* transmits HIV. The law has no specific way of dealing with HIV, short of manipulating other laws...The Health Protection and Promotion Act was never intended to deal with *life-long* infections...Orders to refrain from sexual activity are virtually unenforceable...Finally, public health officials, AIDS experts, lawmakers, and community AIDS organizations will need to sit down together and develop a consensus approach on how to deal with those who deliberately expose others to HIV, short of locking them up and throwing away the key. Confinement...must be a last resort."

8

TERRY HALL HAD AN UNSETTLING CALL from Margaret
Nansamba's estranged husband, who complained that he
had caught Ssenyonga in bed with his wife. He wanted the
police to know that Ssenyonga and Margaret were gone
from her house and were in hiding somewhere. Hall hastily
checked with his surveillance team. Nansamba and
Ssenyonga hadn't budged: false alarm. "They just weren't
opening the door for the husband," Terry decided.

On April 15, 1991, Hall received a call arranged by an
intermediary. A woman, using an agreed-upon code name,
said, "I want to tell you what Ssenyonga did to me."

He asked her to come in and make a statement. Two
days later Al Ciampini and Beth Pimm interviewed the
woman, Danielle Fitzgerald. Danielle told a story of being
date-raped by Ssenyonga and said she was infected with
HIV. Terry arrived around five that afternoon just as she was
finishing and he could tell that his colleagues were pleased
about something.

Danielle Fitzgerald, then thirty-seven years old, was a
prize for the investigation team because she was the only one
of Ssenyonga's known victims who had not consented to

have sexual intercourse with him. If Danielle would agree to testify, Ssenyonga could be arrested for sexual assault.

She said flatly that she would not cooperate. Her brother had just been diagnosed with cancer, her older sister was about to have a baby, her father was recovering from a stroke. The family had enough to deal with. She hadn't informed any of her relatives or friends about her infection and she wasn't going to chance her name being revealed.

Hall didn't press her but he did ask his colleague, the motherly Pat Vooy, to keep checking, gently, to see if Fitzgerald would change her mind. Fitzgerald would be a compelling witness against Ssenyonga. Though spunky and articulate, she was heartbreakingly frail in appearance with a pallor generally associated with serious illness. Indeed, Fitzgerald's immune system was at a dangerously low level. Pat started making the calls, sometimes twice a day, "just checking"; Danielle stood firm: no dice.

Danielle had known about her HIV status for only five months, stoically confiding in no one, and was bursting with unexpressed grief. Her first thought after the diagnosis had not been for herself, however, but for the two men she had slept with after Ssenyonga raped her in the summer of 1988. One of them was a brief encounter. She had loved the other one, with whom she lived for a year and a half and planned for much of that time to marry. Because Danielle had had a tubal ligation, the couple never used condoms.

Danielle was raised mostly by her mother because her father was a travelling man and an alcoholic. She grew up feeling neglected. At eight she ran away from home and at fourteen was considered a wild kid, using street drugs and often coming home drunk. Her mother used to say that Danielle should have been a social worker because she was drawn to people who needed a sympathetic listener. Instead she drifted for years through a series of low-paying jobs, including tobacco picker and hotel maid. One day she resolutely took charge of her life and enrolled in a secretarial training course at community college. At the end of 1987 she was still looking for a white-collar job when she met Charles Ssenyonga. It was soon after he arrived in London and both were working in a community centre that placed unemployed teenagers in temporary jobs in the homes of elderly and disabled people.

Ssenyonga's responsibilities included calling on invalids and the elderly to see if they required assistance. Many times old people would not let him in the door because he was black. When he told Fitzgerald about the humiliation he suffered, she was outraged on his behalf.

A casual friendship developed between Charles and Danielle. He told her that he and his friend Chris Karuhanga were newcomers in London and knew no one. Would she introduce them around? In her friendly, outgoing way, she was happy to oblige. She explains, "I felt I had a duty to be a nice person."

Fitzgerald found Ssenyonga an attractive man, though a bit arrogant, but he didn't appeal to her sexually. She noticed very quickly that he had an easy way with the truth. For one thing, he and Chris were not friendless in London as he pretended: they were part of a large and affectionate Ugandan community, and Charles appeared to be a popular man. For another, he was trying to keep secret the fact that he was moonlighting, working evenings at The African Store, which he and Chris seemed to own.

One evening in June, 1988, a group of co-workers went to a bar. Ssenyonga said he had forgotten his cigarettes at the apartment he shared with Karuhanga on Oxford Street. He invited Danielle to come with him to get them.

"I made a stupid mistake, going with him that night," she says bitterly. She was distressed by the barrenness of the apartment, which was devoid of any furniture except a mattress on the floor in each of the bedrooms. Ssenyonga offered her a cup of tea, and while he was in the kitchen she leafed through some law books he owned. Suddenly he was behind her, putting his arms around her. She protested, but he pushed her down on the mattress, tugging at her underwear and at the same time unzipping his trousers.

"What are you *doing!*" she screamed as he accomplished the rape. She had no weapon to defend herself in that stark room. Besides, she is a tiny woman who weighed less than a hundred pounds at the time, while Ssenyonga was burly and strong. She found his penis enormous; her vagina was torn and for days afterwards was tender.

When it was over she was shocked and incredulous. "Why did you do that?" she asked, fumbling with her clothes.

Ssenyonga replied with a broad, easy smile, "You know you wanted it."

She told no one; it was her way to keep her troubles to herself. Habits of self-reliance were deep in her. She deliberately put the incident out of her mind. A few days later she was dreadfully sick, with a high fever that persevered for two weeks and large red blotches on the upper part of her body. Eventually, after prodding by her mother, she went to a doctor. The doctor called it yuppie flu without examining her and gave her some pills. She was so ill that she was hallucinating, and her mother forced her to see another doctor. This one called her disease red measles and gave her different pills.

Ssenyonga came to visit her while she was recuperating at her mother's house. He looked at her in an odd way and left in a minute or two. "I think he wanted to see if I was going to live," she says bitterly.

When Danielle returned to work, Ssenyonga seemed convinced that she would want to have sex with him again. "You know that you liked it," he told her in a confident way she found repulsive. To her relief, Ssenyonga left two months later to concentrate on working at The African Store.

A year later Danielle suffered an attack of shingles so severe that she was left with scars. She was also troubled by bouts of deep fatigue. The man with whom she was living, the one she intended to marry, told her one day that maybe he had AIDS from a previous relationship in Vancouver. Though their relationship broke up soon afterwards, it stuck in her mind that he might have infected her. When the periods of exhaustion deepened, she decided to be tested for HIV.

Her doctor scoffed at her. "You don't fool around, Danielle," he said. "Why should you need to be tested?"

"Something's not right," she insisted.

On December 4, 1990, she was notified that she was HIV-positive. She was stunned. After years of working at menial jobs that paid around five dollars a hour, she had just landed something better, secretary in an insurance company housed in a luxurious building. She had new furniture in her apartment and was making payments on a car, her first.

"I finally had my life together and then I find I have AIDS," she says, clenching her teeth. What she did about it, immediately after she heard the news, was bury the information and go back to work. Five days later she took a driving test and passed it. "You have to get on with your life," she says staunchly.

She called the boyfriend to urge him to be tested, which he did. He told her the report was negative.

"This is ironic," he observed. "I thought I might have given you AIDS and now you think you might have given it to me. Where do you think you could have got it?"

"I don't know," she replied honestly. The only possibility that came to mind was that the boyfriend was lying about being HIV-negative. Danielle had managed to obliterate the memory of the rape.

When the story of Ssenyonga's infection broke in the London media in March, 1991, a co-worker at the insurance company found Danielle in her office. "Did you hear about Charles Ssenyonga?" he asked. "He's got AIDS. And he's being charged with spreading it."

Another co-worker overheard and saw the shock on Danielle's face. "Did you know Ssenyonga?" she asked.

"Yes," said Danielle weakly. "I used to work with him at a community centre."

The woman studied her. "You didn't go to bed with him, did you?"

"Certainly not," Danielle replied stiffly.

When she heard in April that the Ontario Provincial Police were investigating Ssenyonga, Danielle gamely called Terry Hall. During the statement-taking on April 19, she resisted his efforts to persuade her to charge Ssenyonga with rape. Even Pat Vooy's soft coaxing was rejected. Danielle found that the obligation to describe the rape for the police had opened the wound, leaving her dissolved with anger and grief. She began to have nightmares of helplessness. Her fury was such that one night when she saw a black man she thought was Ssenyonga crossing the street, she had to restrain herself from running him over. That scared her; she wasn't like that. She feared that if she involved herself in long legal proceedings that required her to keep dredging up the memory, she would never recover from her deranged state. Besides, she told herself, the case did not depend on her. The police had plenty of other infected women, enough to put Ssenyonga away; they didn't really need her.

Fitzgerald provided the police with names of her two sexual contacts since Ssenyonga. Both were tested and both men proved negative.

She cried with relief. "That was a big weight off my shoulders," she says, her face bleak. "I would have died if I had given either of them the virus. I wouldn't want to hurt anyone that way."

The stress affected her badly. Her T-4 cell count, by which doctors judge the state of the body's immune system, dropped below one hundred. The normal range for T-4 cells is between five hundred and fifteen hundred cells per millimetre of blood. A count of less than two hundred T-4 cells indicates the onset of AIDS. Danielle Fitzgerald therefore had full-blown AIDS. She quit work, too weakened to continue, and moved to the meagre existence of living on a disability allowance.

On April 16, 1991, the government's application for a Section 101 court order against Ssenyonga was ready. Fletcher Dawson had decided to fight the government on several fronts: first, he would resist the 101 application, and, second, he would seek an extension on the time limitation in order to attack the legitimacy of Section 22 itself. He believed Section 22 was in violation of the Charter of Rights and Freedoms; the government, he felt, had no right to order anyone to stop having sex.

Fletcher was unable to attend the hearing in Toronto before Justice Robert Montgomery. In his stead was a colleague, Tim Morin. The Jane Doe affidavit, which was Joan Estrada's statement, remained sealed, giving rise to Morin's argument that the order should not be granted since there was no evidence before the court that Ssenyonga had violated the Section 22 order. The point was well taken, but the judge compromised. Stating that it was "in the public's interest," he issued a temporary restraining order upholding Section 22. Any breach of this order would be viewed as contempt of court, an offence for which the sentence is a possible two years in prison.

Montgomery adjourned the government's application for a permanent Section 101 without setting a date for the hearing. Dawson, still believing that Ssenyonga was celibate and fuming that a restraint order had been granted without any evidence that it was justified, prepared to appeal. "This raised the most basic concerns of fairness and natural justice," he comments. "It was the first whiff of where this case was going. You could see what was building behind the scenes when the government was trying to keep all the evidence secret."

The civil case was growing complicated. Before the Section 101 application could be heard, the courts needed to dispose of the issues raised by Dawson about unsealing the affidavit. A date was set for that dispute; the government announced that it would be requesting the judge to ban the media from the hearing while the affidavit was examined and afterwards seal the affidavit forever.

Fletcher Dawson was incensed. "They basically want a secret hearing," he fumed. "These are brutal accusations and the Crown is not saying who is making them." He insisted that Ssenyonga's accusor must identify herself.

To mollify Dawson, Wickett allowed him to read the affidavit. The effort at conciliation didn't work. Dawson wanted Jane Doe on the stand so he could cross-examine her on the statements she made; anything less would be unfair to his client.

Public health lawyers went back to Joan Estrada and asked her if she would testify in person. She was horrified, but they promised her total privacy. The media would be barred from the courtroom, they said. When he heard of that proposal, Dawson protested; he was having no part of a closed courtroom.

Joan was caught in the middle of the legal shenanigans. "For a while I was the only person fighting Charles," she says. "Nancy wasn't up, Francine wasn't up, I was the person fighting Charles and I was scared. But also I was mad. I needed to get that anger out. And Charles had infected so many women he couldn't be sure which one was Jane Doe, so I felt he wouldn't be coming after me."

Dawson had the Crown served with a summons to require Jane Doe to appear in court in London to be cross-examined on the affidavit. When neither a Crown lawyer nor Joan Estrada responded, Dawson announced that he would be seeking a court order to make them appear.

Joan, meanwhile, was writing her final exams at Western. Pleading an unnamed illness, with a doctor's unspecific letter to prove it, she was able to avoid three of them. It is testament to her willpower that she received 80s in those she wrote. She had planned to go to graduate school, but she let that go. She did not have a future, she would die soon, there was no point. "I kinda gave up there for a while," she explains.

On May 9, four lawyers put their varying perspectives before Mr. Justice Joseph Potts. The *Toronto Star* and the *Globe and Mail* filed separate protests against the request to close the courtroom; Jane Doe filed a motion asking that the courtroom be closed during her part of the hearing; Fletcher Dawson wanted the judge to haul Jane Doe into the witness stand. Potts had the sensible suggestion that the parties resolve the dispute outside the courtroom and he adjourned the applications indefinitely.

Fletcher was active on another front. He wanted to halt the Section 101 hearing until he could deal with the threshold question of whether Section 22 was unconstitutional because it violated the Charter of Rights and Freedoms. He announced to the media that he was ready to appeal the Section 22 restraint order to Ontario's Health Protection Appeal Board, which is a quasi-judicial panel consisting of appointed lawyers and laypeople. This was the appeal procedure that Marylin McConnell once discussed with Ssenyonga. The regulations, however, stipulate that such appeals should be launched within fifteen days of the issuance of the restraint order; the period had long expired. A Ministry of Health lawyer, Muni Merani, promptly stated that the government would oppose the application on the grounds that the deadline had passed. Fletcher responded with asperity that he intended to ask for a waiver of that requirement.

The ministry had second thoughts. Section 22 had never been tested against a Charter argument and perhaps Dawson was right to question its constitutionality. If Section 22 violated the Charter, the government would need a new law. In any case, nothing was risked in allowing Section 22 to be tested: Ssenyonga remained bound by the interim court order to observe Section 22's prohibition against sex.

It was frustrating to photographers that Ssenyonga did not attend any of these skirmishes. The media were avid for access to the man for a statement and some pictures. Television was using, over and over again, the same single video clip obtained by London television station CFPL. In it Ssenyonga was shown in an open-throat summer shirt, head high, a wistful, embarrassed smile on his face, looking younger than his thirty-three years.

As was their custom, neither Dr. Douglas Pudden nor Dr. Nancy Tuttle of the Middlesex-London health unit were speaking to reporters. Journalists were obliged to find sources more distant from the fray. For a few days after Dawson raised the question, they concentrated on the civil liberties aspect of sex bans. Alan Borovoy, esteemed general counsel for the Canadian Civil Liberties Association, expressed his concern at decrees covering consensual sex practices. "I always worry when state coercion is imposed on people's private activities," he told Greg Van Moorsel of the *London Free Press*. Borovoy wondered what would be the harm if two HIV-positive people had sex.

Ontario Minister of Health Evelyn Gigantes told the media that she had asked Dr. Richard Schabas, the province's chief medical officer of health, to submit a proposal of guidelines that might prevent HIV-infected people from having unprotected sex with unsuspecting partners. A government AIDS advisory committee buckled down to the task. High among the recommendations under discussion was the notion of referring people suspected of knowingly spreading the AIDS virus to a community-based team of counsellors. Theresa Dobko, experienced counsellor at the AIDS Committee of Toronto, and one of the first AIDS counsellors in Canada, was present at many of the discussions and says agreement was never achieved. All accepted that education and counselling were needed, but a way to do that was never resolved.

As the legal skirmishes mounted in intensity, Nancy Gauthier was still waiting in agony for resolution of her indeterminate HIV status. On May 6, 1991, Dr. Janet Gilmour drew another two samples of blood from her, one for Rick Galli in the Toronto lab and one to be forwarded by Galli to the federal lab in Ottawa.

The Ottawa lab became involved in the Ssenyonga case because of a hunch Cheryl Wagner had. She remembered the celebrated case in Florida of a dentist, David Accer, who died in 1990 after infecting six patients with HIV. Microbiologists working at the Los Alamos National Laboratory under the supervision of Dr. Harold W. Jaffe, an AIDS epidemiologist at the Federal Centers for Disease Control and Prevention in Atlanta, had succeeded for the first time in North America in matching sequences of pieces of the DNA in the outer shell of the dentist's virus with sequences in the DNA of the virus in his victims.

In June, 1991, Cheryl called her colleague Dr. Philip Berger about the scientific possibility of doing the same with the Ssenyonga virus. When he encouraged her to follow up, she talked to OPP Inspector Terry Hall. Hall promptly called Dr. Michael O'Shaughnessy, director of the Federal Centre for AIDS in Ottawa. His inquiry was, "Can you match the DNA of the virus in one HIV-infected person with the DNA of another?" O'Shaughnessy said that was an interesting question. The answer even six months earlier would have been no, but the pathfinding work on the virus of the Florida dentist had changed the science. It was possible that a very skilled person could replicate the technique. Luckily, he had a hot-shot on his staff who was keen on genetic research.

Dr. Michael Montpetit, thirty-one, had been hired only a short time before and was looking for a project that would enable him to study the genetic makeup of the AIDS virus. He jumped at the assignment. "It was a great way to start off," he says. It is fortunate that Montpetit relished the task; as it turned out, he spent the next two years of his life working full-time on the Ssenyonga project. "I'm supposed to do pure research," Montpetit explained to Cheryl Wagner the first time they chatted, "and you can't get more pure than this."

Montpetit is a tall, humorous man with a sandy moustache and a gleaming pate. As a scientist working at the outer limits of genetic research, he is assisted greatly by a probing and lively intelligence in the genius range, combined with a capacity for patience and detachment that sees him through the frustrations of his trade. "I like puzzles," he says. "Science to me is a puzzle."

Michael is the son of bilingual parents. With a father in the air force, he was raised at NATO bases in France and Sardinia and then in various places in Canada, ending up in Ottawa. As a child he constructed museum-quality scale models of planes, a hobby that has stayed with him. As a member of the International Plastic Modellers' Society, he has provided drafting and technical illustration for a magazine for enthusiasts.

He found his field, biochemistry, at the University of Ottawa. In 1990 Michael finished his doctorate in the molecular biology of prostate cancer, in the process of which he developed a new animal model for testing recurring cancers.

He has been intrigued ever since by the relationship between viruses and cancer, and that fascination led him into a new field: studying the DNA of viruses. In 1988, still in his twenties, he worked at the Canadian Red Cross Society lab in Ottawa setting up the new diagnostic test polymerase chain reaction (PCR), which burst upon research laboratories in 1985. Montpetit describes it as a sort of molecular photocopier that can generate millions of copies of a specific target with such accuracy that a microscopic bit of it in a large swimming pool would produce replicas of itself in every drop of water.

PCR has significant application for HIV. One important use of it when the technology becomes more available will be earlier diagnosis of HIV infection. At present there is an alarming window of weeks, or even months, between the time of infection and the development of antibodies that can be detected. During that period, infected people test negative when, in fact, they are positive and are infectious.

Montpetit next was employed by a Canadian biotechnology company, Allelix, which had joined with the Canadian government to sponsor certain kinds of research in federal labs. As a post-doctoral fellow Montpetit was put to work studying the papillomavirus that has been linked to cervical cancer.

The keenness of the young researcher's mind caught the attention of Dr. Michael O'Shaughnessy, then director of Health and Welfare's Federal Centre for AIDS, now known as Bureau of HIV/AIDS Laboratories and Research. He hired Montpetit and suggested a range of projects. Montpetit chose to study genetic variations within the AIDS virus in the hope that his research would enable physicians to know which AIDS-slowing drugs work best in individual patients. The cluster of Ssenyonga-infected women was for him an astonishingly appropriate opportunity to embark on that research.

To provide uncompromised blood samples that Montpetit would need for his efforts to match the DNA, Cheryl Wagner and Janet Gilmour drew blood from the women Ssenyonga had infected. In Toronto, that was Jennifer Anderson, Linda Booker, and Francine Dalton; in London, Joan Estrada, Danielle Fitzgerald, and Nancy Gauthier. (Jane Campbell, in Montreal, was uncooperative.) To preclude any possibility that the authenticity of the blood samples could be challenged in court, present at each procedure were a police identification officer and two members of Hall's OPP investigative team. Tubes containing the blood were sealed by the doctors, who identified the donors only as Patients A, B, D, E, F, and G, and then a police seal was affixed on top of that. Terry himself took the tubes to the provincial lab on Toronto's outskirts and put them into the hands of Dr. Rick Galli. All samples sent to Rick Galli in the Toronto lab also went to Montpetit in Ottawa, under the same strict controls.

Rick Galli's willingness to cooperate, so far as medical ethics allowed, was proving an invaluable asset. Galli, indeed, relished the drama into which he unexpectedly had been drawn and could not avoid taking a personal interest in the well-being of the women. On May 19, he called Janet Gilmour with bad news. Nancy Gauthier's Western Blot test had entered the positive zone: she definitely had the virus. Later, testifying at the preliminary trial, Janet Gilmour explained, "The sequence with Nancy is one commonly seen during the early stage of infection. It would tell me that it was a very recent infection, that she likely became infected within the last six months, most probably within the last four months."

A few days later Fletcher Dawson appeared before the Health Protection Appeal Board to ask for an adjournment of about two months. He wasn't yet ready to proceed, he said.

As weeks passed, Cheryl Wagner was worried that the strain of waiting for the hearing was becoming too much for Joan Estrada, who was carrying the entire weight of the prosecution. It seemed to Cheryl, who was talking to Joan on the telephone almost daily, that the young woman was on the verge of collapse. "She was a classic candidate for suicide," Wagner says, "smiling and cheerful on the outside and broken up on the inside."

To spread the responsibility around, she suggested to Tom Wickett, the Ministry of Health lawyer, that other women infected by Ssenyonga might be willing to give Jane Doe affidavits as well, since he had promised confidentiality. She meant Francine Dalton and Nancy Gauthier, both of them eager to see Ssenyonga brought to justice. Wickett, however, was uneasy about continuing to use the Jane Doe approach. In view of Fletcher Dawson's vigorous challenge to the right of Ssenyonga's accusers to be anonymous, Wickett confessed to Wagner that he was not confident that their privacy could be protected after all. He made a gallant promise. "If it looks as though we'll have to give up their names," he said, "the government will drop the case. We won't let that happen."

Meanwhile, Terry Hall continued to search medical records around the province, looking for more women infected by Ssenyonga. He found no reference to Ssenyonga in the files in Toronto, Hamilton, Ottawa, or Kingston. That did not mean that Ssenyonga had not infected women in those cities, only that none had identified him as the source. For instance, no records naming Ssenyonga as a contact turned up in Hamilton, but police were confident from interviews with people close to Ssenyonga that he had infected at least three women and one man while he attended McMaster University. One of the women, the one known to Cheryl Wagner, was his tempestuous lover, Jane Campbell, now living in Montreal with her child, another was a waitress in the university cafeteria, and the third the mother of a year-old baby.

Hall had better luck with doctors who knew Ssenyonga or the women he infected. He and Al Ciampini, Beth Pimm, and Pat Vooy, working in pairs, met with Nancy Reid, who had moved her practice to Kingston, Henry Bendheim, Iain Mackie and Joanne Fox in London, and Cheryl Wagner in Toronto. The four investigators worked full-time and flat-out to gather relevant documents, taking the originals for evidence and leaving the doctors with photocopies.

Occasionally they came across a new name, another woman possibly infected by Ssenyonga, and went calling. One was the woman who worked in a hotel and had intercourse three times with Ssenyonga over a weekend. She said she already had been contacted by Marylin McConnell, and tested negative. The police were puzzled and asked her to be tested a second time: still negative.

"How come?" she was asked.

"I double-wrapped him," she explained. "Two condoms each time." Somehow she had persuaded Ssenyonga that condoms were obligatory. Even though one of the condoms broke, she escaped the infection.

Though Terry Hall was looking for women infected after the sex ban, he was also anxious to interview women infected by Ssenyonga before he tested positive. Their testimony would show a consistent pattern of irresponsible behaviour. When Hall asked Cheryl Wagner about putting him in touch with Patients A and B, the doctor demurred. She preferred that he make the contact through the Parkdale Community Legal Services lawyer, Diane Martin, who would be in a better position than she to protect the legal rights of her patients.

Through Martin, Jennifer Anderson said she would talk to Hall if she could conceal her name and be identified only as Patient A. Hall, thoroughly familiar by that time with the apprehensions of the women infected by Ssenyonga, un-hesitantly agreed.

Linda Booker was even more wary. She would not meet the police in person but she would provide an anonymous taped statement. Diane Martin advised Hall that she would present him with a synopsis of that transcript. He inquired what possible objection there could be to his receiving the whole transcript, since the woman's name would not be on it.

Martin gave him a narrow-eyed look. "I don't know," she said. "I'll have to think about it."

On reflection Linda decided to meet with the police, but only at the home of Cheryl Wagner. On the first of May, 1991, she gave her statement to Beth Pimm and Pat Vooy. At about the same time, Jennifer Anderson gave her statement at OPP headquarters.

The police groaned at what lay ahead. All the women's sexual contacts for a year and a half before their infections would have to be traced and tested. Otherwise Ssenyonga's lawyer would argue that his client might not be responsible.

In fact, Fletcher Dawson was planning exactly that. "The Crown lawyers can't possibly prove that my client infected those women beyond a reasonable doubt unless they are able to rule out that they were not infected by anyone else," he observed. His plan was to ask each complainant one question: "Have you had any other sexual partner?" Each woman, he assumed, would have to respond "Yes." He then would say "Thank you" and sit down.

"I think that would be the end of the prosecution's case," he said with a tight smile.

Terry Hall and his team were obliged to request each woman to name the men in her life, going back eighteen months from the time of their diagnosis. "That was very embarrassing for the women and for the contacts," Terry comments sympathetically.

The women, stiff with humiliation, gave names. Nancy Gauthier at first was still reluctant. "These men were not appropriate for me, especially when I have a child," she says, her mouth drawn. "I couldn't remember them very well. I didn't care about them. And I always made them wear condoms, so they weren't the ones who infected me."

Gently urged by her doctor, Janet Gilmour, Nancy eventually yielded up nine names. That made the total twenty men for the three women. Nancy was mortified to admit to the police that she did not always know the men's last names. Usually she had a helpful lead, such as a bar the man frequented on Tuesdays. One contact she recalled only as a black man known as Flip. Visiting the restaurant where Gauthier had met him, the police observed leaning against the bar a big handsome black man whose friends called him Flip. They followed him to his car in the parking lot and identified themselves as OPP officers. The man grinned. He was a cop himself, but he wasn't the right Flip. It took weeks of patient hunting before they got their man.

Hall's three teammates divided up the workload, each officer assigned to one of the three lists. The drill in each case was approximately the same: "Hello Mr. [name], I'm Beth Pimm of the Ontario Provincial Police. We're investigating a case involving HIV and we are wondering if you might have some contact with it . . . " The women's identities were never revealed. Advised that they might be subpoenaed into court to testify if they didn't cooperate, all the men but one submitted to the request that they have their blood tested by a family doctor. All the tests, to the intense relief of everyone, came back negative.

One contact was a Crown attorney who, unlike the others, guessed it had something to do with Ssenyonga. Another contact was a policeman; one was a nurse; several contacts named by Nancy Gauthier were in the music business.

The police work generated masses of paper. Terry Hall had half a dozen banker's boxes stacked in his office, all of them full. Sometimes secretaries in the OPP investigative branch spent entire days typing statements relating to the Ssenyonga investigation.

Terry was growing edgy. Margaret Nansamba's house on Chester Street was sporting a For Rent sign, and Ssenyonga had not been sighted for some time. If Ssenyonga left the province, the Ministry of Health would have no jurisdiction to return him to London, since the restraint orders applied only to Ontario. Hall sent two police officers in civilian clothes to gain access to Nansamba's by pretending to be prospective tenants. They reported that Ssenyonga was still inside but there were packing boxes everywhere.

Just before noon on April 29, surveillance officers raised the alarm: a moving van had arrived. Word was that Nansamba and her child were driving to Vancouver and Ssenyonga would accompany them.

Hall called for officers in unmarked cars to follow Nansamba and set off himself in pursuit. Keeping in touch with the three other trackers by police radio, Hall caught up to his quarry on Highway 401 near Woodstock and afterwards kept it in sight all the way to Toronto. He parked too late to see Ssenyonga go into a doughnut shop near Dundas and Elizabeth Streets, in the Chinatown district. His first glimpse of his quarry occurred when Ssenyonga emerged. Hall was surprised that Ssenyonga was rather small. He had been expecting someone more formidable.

Ssenyonga returned to the car and set off, driving east in rush-hour traffic. Somewhere around Queen and Broadview, the police lost him in a nest of one-way streets and the cul-de-sacs that curl around subsidized housing developments. Hall is embarrassed to admit it happened. "We didn't have proper surveillance, just a few cars," he says defensively.

The police knew where Margaret Nansamba was going from the change-of-address she left with the post office and the destination she gave the moving company. When they checked the address in Vancouver, they found Nansamba and her child settling in, but there was no sign of Ssenyonga.

On May 15, Hall, Al Ciampini, and Bruce Long met with Brian Trafford in the Toronto offices of the attorney-general. "We don't do anything without a meeting," Hall observes laconically.

The officers laid out the evidence they had obtained to date. The decision was up to Bruce Long, who said he was anxious to get the charges moving, once he figured out what they would be. Trafford observed that criminal negligence causing bodily harm might work. Long responded that it would be good to have a sexual assault charge as well because the identity of the complainants would certainly be protected by the court, but he would have to think about it. Terry Hall briefed them on the testimony they might expect from the six women, if they could be persuaded to testify.

Though Terry gave no names, he was referring to Jennifer Anderson, Linda Booker, Francine Dalton, Joan Estrada, Danielle Fitzgerald and Nancy Gauthier. He knew there were others, such as Jane Campbell, but these six were his best bets. The case was full of holes: blood samples still to be taken, witnesses to be found and, most conspicuously, the cooperation of the women still uncertain.

Terry said he could be sure of only one of them, identified as D (Francine Dalton), but she would insist on a publication ban. His source for this, he said, was a Toronto doctor, Cheryl Wagner. Bruce Long had heard nothing good about her. His impression was that she was obstructing the case, that she knew of the infections and had done nothing. He made a mental note to issue a writ on her and force her to testify. "My first few contacts with Cheryl were a little strained," Long comments ruefully, "because I got this wrong information about her. Someone got her role twisted, maybe through contact with public health in London."

Long realized the case was too complex for one lawyer and decided to parcel out the workload. To make sure that everything stayed on track, he took charge in this initial stage. He couldn't see himself taking it to trial because his responsibilities as chief Crown for eight counties were consuming, but he certainly could get it launched. "Otherwise," he confided gloomily, "the case will evaporate in a morass of problems."

David Arntfield, next to him in authority, would handle the medical and scientific evidence. The third lawyer, chosen to present the complex legal arguments, was new in the department, twenty-eight-year-old Simon Johnson, but already he had shown himself to be a brilliant legal analyst.

Bruce Long confesses that it didn't occur to him to find a suitable lawyer who was black. It never crossed his mind that Charles Ssenyonga was a black man and that everyone involved in the prosecution was white.

Simon Johnson is a tall, handsome, shy, and studious-looking man with owlish dark-rimmed glasses and a shock of thick dark hair. He was born in England and retains an accent. His parents, both teachers, immigrated to a small town in Saskatchewan during a teacher shortage in that province. Non-athletic, he was a loner and a reader as a child and "drifted into law." In law school at the University of Toronto he took part in a mock trial situation and decided he loved criminal law. After that he worked his way through an intellectually patrician post-graduate education at the University of London in England. On his return to Canada he joined the office of the attorney-general because he knew he would get more experience in trial work there than most other avenues open to young lawyers. Though he has exacting work habits, Simon enjoys unexpected pleasures: he plays jazz trombone in a community band and Bach in brass quartets.

The lawyers were aware that pressure was building from an outraged public that saw the government as stalled and impotent. This edge of urgency was a factor, though not the overriding one, in the decision to arrest Charles Ssenyonga.

To swear out a warrant, a justice of the peace would have to be assured that plaintiffs would testify. The lawyers looked to Hall. Would they?

Terry said firmly, "We have to protect the privacy of these women. They can't have their identities exposed. I gave them my word on that. If they agree to testify, we have to be sure that their names won't get out."

"I'll see them and find out where we're at," Bruce Long decided. "Terry, can you get them to my office?"

"It is up to them to decide what they want to do," Terry told him. "I'll talk to them and get back to you."

Hall never wavered in his loyalty to the women infected by Ssenyonga. He says, "They are all nice women, good people, smart." He pauses and adds sadly, "It just happened that Ssenyonga was smarter than they were."

9

THE MEETINGS BETWEEN the Crown lawyers and six of the women infected by Ssenyonga were scheduled for the end of May, 1991. "I knew that unless I established some rapport with the women, the case would go nowhere," Bruce Long says. But first he had to be able to tell them what charges he planned to lay. To do that he needed to find the parts of the Criminal Code that best fit Ssenyonga's activities.

He began the task by contacting district attorneys in the United States and Crown attorneys in Canada to ask about similar cases. Then he and Simon Johnson sat down to brainstorm the problem, a task to which Simon brought a relish for arcane legal quandaries. Also, by a stroke of good fortune, Johnson happened to have done graduate studies in criminal law, which touched on such issues as criminal negligence cases.

The two men spent what Long calculated as one hundred hours in research and discussion, most of it late at night and over weekends. "There was nothing to look at," Long explains. "There were no precedents. There was nothing to start from. You couldn't pick up a text. There's no section in the Code that allows you to say, 'Well, this will cover it.'"

Simon became a familiar figure in the library of the University of Western Ontario's law school. "When it comes to matters of law," Long says, "Simon hears it once and he can extrapolate it to other areas."

The two lawyers, alike in keen-wittedness and patience with legal drudgery, are vastly different in temperament. Bruce has fast reactions and is a pusher; Simon likes to consider carefully. Despite this disparity, a warm amity had developed between them. Bruce, working some nights until almost midnight, was concerned for Simon's health when he stayed in the office until three.

"I would say, 'Simon, you gotta go home'," Bruce says, "and he would say, 'Aren't you the guy who used to fall asleep in law libraries?'"

Simon explains, "I looked at everything I could find in Canadian law, English law, Australian law, New Zealand law, and American law, as far as I could. Clarence, an English case in 1888, said infecting a woman with venereal disease did not amount to assault. And until Ssenyonga that was the leading case in the Commonwealth. So you update that to see if it has been considered in any Canadian cases or any other English cases, or any other Australian cases. Legal research is digging, like any other sort of research. You just have to have an idea where to start."

Most of the research Simon did was manual, but for some of it he could order up a computer search. He discovered that the American military justice system has considered more AIDS infection cases than anywhere else in the English-speaking world, thanks to mandatory testing.

Simon makes a telling comment about the difficulty of finding the right charge to lay against Ssenyonga. "In this case we were pushing the boundaries of criminal law. We were taking conduct that's not traditionally been seen as part of the criminal law and saying that 'Yes, this is criminal.'"

With law books covering the table in the Crown's board room, Simon and Bruce pored over every case they could find that related in the slightest to the transmission of HIV. The pickings were lean, and not always helpful: a handful of ill-fitting precedents in Canada, Britain, Australia, and New Zealand. The United States had a multitude of cases of deliberate HIV infection, but these applied to laws that didn't exist in Canada.

Three of the Canadian trials involving criminal charges around the transmission of the AIDS virus were of little help because of guilty pleas. The HIV-infected man in Ottawa who donated blood pleaded guilty to a charge of common nuisance; the men charged with criminal negligence causing bodily harm in Halifax and Calgary also pleaded guilty. Consequently, it was never established what kind of evidence would have succeeded in obtaining a conviction. Denver Lee, the Toronto intravenous drug user and bisexual who pleaded not guilty to aggravated sexual assault, was acquitted because the woman with whom he had sex had agreed to the intercourse. None of this was particularly helpful to Johnson and Long.

The women infected by Ssenyonga had hoped for something dramatic in the way of charges. Since they saw themselves as the walking dead, they wanted Ssenyonga arrested for attempted murder. Long and Johnson spent no time on that consideration, however. Due to an ancient common law rule still in the Criminal Code, the prosecution probably would have to prove that the accused person intended death to occur within a year and a day of the event. In the first place, there was no evidence that Ssenyonga had murder in mind when he had sex, and in the second, all the women infected for a year and a day were still alive. A manslaughter charge was out of the question: no woman yet had died.

Working down the scale of serious offences, they came to aggravated sexual assault, the most grave of the three classifications of sexual assault in the Criminal Code. It applies when the sexual assault causes wounding, maiming, disfigurement, or puts someone's life in danger. The problem was that all the women, with the single exception of the one who was raped, had agreed to have sex with Ssenyonga.

"The consent issue really had us going back and forth," Long recalls. For Simon, it meant months of slogging in law libraries. Providentially, Long had some expertise in the legal interpretation of consent to intercourse: it had been a law school project. Certainly the women consented to sex, but had they consented to being infected with something that would kill them?

In discussions of the legal meaning of consent, lawyers and judges use the word *vitiate,* meaning the consent was invalidated by some other factor in the situation. In practice, however, courts tend to be dogmatic about consent: it is given or it isn't, with not much between. After much research and discussion, the two lawyers decided that aggravated sexual assault was a good charge if they could prove that consent was vitiated in one or more ways. One was fraud, the argument that had failed in the Denver Lee case in Toronto. Simon Johnson was prepared to argue the legal nuance again in the hope of a better outcome: he would present the case that consent was obtained by fraud because Ssenyonga deceived the women about his HIV status. Johnson thought a good argument could be made as well on the issue of public policy. The law holds that there are certain classes of harm that people cannot consent to having inflicted upon them. A third argument moved the focus from harms to risks. Courts have held that consent to certain activities is a consent to some, but not necessarily all, of the risks that the activity involves. The Ontario Court of Appeal once pondered on this subtlety in the case of a hockey player injured in a brawl. It decided that the hockey player in the legal sense consented to being hurt in regular play, since he knew his sport is brutal, but he did not consent to being injured in a fight. Simon felt that this principle, developed for contact sports, could hold true in other activities: a person could consent to intercourse without consenting to the risk that AIDS would be the result.

The preliminary hearing judge might throw out the reasons for vitiating consent, but the prosecution had to try. The sexual assault charge would grant automatic protection of the identity of the complainants. Terry Hall and Cheryl Wagner had indicated that the women wanted more than that. They were asking that the courtroom be closed while they testified. Such rulings are uncommon but not unknown. Judges have barred the public when national security is involved or the safety of witnesses would be threatened if they showed their faces in public. The poignancy of the women's situation might persuade a judge to take that unusual step. The lawyers hauled out more case law, looking at every closed-courtroom situation on the record for points of similarity. They found little to give them comfort, but they didn't give up on the notion. Something might be bent to fit.

Another possibility occurred: perhaps the judge would accept the use of initials or pseudonyms rather than the women's full names.

In case the judge threw out the aggravated sexual assault charge, which carries penalties ranging up to life imprisonment, the lawyers needed additional charges. These would not bring the benefit of a mandatory publication ban on the identity of witnesses, but Bruce Long reasoned that whatever charge the Crown laid would relate to sexual acts and might therefore entitle the women to protection. A judge might disagree, but Long was confident he could present compelling arguments.

The charge most often laid in other AIDS-related criminal trials was criminal negligence causing bodily harm, which is just one step down from a manslaughter charge. One difficulty with crim-neg, as lawyers call it, was the necessity to prove that Ssenyonga, and no one else, was the source of the women's infection. Another difficulty was a deep uncertainty, extending right up to the Supreme Court of Canada, over what state of mind the Crown had to prove to establish criminal negligence. Serious crimes require the Crown to show both conduct and the state of mind, or what lawyers refer to as *mens rea*, of accused persons at the time of the alleged crime. Criminal negligence requires conduct that shows wanton and reckless disregard for the lives and safety of others. Bruce and Simon were sure they could prove disregard at that level, but it wasn't clear to them whether they would also have to prove that Ssenyonga knew for certain that he was exposing his partners to risk. Maybe, the lawyers speculated, it would be enough if the Crown showed that a reasonable person in Ssenyonga's position would have known. Hosts of lawyers and judges can dance on the heads of those pins.

"Who knew what criminal negligence meant any more?" asks Bruce Long. "It was in flux in 1992, whether there would be an objective standard, a subjective standard, reasonably foreseeable, all those kinds of things."

Still, Long and Johnson decided on a charge of criminal negligence causing bodily harm and another charge, later discarded as redundant, unlawfully causing bodily harm. They added a third charge, committing a common nuisance, used against the Ottawa man who donated his HIV-infected blood to the Red Cross. The last is intended to address acts that endanger the lives and safety of the public.

Conferring with Hall, Ciampini, and David Arntfield, his deputy, Bruce Long decided to add another charge, administering a noxious thing. That was Simon Johnson's inspiration, the fruit of some work done on that law while studying in England. "Essentially it's a poisoning charge," Johnson explains, "and I don't think it's a stretch at all to say that what we have here is a poisoning. I thought it fit."

Throughout the exhausting hours of exploring the alternatives, Long and Johnson were haunted by the knowledge that their work would have been for nothing if the women did not agree to testify. There would be no trial. Long had the legal authority to force them to testify by issuing subpoenas and then, if they failed to appear in court, asking a judge to issue a writ for their arrest. He never gave that option any consideration. "I wouldn't do that," he said flatly. "It was the only time in my career that I didn't subpoena victims. I always do as a safeguard but in this case I would not coerce the women into court."

Lawyers involved in a novel case such as Ssenyonga's are stimulated by the opportunity it offers to change the way laws are interpreted by courts, in effect to write new laws. The law is not as static as it might appear. In lower courts, judges customarily take a literal view of the way the law is written and follow the precedents, but decisions in controversial matters usually are appealed, and can be appealed again all the way to the Supreme Court of Canada. In the end a law that once meant one thing is transformed to mean something lawmakers did not anticipate. That way, courts shape the law to meet situations that didn't exist when the law was enacted.

The legal and ethical crisis of Ssenyonga's behaviour could either result in a new way to apply the existing Criminal Code to cover aberrant sexual behaviour by HIV-infected people, or would push the government to write a new law. In normal circumstances, Long and Johnson could look forward to making legal history however the lower courts decided, but these were not normal circumstances. With the accused and all the complainants infected with

HIV, it was unlikely any would live long enough for the appeal process to be completed.

The Crown's final task was to prepare motions to protect the witnesses. Simon Johnson was assigned to research supportive material to ask the judge to restrict identification of complainants, to restrict publication of evidence, to exclude the public, and to allow the infected women to use pseudonyms or initials.

The theatre for all this activity would be the preliminary hearing, where the Crown would present its case to a judge who would rule on whether the motions were acceptable, the charges appropriate, and the evidence sufficient to commit Charles Ssenyonga to trial.

It was time for the lawyers to meet the women Ssenyonga had infected. Two days, May 28 and May 29, were set aside for these critical sessions. Terry Hall made the arrangements as the lawyers waited, filled with apprehension. They expected the women might look very ill, and even appear close to death. The encounter promised to be harrowing.

The night before the meetings began, Simon Johnson could not sleep. "The hardest thing I have ever had to do as a lawyer," he says, "was to sit down and meet these women, cold, at a point when we didn't even know their names. You just can't admire strongly enough what those women were willing to do to help the prosecution."

Terry Hall warned Bruce Long that the women were nervous. Since everything hinged on their cooperation, Long was anxious to put them at ease. He gave thoughtful consideration even to furniture arrangement. For the sake of informality, he moved one desk out of the room, pushed another against the wall, and rounded up all the comfortable chairs in the department, arranging them roughly in a circle.

Long is blunt and vigorous in his style, not yielding much to the politics of finesse. His demeanour with the women witnesses, however, was consistently gentle and patient, and he readily fell in with any suggestion to make them feel more at ease. His deputy, David Arntfield, invited Ruth Rutherford to the meeting. She is head of the London court's victim-witness assistance program, and experienced in calming agitated witnesses.

The meetings were scheduled in the late afternoon and evening so the women would encounter as few people as possible, and were spaced so they would not meet one another. The OPP's Pat Vooy and Al Ciampini ran a sort of taxi service, meeting planes at the London airport to pick up Jennifer Anderson, Linda Booker, and Francine Dalton, and collecting Joan Estrada in Hamilton by car. Danielle Fitzgerald and Nancy Gauthier, already in London, were picked up at their homes. "It was all very cloak and dagger," Jennifer says.

Ruth Rutherford, thirty-six, a composed and gracious woman, sat on a couch to allow the victims to sit beside her, the only other woman in the room. Also present were Long, Johnson, Arntfield, Hall and Ciampini.

Francine Dalton had the first appointment. Bruce introduced himself and the others, not asking or expecting her to give her name, and launched into a recital of his activities since beginning the case two weeks earlier. Francine's face lit up when he told her what criminal charges were being considered.

Taking his cue from Terry Hall, Long was candid. He told Francine he desperately needed her to testify. She was one of the three women known to be infected after Ssenyonga was notified he was HIV-positive, so the case would be diminished without her. However, he could not guarantee that her identity would be protected. He would do his best to close the courtroom and obtain a publication ban, but he could give no assurance that he would succeed: that was up to a judge and out of his hands.

"This will be over in a year," he assured her. "The preliminary will be held in six to nine months and the trial three months later. It will be wrapped up by the summer of 1992."

Francine is hesitant to make decisions in the best of circumstances. At the conclusion of Long's explanation, she appeared taken aback and confused. She said in her wispy voice, her large glasses sliding down her nose, that she wanted to testify against Ssenyonga but she needed more time to think about it.

Jennifer Anderson arrived next. Although her infection occurred before Ssenyonga was advised he was HIV-positive, she was valuable to the prosecution because her testimony would show the consistent pattern of Ssenyonga's behaviour. "I felt very defensive," she admits. "I felt overwhelmed by all these people who obviously had read my statement and knew every detail of my sexual relationship with Charles."

Cautious and reserved as ever, she too was not ready to make a commitment. She was angry to learn that the statement she made to the police had been released to Ssenyonga's lawyer. "I felt I was on a roller coaster where I no longer had any choice about cooperating. It was 'go with the flow.' I didn't feel those people were on my side."

She told them sharply that she was leaning in the direction of withdrawing from any legal action. "You aren't able to guarantee me any confidentiality," she explained. "If this gets out about me being infected, it will kill my father." At the same time, though, she felt a moral obligation to testify if it would help convict Ssenyonga. She said she would think it over.

Linda Booker was there to size up the Crown lawyers. She was not going to cooperate if it turned out they were lightweights. "I was impressed first with the police," she says in her firm, rational way. "They were not crackpots. They did a proper job of investigation. If the lawyers hadn't also impressed me as being capable and intelligent, I wasn't going to have my life turned inside out for something with no impact."

Of all the women, she seems to have had the best sense that the case would not be an easy one to win. "I was not optimistic about the outcome," she admits, "but I saw that the lawyers were top-notch people. They had integrity. I have a feeling that the brightest and best were drawn to this project."

Joan Estrada came the next morning accompanied by her lawyer, Malcolm Bennett. "Nothing like having ten people in the room when you have to spill your history," she comments laconically of the ordeal, "but they were very professional."

She was firm of purpose; she would cooperate. However, her recollection is that Long didn't stress with her the element of doubt about closing the courtroom. She depended instead on Terry Hall's promise that she could back out, even at the last minute.

Danielle Fitzgerald came next. As the rape survivor, she was potentially the Crown's best witness. "It was scary, all those men," she says. When they explained that they would need to bring evidence about her other sexual partners in order to establish that Ssenyonga was the only one who was infected, Danielle was appalled. It seemed to her that she would look like "some kind of slut." Shaking, she agreed to do it, but a few days later changed her mind. She told Terry Hall, "I can't go through with it."

He hid his disappointment. "I understand," he told her without hesitation.

Danielle was followed by Nancy Gauthier. In preparation for her entrance, Hall and Ciampini, grinning in anticipation, adjusted their chairs to fade into the background. Gauthier strode in, dressed in her best, and fixed Long with a savage glare. She crossed the room, pointed her finger in his face and yelled, "You'd better be fucking good!"

Simon Johnson, a proper young man whom Hall once described affectionately as looking "like a preacher reading from the Bible," was seen to quiver. He was even more shocked a few minutes later when Gauthier, misunderstanding something that he was gravely explaining about sexual assault charges, yelled at him, "I'm HIV. Would you fuck me?"

Terry rose to his feet and gently led Nancy from the room to calm her down. When she returned with him a few minutes later, her good humour was restored and her eyes were dancing with mirth at the stir she had created. That cheery mood lasted only until Johnson politely referred to Ssenyonga as "Mr. Ssenyonga." Gauthier jumped up, outraged. "Don't you call him fucking *mister!*" she shouted at the hapless lawyer.

Johnson was discomfited but moved by the tragedy of the women's infections. "I had never met anyone with HIV," he says quietly. "Dealing with them has made it a very difficult case."

The waiting that followed the interviews was a low point for Bruce Long. "It still wasn't clear that any of them would testify," he says. On May 31, Nancy called him to say she feared for her daughter's future and had not made up her mind. "Still not clear," he noted bleakly in his journal. "Try to get a pseudonym."

It was two weeks before the prosecution knew what it had. Francine Dalton and Linda Booker certainly would testify, Jennifer Anderson, Joan Estrada, and Nancy Gauthier were on the fence, with Anderson the most skittish, and Danielle Fitzgerald was definitely out.

Terry Hall grew impatient, pushing Long to prepare the charges. After a telephone conversation early in June, Bruce Long made a weary note, "I can't move faster. I won't be able to review all the law before Friday morning." Despite the consuming demands of preparing the Ssenyonga case, Long was struggling to keep up with the workload demanded of the head of all the Crown lawyers in eight counties.

The three women infected after Ssenyonga was tested in early 1989 were known in Long's office as complainants or, more frequently, "victims." Jennifer Anderson and Linda Booker, infected before Ssenyonga was tested, were described as "pre-notification witnesses." Their situation, in fact, was even more precarious than that of the victims. Because they would not be named in the sexual assault charges, they had no automatic right to have their privacy protected.

The Crown, however, would not have all its ducks in a row for many months, despite Long's initial optimism about the quickness of the trials. With many of the previous sexual contacts still to be found, the preliminary trial might be a year away. Bruce Long worried that the resolution of the witnesses could waver under the strain of a long delay. That was where Ruth Rutherford became an invaluable asset. The victim witness assistance program, designed to help traumatized victims of violent crimes, would serve the women infected by Ssenyonga well.

The program, which has spread across Ontario, was pioneered in London by the Salvation Army. As rape and family violence cases exploded in numbers, Crown lawyers found that victims, almost always women and children, were often overwhelmed by the prospect of testifying. In 1980 the attorney-general's department took over financial responsibility for the program.

Ruth Rutherford, a lay member of the Salvation Army, was a volunteer with the program at that time, and though only in her twenties she was named its first director. Rutherford, a striking brunette, says her job enables her to fulfil her religion.

At the time of the Ssenyonga trial, the London program was helping some six to eight hundred people a year, victims and witnesses traumatized by their involvement in violent crimes. The function of staff and volunteers was to prepare the Crown's witnesses for the intimidating, abstruse rituals of a criminal trial and to offer reassurance throughout the legal process.

The program office is in a corner on the main floor of the lugubrious London courthouse. In contrast to the gloom of black glass, dark walls, and cold tiles that subdue arrivals at the main doors of the building, Rutherford's space is bright and crammed with the softening delights of child-size furniture, stuffed animals, and posters. Coffee and cookies are set out on the counter, and no one waits long to be greeted.

"The Crown thought the Ssenyonga victims would need help from this office," Rutherford explains. "Most people feel so lost in the court system. The police were very sensitive, very caring — the women see them as heroes — but it was difficult for the women and they needed support."

For months after her first contact with them, the women infected by Ssenyonga told her that they didn't really want to testify and might back out. "They were very hostile, angry women," she says. "Their fear was that their names would become known. Over time I saw them change. They started to see themselves as women who have a voice, who have something to say, who need to tell what happened so other women will recognize that this could happen to anyone."

In addition to the support Rutherford and her office was providing the women, Bruce Long informed each of his witnesses that she could call him any time with questions or concerns. Francine Dalton and Joan Estrada were on the phone a few times a week to ask what was happening, but Nancy Gauthier, frantic after the excruciating ordeal of watching her blood gradually test positive, was in a state close to hysteria. She telephoned Bruce Long as many as eight times a day, and Terry Hall the same.

Sometimes she called to be reassured that efforts would be made to protect her identity. Sometimes she called to ask what was happening. Sometimes she had a perky idea. Instead of calling her Jane Doe in the Section 101 action, how about Marilyn Monroe? Sometimes she called just to chat about whatever was on her mind. Once she called Bruce Long to thank him for being truthful with her. In his note of that call he reminded himself, "She has a right to pull out *any* time. *Try* to get a pseudonym."

Both men took every call. Long says, "I am not exaggerating. I'll bet there were a thousand calls." Then he checked: detailed journals are his hallmark. "Wrong. I kept a record of all the calls and there were four hundred." It just seemed like more.

Terry and Bruce remained affable and gave what comfort a sympathetic listener can provide. Hall slept with his pager beside his bed because Gauthier or another of the women sometimes needed a friendly voice in the middle of the night. Neither showed any resentment of the demands on them during that period. Terry came to regard the women fondly as "my other family."

Francine Dalton, though firmly committed to testifying, grew nervous about her decision. She called one day with a demand: she wanted written assurance, signed by Long, that the trial would be *in camera*, that there would be a publication ban, and that she would be allowed to testify under a pseudonym. Long repeated what he said in the beginning: he could offer no guarantees.

Frustrated and distressed, she consulted Diane Martin at the Parkdale clinic. Martin told her that Bruce Long was right. He couldn't give guarantees because the matter wasn't in his control. All he could do was ask: the judge would decide.

Cheryl Wagner understood their fears. "For the women, it was like stepping off a cliff. They didn't know what would happen."

Joan Estrada, busy with her new job as a phys-ed teacher, called less frequently, but her isolation concerned everyone. She was living and working in a community where she knew no one, and she still had not informed her family or friends that she was infected with HIV. "She was all alone," Hall comments. "We worried about her."

Joan was the slowest to decide to testify. She called Bruce Long one day, her voice strained, to ask if he could be certain that the judge would close the courtroom. He repeated regretfully that it wasn't up to him; he would do his best to get a closed court but Fletcher Dawson was sure to object. She was disappointed, but indecision was wearing her out. "I'll do it," she said with a sigh.

Bruce Long had resigned himself to staying with the case, despite the crushing burden of the extra work. "Since I was the one who had looked the women in the eye and made the promises," he explains, "then I had to be the one who went to court with them."

The courage of the women who testified bears commendation in whatever hall of fame exists for citizens who act out of principle for the public good. The panic they felt over the possibility that their HIV status would be discovered was intensified by the dread that consumed them all: their approaching deaths. Each woman had a different way of handling that horror. Nancy Gauthier's fears spilled out in diatribes about Ssenyonga and her despair that her child would be raised by others; Jennifer Anderson remained buttoned-up and tried to forget that she was ill. The others were somewhere on that continuum, breaking down occasionally, the middle-of-the-night waking periods being the loneliest, but outwardly matter-of-fact. All saw their doctors regularly and waited with suspended breath for the results of the T-4 cell count. They wrote their wills. All suffered fright at the onset of a cold or stomach upsets, seized by panic that it was the beginning of AIDS. Francine Dalton, who like

Danielle Fitzgerald already had AIDS, watched the relentless march of her deterioration: night sweats that soaked her bed, rashes, throat infections, diarrhoea.

Meanwhile, a case very much like the Ssenyonga one was developing in Newfoundland, though none of the facts were yet public. Raymond Mercer, twenty-seven, the town ne'er do well, had been found HIV-positive and was given a warning by public health that he must always wear a condom. Mercer, as authorities learned too late, continued to have unprotected sex and told his many partners that he had tested negative for HIV.

Terry Hall stopped searching for more people infected by Ssenyonga. His tally had risen to seventeen, one of them male. He didn't count rumours, however reliable the source. For instance, many in London believe that Ssenyonga infected more than one man. Francine Dalton guesses that Ssenyonga infected one hundred people.

"He was in Canada for ten years and he was never without a woman," she says. "And the women overlapped. There was one time when he slept with me and Nancy Gauthier on the same day."

Six weeks had passed since Ssenyonga vanished from Toronto's east end. On June 11, 1991, Terry Hall had a conversation with Bruce Long. He knew that Ssenyonga had driven with Margaret Nansamba to Vancouver, but he still didn't know where their quarry could be found in that city. Long worried that Ssenyonga might be infecting someone else, and Hall agreed it was certainly possible. Moreover, Ssenyonga was free legally to do so: the celibacy order served on him did not apply outside Ontario. Terry was worried that Ssenyonga was preparing to flee the country.

It was time to move. With assurances that at least some of the women would testify, Long was in a position to lay criminal charges. The first step was to apply to a justice of the peace for a warrant. The next step would be to locate Ssenyonga and arrest him.

Hall was confident he could find Ssenyonga. He knew a resourceful police officer on the Vancouver force, Detective Grant MacDonald, who would help. Terry's years of working with international police forces to combat drug traffic had provided him with an impressive global network. Like veterans of a nasty and brutish military campaign, they shared a bond. When Terry Hall needed assistance, he got it. Within two days MacDonald had Ssenyonga's address, a rundown Burrard Street hotel where the welfare department paid the rent for homeless people.

On Friday June 14, 1991, Hall and Ciampini conferred with Bruce Long. The decision was made to send the two OPP officers to Vancouver to arrest Ssenyonga on the four charges and bring him back to London. That afternoon the officers picked up arrest warrants to be presented to a justice of the peace in Vancouver. On Monday, they flew to Vancouver.

Hall and Ciampini got their warrant and went the next day to stake out the hotel. While Ciampini watched the front door, Hall went around to the back and eased into a spot near the rear exit. Two Vancouver police, MacDonald and his partner, went into the hotel and knocked on a door. They asked the man who answered if he was Charles Ssenyonga. Ssenyonga acknowledged that he was, and was arrested.

Ssenyonga was cool and polite. "What is this about?" he inquired civilly.

Mindful of Ssenyonga's rights, Hall tried to contact Fletcher Dawson, but time-zone differences made it difficult and he failed to reach the lawyer. The following morning the three men pre-boarded a plane to Toronto, taking the last row of seats in the tail with Ssenyonga between the two officers.

There was little conversation during the five-hour flight. A flight attendant, aware they were police officers with a prisoner, whispered to Hall that there was no plastic cutlery aboard, only metal. Would it be safe to give the prisoner metal cutlery? Hall assured her it was.

"What was that about?" Ssenyonga asked.

"She thought that you might use the knife as a weapon," Terry explained. "The only weapon I'm concerned about is in your pants. You just keep it there."

Hall hustled Ssenyonga into a police car waiting at the airport and drove to London. On the way Hall used his cellular telephone to reach Dawson with the information that his client had been arrested. He also called the women who would testify. Joan Estrada found the message on her answering machine when she returned from work that day: "We've found him, and he has been arrested."

She says, "The feeling of that was just victorious. I could have hit the roof."

An enterprising *London Free Press* photographer, Sue Reeve, caught Ssenyonga entering the Elgin Middlesex Detention Centre. He was wearing a loose black suit over a white T-shirt and his hands were handcuffed before him. A tousled-haired Al Ciampini was leading him by the arm.

The AIDS Committee of London, meanwhile, was distressed. Clarence Crossman, the education coordinator, comments that many people in the organization thought that the police and the media were behaving with undue severity. "We wondered if they were handling the situation that way because he was a Ugandan black man," Clarence says. "We feared it might have been very different had he been a white, middle-class man born in Canada. There seemed to be a punitive dimension to everything they were doing."

Michael Sauer, fund raiser at the AIDS Committee, concurs. "There seemed to be a lynch mentality. The attitude was that the problem of irresponsible transmission of HIV was solved by blaming this man."

Fletcher Dawson arrived at the jail a half hour after Ssenyonga was locked in a cell. After meeting with Ssenyonga, Dawson spoke to reporters waiting for him. He told them that his client had not run away. In fact he had returned to London the month before to talk to his lawyer. His purpose in going to Vancouver was to seek better medical attention than was available in London and to visit friends. Ssenyonga would have returned voluntarily if the police had asked him.

Dawson added indignantly that he had yet to see "a twit of evidence" that Charles Ssenyonga had continued to have sex after learning he was infected.

Nancy Gauthier, reading this in the *Free Press,* took umbrage. She telephoned Dawson with the intention of asking him if he was calling her a twit, but the exchange got out of hand. Though Fletcher tried valiantly to end it, and committed the call to tape, Nancy was too upset to contain herself.

"You're just trying to get famous. Ssenyonga is not going to win this case," she shouted, "and when he goes down, you'll go down too. Don't be standing too close."

Dawson, shaken, asked, "Are you saying that you are going to shoot my client?"

Nancy was taken aback. "No," she responded, confused.

Dawson reported the threatening call to the police, who paid Nancy a visit. Bruce Long, embarrassed by the incident, sternly instructed her not to call Fletcher again.

It is impossible to know if the police and media would have behaved differently if Ssenyonga had been a white man. Comparisons with the case in Newfoundland, where Raymond Mercer escaped much media attention, are not useful. The period between Mercer's arrest and trial was brief, and the trial a quick one because he admitted guilt; it was over almost as soon as it began. On the other hand, more than two years elapsed between the time Charles Ssenyonga first emerged in the public eye and the end of his long trial. Ssenyonga's possession of a passport and Nancy Gauthier's assurance that he had a plane ticket to Uganda raised legitimate concern that he planned to leave the country, so the arrest in Vancouver was not gratuitous.

Across the country, AIDS organizations were backing off. The Ssenyonga case was proving to be a nettle only a fool would grasp. A press conference in Toronto that would have involved major AIDS organizations was cancelled when the spokespeople got qualms. The London AIDS Committee, however, was still responding when asked for comment. Clarence Crossman explains, "We thought playing it safe would not serve the needs of people with HIV and AIDS. If we could say something balanced, that would be helpful. The quotes coming from our office were along the lines that this was a more complicated issue than it appeared on the surface. We were not comfortable to simply blame Ssenyonga. Neither did we think it appropriate to blame the victims."

The Ugandan community in London was in a similar state of confusion. While appalled at the notoriety their countryman had attracted and how it reflected on all Ugandans, they resolutely decided to support him. Chris Karuhanga, representing them all, went to see Ssenyonga in jail. Though the relationship between the two former partners was chilly, Chris sincerely offered comfort in the crisis Ssenyonga faced. He expressed his regret that he could not attend the bail hearing. He was scheduled to leave the next day for west Africa and his travel plans could not be changed on such short notice. Connie Neill volunteered to be Karuhanga's replacement. She met members of the Ugandan community to discuss raising bail money and finding a place for Charles to stay upon his release from custody.

Fletcher Dawson cautioned the Ugandans that the person offering shelter would have to impress the justice of the peace as being a solid citizen. The Ugandans were not certain that any of them would qualify as such to a white official. Nina Rochon came forward to offer her address. She was a perfect candidate, a nurse who was a medical missionary in Uganda and was planning to return to Africa in two months. Ssenyonga, she said, was welcome to stay with her and her missionary friends until that time. A Ugandan couple was found to post the bail.

Ugandan custom requires that the elder of the community attend in times of trouble, but the elder in London had a daytime job he couldn't leave. It was unthinkable that Ssenyonga be left alone, but no Ugandan was available. Connie offered to fill the gap. As she was known as Chris Karuhanga's girlfriend, the arrangement was acceptable in the emergency.

When the Ugandan couple found themselves unable to provide bail money after all, Connie leaped to help with that too. She delivered to Fletcher Dawson's office an inventory of the stored goods from The African Store, which could be offered as surety on the bail. One piece alone, a chair, was valued at more than $3,000.

Early on the morning of the bail hearing, Connie received a telephone call from a lawyer in Dawson's office. Someone was needed to post cash as part of the bail package. Could she help? She gathered what she had, $300, and went to court. She says simply, "I have always been there for Charles."

According to Connie, Ssenyonga was relieved that no Ugandans were present at the hearing. When Ugandans realized that he didn't want them around, some were puzzled and others offended. Whatever Ssenyonga's reasons, and shame must have been a factor, from that day on he seemed content to depend entirely on Connie Neill. Ugandans withdrew.

"He didn't want to embroil any of them in his problems," Connie explains sympathetically. "He didn't even want them to post the bail."

The bail hearing took place the next morning before a justice of the peace, James P. Zavitz. David Arntfield, acting chief Crown in the absence of Bruce Long, opened the proceedings by requesting a publication ban on the identities of the three complainants, though their names were not specified in the charges. Fletcher Dawson had no objection to a publication ban but found it absurd that such an order was being requested without the Crown producing any of the names to be protected. He said to Zavitz, "My friend is really asking your worship to make an order in the dark, and then to make an order which is not enforceable because it doesn't name anybody... You are being asked to make an order no one understands."

A day of arguments followed, with Dawson fighting to have the names entered into the record before the ban was issued. The hearing resumed the next morning with a new Crown lawyer, Geoffrey Beasley, a loose-limbed, lanky, freckled redhead. Arntfield was absent on another matter and Beasley was filling in. By a coincidence that happens not infrequently in courtrooms, Beasley and Dawson are friends and golf together.

Geoff Beasley was an auspicious substitute: he shines in cases involving scientific or psychiatric evidence, and the Ssenyonga case was to consist heavily of both. An "army brat," as he puts it, Geoff was raised on army bases in Canada and Germany. He's a gangly six-foot-five man in his early forties with an easy-going nature that belies the acuity of his intellect. After dropping out of university he worked a number of jobs, including prison guard and clerk. Then he enrolled in a community college, studying photography. "When my colleagues see my scholastic record," he notes, "they shake their heads."

Photography jobs being scarce, he began work on an undergraduate degree at Carleton University which included an introduction to law course. He decided law was fun. On an impulse during his second year of university, he wrote the admission exams for law school and scored so spectacularly that he was accepted at two universities, one of them the University of Western Ontario in London. He was twenty-seven when he entered law school at Western without having completed an undergraduate degree.

After his call to the bar he worked in a mixed practice for a while and then in 1985 joined the London office of the attorney-general. Early on Geoff prosecuted a string of arson cases, where he developed a fascination for scientific evidence.

"With arson you have to understand the use of accelerants and the basic rules of fire," he says. "It's more complicated than just 'the house burned down.'"

His next areas of specialty were trials and inquests involving medical and psychiatric evidence. That leap occurred when a diplomat died in a London hospital and Geoff was the Crown lawyer at the inquest. To prepare, Geoff spent two days at the Ottawa Heart Institute learning about heart surgery. As a souvenir, he has a thoracic catheter on his office wall.

"I've had crash courses in a lot of areas of science since then." He grins happily.

Fletcher Dawson, treating his friend with icy courtesy, announced at the bail hearing that the Crown, through Beasley, had offered him a compromise. The Crown would continue to conceal the identities of the women for the purpose of the hearing but Dawson had received the women's names and copies of their statements.

Dawson told Zavitz, the justice of the peace, that he accepted this offer though, as he added testily, he wasn't given much time to consider. He declared, "There is a real danger that this case is being treated differently than others in our system. It raises the spectre of unequal justice." He said he was conceding only because his main concern was to get his client out of jail.

Fletcher gave no inkling that he had received an unsettling surprise. When he read the three affidavits, he could not escape the realization that his client had lied to him about being celibate. It was clear from the consistency of the stories and their damning detail that Ssenyonga had violated the Section 22 order. When Fletcher confronted Ssenyonga about being untruthful, Ssenyonga denied it. He continued to insist that he was being wrongly accused. Dawson admits now, without expression, that his client didn't acknowledge guilt "until well along in the criminal process."

Dawson accepts that being misled by a client is an occupational hazard. "When you do this work for years and years and years, it's part of what you do," he says. "Criminal lawyers know that they are going to see something on the Crown's side that they haven't learned from their clients. I wasn't surprised and shocked. But then I am never surprised and shocked."

With Ssenyonga staunchly maintaining that someone else had infected the women, Dawson had to agree that it was not outside the realm of possibility. Although "things appeared to be fitting together from the prosecution's side of the case," as Dawson put it delicately, meaning that the roof was crashing on the defence, he clung to the element of reasonable doubt that Ssenyonga was the source of the infection. The onus was on the Crown to prove otherwise, and Fletcher couldn't see how that could be done with any certainty.

Just the same, Dawson now had a very different situation on his hands. His client was not the totally innocent man he had believed he was representing. That did not mean, however, that Ssenyonga was not entitled to the best defence Dawson could devise. Reviewing his diminished options, Dawson decided that the weakest elements of the Crown's case were the charges themselves. He thought they were all a house of cards except for one, criminal negligence causing bodily harm. There wasn't a shred of evidence that Ssenyonga had set out to harm anyone, and the fact that the sex was consensual should knock out the sex assault charges.

With the help of law students, paralegals, and other lawyers in his firm, Dawson began researching the legal ramifications of consent.

10

DETECTIVE-SERGEANT ALBERT CIAMPINI of the Ontario Provincial Police was the first witness in the bail hearing before Justice of the Peace James P. Zavitz to determine if Charles Ssenyonga would remain in jail. The burly officer testified that Ssenyonga was arrested because the police had reason to fear that he was planning to leave the country for Uganda. He then outlined the evidence he and Terry Hall had obtained from women, not named, each of whom described an affair with Ssenyonga and infection with HIV.

Fletcher Dawson's cross-examination was aggressive. He drew from Ciampini the admission that police had not found Ssenyonga in possession of a ticket to leave the country, the inference being that they had no reason to put him in jail. This was a stretch, since Ssenyonga informed a number of people that he had an airline ticket, but the defence lawyer's suggestion that police overreacted hung in the air.

Fletcher noted scornfully that the infected women gave their full consent to the sex acts. Therefore, he declared, the charge under which Ssenyonga was deprived of his freedom did not fit within the legal boundaries of sexual assault. "This is different from any sexual assault case you have been involved with as a police officer in all these years?" he said smoothly to Ciampini.

The officer could only reply, "Yes."

"You must be aware in fact that there have been higher court decisions in Ontario that have indicated that sexual assault charges cannot be made out where you have consent to the sexual act."

"Yes."

"And you are probably aware that courts of appeal in other provinces have ruled to the same effect."

"Yes."

"So really it is fair to say that what we've got potentially in this case is something pretty new?"

"Correct."

"It is new to everybody. It is new to the police."

"Correct," said Ciampini stolidly.

"And it is undoubtedly new to the lawyers on both sides of the case?"

"Yes."

"Undoubtedly new to people who might find themselves sitting where Mr. Ssenyonga is sitting?"

"Yes."

Dawson's questions implied that many of the women had hotly pursued Ssenyonga and therefore bore some responsibility for their misfortunes. Next, he hammered away at the possibility that the women were infected by someone else, not Ssenyonga. Ciampini unhappily plodded through his replies.

Then Ssenyonga took the stand. He gave his name as Charles Muleka Ssenyonga and his age as thirty-four. He was steered by Dawson through a chronological account of his life in Uganda and his coming to Canada. He described his long struggle in Canada to escape poverty, culminating in the collapse of The African Store.

"We couldn't pay ourselves out of the store so it was a matter of struggling to have other jobs on the side," he said.

"I did some kind of social work. I worked for Canada Post on a casual basis, sorting mail at night." Between December 1989 and February 1990, the store was closed. It reopened briefly and then collapsed for the second and last time. During this period Ssenyonga said he was active in the community, appearing on television and radio to talk about Ugandan music and art.

The questions moved to his decision to live in Vancouver. Ssenyonga testified that his relationship with Margaret Nansamba was platonic. He went with her to Vancouver, he said, to seek medical treatment.

Ssenyonga emerged under Dawson's deft questioning as a helpless, good man who was being persecuted by police, Crown lawyers, and the media. The arrest in Vancouver was unnecessary, Ssenyonga was saying, and the publicity in London was undue. Dawson commented on Ssenyonga's "name being published again and again in the newspapers after the *London Free Press* decided it should publish it, is that right? And the photographs of you were published?"

"Yes," said Ssenyonga.

"You became aware that even on the television news, your picture was there?"

"That's right."

"Did that make life difficult for you?"

"It made it very difficult. It made it difficult in terms of my relations with people and made it difficult for me socially. But it is harder, it is impossible to find work. More or less impossible. The moment I would approach an employer they would ask me if I was the person they had seen on the news."

Ssenyonga said he went to Vancouver because "it was going to be impossible to live the life I'd known in Ontario, in London specifically. I would find it hard to get medical treatment that I would feel comfortable with. In London my whole medical situation was tied up with the assertions and claims of the legal proceedings. I wanted to find a doctor I could approach as just me."

Geoff Beasley conducted the cross-examination, this time as a permanent replacement for David Arntfield. Arntfield was dropping off the prosecution team after spending a prodigious amount of time on the case because he was carrying an added burden of filling in for vacationing Bruce Long as regional director. Beasley was intrigued by the assignment. "These victims were different from any victims in any other kind of case," he comments. "They had been victimized in a way that made them stand apart. Basically, I suppose, they were given a death sentence. We didn't know much about HIV at that time and we thought they would not live long, maybe not long enough to testify."

Geoff Beasley's cross-examination of Ssenyonga was intended to show the judge that the accused was not as honourable and upright as his testimony had indicated. The Crown lawyer drew from Ssenyonga the information that he owed more than $6,000 in London, the largest creditor being the Royal Bank. Ssenyonga admitted that he had applied for welfare in Vancouver and had requested that his unemployment insurance payments be forwarded to him from Ontario. Beasley challenged Ssenyonga's explanation that he was in Vancouver to seek medical expertise. Was Dr. Iain Mackie not a leading authority on AIDS? Ssenyonga replied that he wanted to find someone who was not as busy as Mackie, someone to give him "personal attention" and "address my problem on a one-to-one basis."

And was Ssenyonga aware that a celibacy order in Ontario would not apply in British Columbia?

"That never occurred to me at all," Ssenyonga, a law student for four years, responded evenly. "I actually had imagined that the order applied everywhere."

Nina Rochon, a twenty-four-year-old nurse and medical missionary, then testified that Charles Ssenyonga could live at her home if the justice of the peace released him from jail. She met Ssenyonga soon after she returned from Uganda, she said, where she was with a team immunizing children. She did not have a sexual affair with him, she said, but they were friends.

When Beasley tried to shake her faith in Ssenyonga's honesty, she spoke up spunkily. "I believe that if he agreed to something, he would do it."

The bail hearing continued after the lunch break, with Michael Thompson replacing Dawson, who was needed in Toronto to argue another Ssenyonga matter. The justice of the peace was ready with his decision. Zavitz announced that after carefully balancing the rights of the public and Ssenyonga's rights as an individual, he was releasing the accused. He then made a curious statement that disconcerted Crown lawyers.

"I would not want to be the prosecutor in these matters," he said, "because I feel the probability of conviction is really not strong in the majority of the charges, and that has had a lot to do with my final decision."

Zavitz released Ssenyonga from jail and ordered him to surrender his passport and remain in Canada, reporting to the London city police "each and every Sunday." Also, Ssenyonga was not to "indulge in any sexual intercourse with anyone."

"Do you understand, Mr. Ssenyonga?"

Ssenyonga said, "I do, Your Worship."

"And will you comply?"

"I will."

Bail was set at $5,000. Connie Neill filled out the form — "Bail $300; without deposit $4,700" — and signed it. She turned over the $300 she brought with her, and Charles Ssenyonga left a free man.

When Nancy Gauthier heard that Ssenyonga had been released, she was furious. Her wild emotional state had an adverse effect on her immune system, causing a collapse that evidenced itself as a severe case of hives, a not-uncommon reaction in HIV-infected people.

Martha Allen, Ssenyonga's seventyish retired school-teacher friend, was relieved that Charles was out of jail. The newspaper photograph of him in handcuffs was her first intimation that he was in trouble. The allegations against him bewildered her. "This is a pity," she thought. "This is a very bright man." Some time later Martha saw Charles in a supermarket and greeted him kindly. He seemed touched and grateful that she didn't snub him. She felt it would be "rotten" to hurt him that way.

Fletcher Dawson, meanwhile, was fighting for Ssenyonga on all fronts. The afternoon of the successful bail hearing, he drove to Toronto to appear before an Osgoode Hall judge to ask that Ssenyonga be allowed to appeal the interim Section 101 order banning him from having sex. He argued before Justice Douglas Lissaman that the order should not have been made because the Crown had produced no evidence to prove that Ssenyonga was not celibate as he claimed. Lissaman adjourned to think about it. The next day be delivered his verdict. Dawson was right: Ssenyonga had grounds to appeal the order.

Cheryl Wagner, fascinated with the novelty of the biochemical research that Michael Montpetit was doing in Ottawa, often talked to him about his progress. He was discouraged, he said. The method used to break down the DNA of the virus found in the victims of the Florida dentist simply didn't work on the virus from the women Ssenyonga infected, and he didn't know why.

Early in July, Al Ciampini was replaced as Terry Hall's sidekick by Detective-Sergeant Christopher Lewis, a husky, laconic redhead with watchful eyes, a newcomer to the investigative branch. With Pat Vooy about to go on maternity leave, the critical assignment given the reconstituted OPP crew was to repeat the HIV tests on the previous sexual contacts of the women who would testify at Ssenyonga's trial. All but one of the twenty former sex partners had given blood samples to their family doctors, and all of them tested negative, but this would not be good enough at the trial. An alert defence attorney, and Dawson certainly was that, would protest that the blood samples could have been switched with others in the doctors' offices. The tests would have to be repeated with Terry Hall present to guarantee the integrity of the process.

This time the police team left nothing to chance. Each man was photographed in the act of giving a blood sample, with Terry Hall standing in the picture. Hall then took personal charge of the blood sample and delivered it himself to Rick Galli.

It was a costly undertaking. One man had moved to Honduras; one to Mexico. The one in Mexico could not be brought back to Canada for the test because of his immigration status. Terry Hall called a friend of his in United States customs, another old buddy of the drug wars, and the sexual contact was flown to Atlanta, Georgia, where Hall witnessed his blood being drawn.

One man was flown to Toronto from the United States. Terry Hall met him and telephoned Cheryl Wagner from the airport. "We'll be right there," he said. "Can you be ready to take his blood?" She said she would wait in her office. It was a long wait. Hall and his bewildered subject were tangled for hours in the security measures at the airport for the arrival of another American, President George Bush.

With one exception, all the men cooperated, though none was obliged to assist the investigators, and all nineteen who gave blood signed releases. The single holdout was a tense, excitable man, his unsteady frame of mind owing to a severe head injury, who said he would never, never give his blood. He saw in the request some kind of a plot against him. Somehow, in the confusion of preparing for trial, he was forgotten.

Meanwhile, the Crown was trying to put Ssenyonga back in jail. Geoff Beasley appeared before Judge J. F. McGarry on July 15, 1991, with a motion to have Justice of the Peace Zavitz's controversial bail order revoked. The hitch in the proceedings was that Dawson couldn't attend and Ssenyonga refused to accept the substitute he sent, Michael Thompson.

"The case is unusual in many respects," Beasley said in his easy-going manner, "not the least of which is that the charges are somewhat unique. I suppose that Mr. Ssenyonga naturally would want Mr. Dawson to have carriage," meaning, the Crown could understand that Ssenyonga preferred to have Dawson present because the case raised so many complex and novel legal questions.

The matter was adjourned to August 9, when it was heard by Judge William A. Jenkins. Bruce Long appeared for the Crown to argue that Ssenyonga be returned to jail to await the preliminary trial, scheduled for November 12, citing as a compelling reason the need to protect the public.

Fletcher Dawson objected, pointing out that the Crown still had produced no evidence to show that Ssenyonga was having sex with anyone.

"I had to fight like crazy to get him out of jail," Dawson recalls grimly. "The Crown wanted to keep him there."

Fletcher succeeded. Jenkins upheld the Zavitz decision in every particular. "I agree with the view expressed by the learned justice of the peace," he said, to the horror of the prosecution team. "The Crown will have difficulty obtaining convictions on some or all of these charges." Further, he agreed with Dawson that in the absence of any evidence that Ssenyonga was not complying with the celibacy order, he deserved to remain free.

Many lawyers were surprised that a judge would predict the outcome of a trial. Jenkins's pessimism about the worth of the Crown's case threw a pall over spirits in Bruce Long's office. As a direct consequence, the investigation became more extensive, more time-consuming, more painstaking, and much more expensive. Despite the scepticism of a justice of the peace and a judge, Bruce Long was determined to make the charges stick. Investigators became almost fanatical in the precautions they took to protect the sanctity of evidence that was being gathered.

The women Ssenyonga infected also were appalled by the judge's comments. It chilled their opinion of the justice system, already far from cordial. "He is going to go on infecting people," Nancy Gauthier wailed. She was seething at the judge and enraged too at the Middlesex-London public health unit, which she blamed for her infection. As she saw it, the authorities knew Ssenyonga was infected, and knew he was having unprotected sex, and still left him free to infect her.

London public health officials asked for a meeting with Nancy to talk about her Jane Doe testimony. In a belligerent mood, and accompanied by her lawyer, Malcolm Bennett, she listened patiently as the public health protection act was explained to her.

"Excuse me," she said when the summary ended, "but I don't understand how I was left to be hurt in 1991. The sex ban that you had on Ssenyonga made a joke of my life. And as far as I am concerned, public health can kiss my HIV foot." With that, she left and slammed the door behind her. Since then, her relations with the Middlesex-London health unit cannot be described as cordial. (In May, 1994, Gauthier sued the health unit for $3,000,000 for failing to protect her from Ssenyonga. The unit, with a new and accessible Medical Officer of Health, Dr. Graham Pollett, fought back. In November, 1994, the health unit went before a judge in

London to argue that Gauthier's suit missed the statutory limit of six months and therefore should not proceed. Justice Michael Meehan agreed instead with Gauthier's lawyer, who pleaded the extenuating circumstances in a most unusual case, and said the suit could proceed to trial.)

On August 27, Ssenyonga appeared before the Ontario Health Protection Appeal Board. Before he could argue that Section 22 violated the Charter, Fletcher had to get the board's agreement to hear the appeal despite the fact that the time permitted for filing had expired. The Ministry of Health had decided not to oppose his application, but the three-person panel, consisting of two lawyers and a school-teacher, wanted to explore the precedent of allowing a late appeal. Most of a day was taken with this question.

Ssenyonga testified on his own behalf, earnestly pleading that he be allowed to resume sexual relations. He wished to marry a woman who knew of his HIV infection and wanted to marry him. The sex ban "diminished what little hope there is," he said. He made an extraordinary comment: he said that celibacy offended him because it was "something that goes against what being human is all about."

He added sorrowfully, "The issue right now is, how can I do that [get married] without offending society?" Asked why he did not appeal the ban sooner, he replied that he was too "flabbergasted" by the celibacy order. Witnesses to the hearing were struck by Ssenyonga's charm, a word used by almost every woman who ever knew him. One reporter recalls that Ssenyonga had "dynamism."

The hearing was covered by one of the London Free Press's brightest young reporters, Debora Van Brenk, who afterwards made the Ssenyonga case her own. Her crisp, clear, authoritative coverage of the Ssenyonga drama for her newspaper and on Peter Gzowski's CBC radio show "Morningside" were widely admired in the business. A whip-thin, athletic twenty-seven-year-old with an expressive face and gamin grin, Debora brings to journalism integrity, detachment, inquisitive intellect, and acute observation.

She had been with the *Free Press* for four years when the Ssenyonga case broke. When the Health Protection Appeal Board hearings opened, editors were faced with a dilemma. No one knew whether to classify the story as a health and environment subject, or a justice subject, or a breaking news story. Because of the strong AIDS component, the decision went to health, and Debora got the assignment since she was covering that field.

She began promisingly with a scoop, the first and only press interview Ssenyonga ever gave. During a recess, she spotted him standing by himself and approached with a question about his marriage plans. He replied that he had no comment. She said, her face a mask of innocent interest, "Why not?" Ssenyonga became loquacious. She found him exceedingly self-assured, and while he seemed bewildered by the process, he also gave the impression that he considered the whole uproar a mere misunderstanding that would soon be resolved. At one point he said sadly, "This continues to be a very difficult situation for me and for those who are close to me."

Ssenyonga seemed prepared to go on chatting, with Debora taking notes, but Fletcher Dawson saw what was happening and led him away.

Paula Adamick, a stringer for the *Toronto Star,* covered the same hearing. Her account of it noted Dawson's explanation to the tribunal that his client didn't understand the seriousness of the celibacy order because it was issued by the Health Ministry, not the courts. Ssenyonga also said he was so upset to find himself HIV-positive that he was not thinking straight. It was a hint that Ssenyonga planned to present himself as a simple, confused man.

It was a lively hearing. John Judson, lawyer for the Middlesex-London health unit, called Ssenyonga a liar and described him as "a deceitful person, a seductive person." Fletcher Dawson retorted that Judson's comments were "outrageous."

The three-person tribunal decided to allow Ssenyonga to appeal the Section 22 ban. The appeal hearing was scheduled for January, 1992, two months after the commencement of Ssenyonga's preliminary hearing on criminal charges. Pending also was the appeal of the interim Section 101 order. Fletcher Dawson was obliged to prepare simultaneously on three fronts.

He had scarcely begun research when Geoff Beasley notified him that Dr. Michael Montpetit, an Ottawa biochemist, was working on the DNA of the virus found in the blood of the complainants and might be ready to testify at the preliminary. Fletcher then was obliged to learn about molecular biology. He made a few calls to major laboratories and university research centres around the continent and was stunned by what he found. "There were only about five people in all of North America who understood what Montpetit was doing," he groans.

The woman Ssenyonga described to the media as his fiancée was Constance Neill, then twenty-five. Abruptly, while Chris Karuhanga was still in Africa, she had decided her relationship with him was over. She was not moving with Chris to his new teaching job in another city, as the two had planned only weeks earlier. She had fallen deeply in love with Charles Ssenyonga.

It started when Connie drove Ssenyonga from the jail after his release. She took him to the home of Nina Rochon and helped him get settled there. He called the next day to thank her and she invited him to dinner. He said that would be wonderful. Rochon had numerous cats and he was allergic to cats, so he was suffering. She told him her apartment had an empty bedroom with its own bathroom. If he wanted to stay overnight, he was welcome. He arrived with luggage and spent the next few days with her. Ssenyonga showed surprise and appreciation when she cooked Ugandan food for him: raw peanuts boiled slowly for two hours, rice, green bananas cooked and served like potatoes, lamb.

His emotional state alarmed her and brought out her maternal instincts. In contrast to his normal lucidity, he was rambling, and some of the things he said made no sense. She wondered if AIDS was affecting his brain. Ssenyonga returned to Nina's but complained of the cats and the throngs of guests in that hospitable household. Connie invited him to move in with her and he accepted gratefully.

"Charles was a vagabond," Connie says. "He was always moving, sometimes living in apartments he couldn't afford, sometimes in dumps, often sleeping in The African Store car in some parking lot. He belonged nowhere. He was in such a state I wanted to take care of him."

Connie says she was having doubts about Chris Karuhanga even before Charles Ssenyonga touched her heart. She felt Charles was a more sophisticated man with broader interests. He was stimulating on such subjects as religion and philosophy, both of which fascinated Connie, who was avidly learning about Buddhism and the Koran. "Chris was just too much a Roman Catholic for me," she explains.

The decisive moment came when Ssenyonga accidentally, it seemed, referred to the girlfriend and child Chris had left in Ottawa. Connie was shocked. Chris had never mentioned these people, and she was furious that he had not been open with her. She decided she would break it off with Chris as soon as he returned.

Ssenyonga settled into the apartment and she became his constant attendant, driving him to medical and legal appointments. Since Connie was working night shifts at Grace

Villa Hospital, her days were free to assist Ssenyonga, who appeared to be seriously disoriented. Charles couldn't seem to remember his doctor's instructions or grasp what Fletcher Dawson was saying to him. Connie became note-taker, decision-maker and keeper of the agenda.

Leslie-Anne Jenkins, when she heard of the overseer role that Connie played, was mystified. "That simply wasn't like Charles," she said, shaking her head. "He was always very independent, very much in charge of what he was doing."

Some speculate that Charles Ssenyonga was pretending to be helpless and confused in order to evoke Connie's sympathy, but it also is possible that the shock of his arrest and confinement had triggered a reaction in his vulnerable immune system, destabilizing him emotionally. Confusion is a common symptom of AIDS. Whatever the cause, his shaken condition was appealing to Connie.

Martha Allen, an astute, humorous woman, once said of Connie, "Connie's one for causes. She's like Clara Barton and Florence Nightingale rolled into one. She'll get over it, if she survives."

"I stayed with Charles out of human compassion," Connie explains with shining eyes. "I felt a calling. Charles had no one and he was facing so much. His behaviour at that time was very weird, very strange. Something told me, 'This is where you are needed' — and I answered the calling."

When Chris returned late in August from Africa, he was desolate to learn that Connie was ending the relationship. For a while he slept in their old bedroom and Connie moved to a couch in the living room. People close to Karuhanga at the time speak of his grief. Chris had nowhere live until the end of September when his place in the nearby city would be available, so Connie accommodatingly offered to move out with Ssenyonga. She went looking for something cheap to rent.

She was indifferent to the fact that Ssenyonga had AIDS. His HIV status was not even discussed between them, she says. "It was never an issue with us. For me, I would never leave a relationship because a man was HIV-positive, whether I was positive or not. I would never want to know whether I am positive or not. I am not interested in getting tested." She did check her T-4 cell count, however, and found her immune system was in the normal range. She decided that was all she needed to know about her health.

Her blithe attitude came from something she picked up from Ssenyonga, a belief that HIV was not the direct cause of AIDS. Following his arrest he became a strong proponent of the radical theory that passing along HIV infection doesn't in itself harm people. He convinced Connie that she had nothing to fear from HIV: HIV-positive people who take care of themselves will never get AIDS.

At his urging, Connie began reading books and articles by a handful of scientists who maintain that the cause of AIDS is unknown. A leading champion of this view is Peter Duesberg, a California expert on retroviruses, of which group HIV is one.

"Getting AIDS has to do with your lifestyle choices," Connie asserts firmly. "It has to do with your nutrition, your substance abuse, it's all those things. And Charles and I were not in those risk groups."

The couple rented a lovely beach house in Port Stanley on Lake Erie, where they lived until winter. Connie found work in a nearby nursing home and Ssenyonga applied for welfare. Because his immune system had vanished off the scale, registering a T-4 cell count of zero, he had no difficulty qualifying as a disabled person. Despite his insistence that HIV did not cause AIDS, Charles Ssenyonga had full-blown AIDS. Connie was not daunted. She believed she could restore Ssenyonga's immune system with good food and daily exercise.

Nina Rochon insisted that Ssenyonga get in touch with the AIDS Committee of London for counselling. Despite the agency's prestige, Ssenyonga was reluctant to approach the group. The organization was for gay men, he said, and he emphatically wasn't gay. Informed that one of the staff, Michael Sauer, was heterosexual, Ssenyonga agreed to see him. Sauer came to Connie's apartment in London just before the Port Stanley move.

"Mike became our friend, really," Connie says warmly.

Mike Sauer is an assured, attractive man in his forties who was raised in a low-income area of London and holds three university degrees. He taught high school English briefly and then worked in a cross-cultural learning centre helping Southeast Asians settle in London. Then, because of his experience as a community worker, he was hired by the Oxford county board of health as an AIDS educator. That put him in close communication with the AIDS Committee of London, where he later went to work as a fund-raiser.

He is such an anomaly in that organization that sometimes gay men make sexual overtures, assuming he must be gay. Mike has various responses depending on the situation, but usually he says with a friendly smile, "I'm straight, but don't hold that against me."

Married to a Chinese woman from Singapore, Mike is accustomed to the complexity of cross-cultural relationships. He has sympathy for Ssenyonga's difficulties in a society dominated by whites. He thinks Ssenyonga may not have accepted, in his core, that he was infectious. Other cultures have very different beliefs about diseases, he explains. "The modern Western model of disease transmission is new in the world. It's only a few generations old. The overlayering of Western thinking about infection, even among sophisticated Africans, doesn't always work."

In Port Stanley, Constance Neill and Charles Ssenyonga became lovers. Safe in her conviction that a healthy lifestyle would prevent AIDS, Connie had no fear of becoming infected with HIV. For his part, Charles appeared to be indifferent that he was under the Section 22 restraining order and the interim Section 101 order not to have sex.

11

PRELIMINARY HEARINGS ARE NOT TRIALS: they are test runs of the Crown's case designed to give the defence lawyers a look at what they are up against. A decision in 1991 by the Supreme Court of Canada tightened the rules of prosecutorial disclosure, with the result that defence attorneys emerge from preliminary hearings better prepared, which makes trials speedier. Judges at preliminaries must determine if the Crown has a case solid enough to justify sending the accused to trial. The judges also decide if the charge or charges are appropriate for the alleged crime.

In the weeks leading up to November 12, 1991, the date set for Ssenyonga's preliminary, the accused man presented a calm, assured exterior but, according to Connie Neill, he was drained. "What gets mistaken as aloofness in him is really exhaustion," she explained. "At the time of the preliminary trial he was exhausted physically, emotionally, intellectually, with having to grapple with what was happening to him."

Preparing Ssenyonga for the ordeal, Neill compelled him to go for long walks with her every day and she fed him foods she believes have properties to boost the immune system. She persuaded him to quit smoking cigarettes, which she detests; he took up a pipe instead. She noted with amusement that Charles had grown attached to a baseball cap that concealed his thinning hair.

She was always with Ssenyonga when he met with Fletcher Dawson because the two men, both with legal training, often disagreed. She explains, "Charles and Fletcher were not on the same wavelength." Sometimes she had to prod Charles to return Fletcher's telephone calls.

Fletcher told them he was confident the judge at the preliminary would dismiss all the charges but criminal negligence. The others, he said, were ridiculous.

"I think the Crown just threw in every charge they could think of, including the kitchen sink," he comments. "This is one of those cases that comes along where there is a lot of public interest and political pressure behind the thing. And the orders come down from the top so everybody starts to play hardball and they pull out the stops."

The noxious thing charge, he felt, was faulty because the Crown would never be able to prove that Ssenyonga intended to harm the women. The common nuisance charge was wrong because it requires proof that the offender endangered the public. "It just didn't really apply," Dawson says with exasperation. "There was not a shred of evidence that my client intended to endanger the public or deliberately pass this virus."

Dawson was most impatient with the aggravated sexual assault charge. "There was consent. My client had real relationships with those women. They weren't one-night stands. They consented to sexual contact."

Besides, he couldn't see how the Crown with any certainty could prove that Ssenyonga caused the infections. "How do you prove that a particular person was infected by a particular accused?" Dawson asked. "You have to find every one of the victim's sexual contacts, get in touch with those persons, get a sample of their blood, show that they are not HIV-infected, and on and on and on."

Ssenyonga from his years in law school knew something about causation. Anyone could have infected the women, he told Connie. In Ssenyonga's opinion, the women got together with Cheryl Wagner to plot against him out of revenge.

Fletcher toiled away on other lines of defence. One promising avenue was the nuances within *mens rea*, the state of Ssenyonga's mind when he infected the women. Perhaps Ssenyonga didn't know that women could be infected by vaginal sex. Perhaps he thought HIV would not harm them. Perhaps he was confused, distraught, maybe not responsible because of some psychological or neurological impairment. Perhaps Ssenyonga was simply unable to grasp the seriousness of his behaviour.

Bruce Long was expecting something like that. A clever defence for Ssenyonga, he thought, would be to pretend that he was an unsophisticated man who couldn't understand what public health officials and doctors were telling him. Long already was planning his cross-examination. He intended to show that a man with eight years of university education was not simple-minded.

Dawson had a different perspective. Asking himself if a sane, cognizant person would deliberately, knowingly infect another, he came up with a *no*. Ssenyonga therefore must have some emotional scar that prevented him from being fully in control of his sexual behaviour. If that was the case, Dawson could consider a Section 16 defence. The old provision of the Criminal Code used the phrase "not guilty by reason of insanity," but that had been replaced by "not criminally responsible." Ssenyonga might be innocent because he didn't appreciate the consequences of his actions.

Dawson proposed that Ssenyonga undergo psychiatric examination to explore his sexuality. Ssenyonga bridled at the suggestion that he was somehow unbalanced. He would not consent to having any shadow cast on his sanity, he told Connie and Fletcher indignantly; it was out of the question.

Two or three times, Martha Allen came to tea and once to dinner with Connie and Charles. Connie's flair for decor was evident, and Ssenyonga had done some carpentry to transform a shabby space into something appealing. They made an attractive couple; Connie was ardently affectionate with Charles and he seemed appreciative of her. The conversation covered the state of Marxism in Cuba and the tribal similarities between the Irish and Africans but did not touch on the upcoming preliminary. Martha was not interested. The Charles Ssenyonga she knew was not the one portrayed in the media.

Only once she scolded him. "Charles, you behaved like a damned fool," she said.

"Yes," he said contritely.

"I'll drop it now," she told him, "but I wanted you to hear that."

In retrospect, Martha sees that "damned fool" didn't address the magnitude of Ssenyonga's behaviour. Until the full story emerged, she says she could not believe there was any duplicity in his nature. She believed him guilty of no more than impetuosity in his sexual relations.

The women who would testify against Ssenyonga were obsessed with fears about their upcoming ordeal. Ruth Rutherford, director of the court-funded victim-witness assistance program, hoped to allay some of their concerns by making them familiar with court procedures. She invited the witnesses to come one by one to the courthouse in the evening when the building was almost deserted. With the permission of the security staff, she showed the women the room where they would be testifying and had them stand in the witness box, which, she pointed out, gave them a commanding position — higher than anyone else except the judge. "It gives you an element of control," she told them.

At her direction, they practised deep breathing exercises to help them relax while testifying. What troubled every woman was the prospect of seeing Charles Ssenyonga again. Joan Estrada had been sleepless for three weeks at the thought of it, her insomnia so severe she had hallucinations. Rutherford's advice was: don't look at him.

Linda Booker, infected the earliest of all the witnesses, was apprehensive that she would have difficulty remembering details of the few months of their affair in 1986. She was not impressed with Nancy Gauthier, Francine Dalton, and Joan Estrada as credible witnesses, writing them off as "pretty well basket cases." She saw the responsibility to convince a judge as hers. "I felt a sense of mission about testifying," she says with glittering eyes.

Joan Estrada was appalled to see rows of spectator benches in the courtroom. "What if someone from work just happens to drop in?" she thought. Almost no one knew of her infection and she wanted it to stay that way.

Ruth then escorted the women along a back route to the courtroom that would allow them to encounter as few people as possible, and on the way pointed out the location of the washrooms.

Cheryl Wagner was concerned for the emotional state of her patients. She feared that none of them would be able to tolerate the multiple stress of the Public Health Appeal Board hearing, the preliminary hearing, and the criminal trial that lay beyond that. Accordingly, she sent Francine, Joan, and Nancy to be assessed by a Toronto psychiatrist, Peter Collins, of the Clarke Institute of Psychiatry. Collins was troubled by what he found. He told Bruce Long that he was prepared to testify that the women would suffer grievously if the courtroom was open to the public.

As date of the preliminary hearing approached, all the women were flooded by fresh fears that their identities would be revealed. Terry Hall, Bruce Long, and Ruth Rutherford took calls daily from women wanting reassurance. Nancy Gauthier called a half dozen times a day and then her nerve cracked. She told Ruth she was withdrawing.

Ruth took her to lunch, not to pressure her but to help her steady herself. "It's your choice," she assured her. "I'll stand by you whatever you decide." Gauthier gave her a gift: a stained-glass dove.

Later that same day Rutherford was in a frightful car accident that turned her automobile into junk. Trapped in the tangle of metal while awaiting the "jaws of death" rescue team, she watched the dove swinging on her rear-view mirror and thought affectionately of Nancy. Almost the first call she received in her hospital room was from Nancy, who said, "I have changed my mind. I have decided to testify."

Rutherford grins. "God moves in mysterious ways..."

Though stiff and sore and still on sick leave, Rutherford attended the preliminary to support the witnesses. Her presence had an unexpected benefit. In their concern for her well-being, the women almost forgot their own terrors. "They appreciated that the case was very important to me too," she says gratefully.

The judge assigned to the Ssenyonga preliminary hearing was Deborah Livingstone, thirty-nine years old, and less than two years on the bench in the Provincial Division of the Ontario Court. Livingstone is a lanky triathlon athlete married to Roland Haines, another lawyer who was appointed judge soon after she was. An able, intelligent woman with a direct manner and a store of common sense, she has a firm place in the London community. She was active in social work with Big Sisters and once served as president of the Canadian Club.

The justice of the peace who assigns judges asked her if she would be interested in sitting on the Ssenyonga preliminary. She jumped at the chance. "It was a landmark case," she explains. "The medical aspect of the case fascinated me, the moral aspect of the case fascinated me even more. It isn't often that judges get to deal with absolutely new law, particularly at this level [lower court] where we are so precedent-bound."

Fletcher Dawson had a meeting with the AIDS Committee of London to seek support. Closing the courtroom was an extreme act, he said, and the agency might want to protest by sending someone to testify at the hearing. The agency was plunged into debate. Clarence Crossman, education coordinator, a pale redhead with a grave, gentle manner, says that the staff was torn between protecting the witnesses and the possibility that a closed courtroom would suggest that there was something repugnant about people with HIV and AIDS.

As is their habit when ethical or policy issues arise, senior staff met several times. Consensus eluded them. Executive Director Betty Anne Thomas comments that the agency was in a delicate situation. The mandate is to support people with HIV, so the committee had a responsibility not only to the infected women but also to Ssenyonga. "Actually," she adds, "we're really quite good at not judging folks. You never know why people do what they do." In the end the agency decided not to testify.

The preliminary hearing opened with Ssenyonga sitting composedly beside Fletcher Dawson, who appeared tense. The three Crown lawyers took chairs at a table piled high with legal documents: Bruce Long looking determined and fierce, Geoff Beasley loose-limbed as a puppet with its strings cut, and Simon Johnson, already crouched over a legal foolscap pad, scribbling notes.

Dawson rather liked being one lawyer against three. He believes consistency can suffer when more than one lawyer has carriage of a case. But he was not the lonely figure he appeared. "Lots of people helped me on this case," he explains. "In the beginning Tim Morin, a lawyer in our firm, did a lot of work. I think four different law students put in a lot of time, along with various paralegals. I did the court work myself because I like to maintain control."

The first issues to confront Deborah Livingstone were the Crown's applications for a publication ban on the identities of the women who would testify that Ssenyonga infected them, the use of pseudonyms or initials for the women, and a closed courtroom while they testified. Livingstone, warned of this, was prepared with her own research.

Closed courtrooms have become highly controversial in Canada, particularly since the publication ban in 1993 on the Karla Homolka trial in St. Catharines. It was imposed by a judge who believed that Homolka's estranged husband, Paul Teale, would not otherwise have a fair trial. Until the nineties, closed courtrooms were rare, allowable only in such dire circumstances as national security or when it could be demonstrated that a witness's life would be endangered by testifying in public.

Livingstone comments, "Open courts are matters of principle and also of law. The Criminal Code provides that courts should be open to the public, but there are allowable exceptions. One such is protection of the identity and the sanctity of the witnesses when the charge is of a sexual nature. That is the public policy, that's the common law, and that is in the Criminal Code."

Arguments about closing the courtroom lasted for two days. A strong element in the Crown's case was the evidence from Dr. Peter Collins. He presented his view that the women's unsettled emotional states were such that they would suffer greatly if their names were read out in an open courtroom. It would soften the ordeal for them, he said, to use initials and keep out spectators.

Fletcher was unimpressed. "There are lots and lots of others who would rather not testify in public or have their names made public," he declared.

On November 13, 1991, Judge Livingstone adjourned the hearing to consider her decision. In the interval another woman infected by Ssenyonga came forward, Katie Newman. On the day of the adjournment, Katie was in Brantford visiting her parents. She switched on the radio in her parents' car and heard a news broadcast about the preliminary hearing of Charles Ssenyonga, a man accused of infecting some women with HIV. She was incredulous. She called the radio station to ask if she had heard the name right. Then she went straight to the Brantford police station. "I want to lay a complaint," she said. "Charles Ssenyonga infected me too." Within hours, the OPP's Terry Hall was on her doorstep.

Katie, a slim, tall, bright-eyed woman in her thirties, told Hall and, later, the judge at the preliminary trial, much the same story as Ssenyonga's other dates, except that she never loved the man. For her the pleasure was sexual. A Queen's University graduate who majored in psychology, she moved to the Caribbean. She was in London in February, 1988, and visiting The African Store, where a mutual friend introduced her to Charles Ssenyonga. She went to bed with him that night and they had sex twice, maybe three times. He didn't wear a condom but she was not concerned. She had been informed by people she believed knowledgeable about AIDS that women were not at risk from sex with heterosexual men.

Over the next three months Katie and Charles slept together about ten times, mostly in hotels where she paid for the room. "I really liked him," she said. She returned to the Caribbean in September, and there met a man she married. After a difficult pregnancy, their baby, a boy, was born in July, 1989. He was sickly from birth. When Katie went home to show him to her parents, she took the infant to the Brantford General Hospital. Meningitis was suspected, but complete blood tests were done and the baby was found to have HIV antibodies. Katie, suffering from chlamydia, a vaginal infection, and abscesses on her legs, was tested as well, and subsequently notified that she had AIDS.

Katie went with her baby to the children's HIV/AIDS clinic at the Hospital for Sick Children in Toronto. A nurse there gave her some reassuring information. Babies born to HIV-infected mothers will carry the mother's HIV antibodies in their blood for a year or so, but only about a quarter of them have the AIDS virus as well. Chances were that her son was well.

The nurse asked Katie if she knew the source of her infection. Katie said she thought it might be a Ugandan man who ran an African shop in London. The nurse sat bolt upright. That made two people on her caseload infected by a Ugandan who ran an African store in London. The other was a teacher and her child in Hamilton.

Katie telephoned Ssenyonga and arranged to meet him in a bar in Brantford. From there they went to the home of her parents, who were away for the weekend. She asked him if he had ever dated a teacher in Hamilton. Ssenyonga appeared shocked. He wanted to know who was spreading lies about him.

"This is very difficult for me to say..." Katie began.

"Is it AIDS?" he asked quickly.

She nodded. She told him she had AIDS. Ssenyonga put his arms around her and said he would be there for her through everything. She said she was concerned for him, and he told her he would get tested.

This was almost exactly six months after Ssenyonga heard from Dr. Henry Bendheim that he was HIV-positive.

Ssenyonga then asked if it would be safe for them to have sex.

"I think it would be risky for you," Katie protested.

"What about oral sex?" he persisted. "Would that be risky?"

He stayed the night and, at her insistence, they confined their sexual activities to mutual masturbation.

Two weeks later he telephoned Katie. He told her his HIV test was negative. He was much relieved, he said, because he was deeply involved with a woman in Toronto (this would be Francine Dalton). Newman was baffled. If Ssenyonga didn't have HIV, she couldn't imagine who could have infected her. The likeliest possibility was a bisexual man with whom she had a two-year relationship. She notified him of her infection and he promptly went for testing. He was HIV-negative, and so, fortunately, was her husband.

She returned to her husband in the Caribbean but was back in Canada two years later, again to visit her parents. She was beginning to be ill, with heavy vaginal bleeding that doctors in the Caribbean could not control. The news on the radio that Charles Ssenyonga was charged with infecting women with HIV made her furious. He had lied to her. When Terry Hall asked if she would like to testify at the preliminary, she said she certainly would. Hall asked her to give a blood sample to Dr. Janet Gilmour in London.

On November 26, Katie Newman saw Gilmour, who obtained a medical history and performed a physical examination. The doctor drew blood and sent samples to Rick Galli in Toronto and Michael Montpetit in Ottawa. Newman proved to be positive for both ELISA and Western Blot. Indeed, AIDS was advancing rapidly in her, and her T-4 cell count was very low. As Gilmour was to testify at the trial, Newman was "quite symptomatic" and "at significant risk for developing opportunistic infections" such as pneumonia.

On November 29, the preliminary hearing resumed with a decision from Judge Deborah Livingstone. She issued a ban on publication of the six women's identities and a ban on publication of any of the preliminary testimony until after the trial, but she required the real names of the women to be used in their testimony and opened the courtroom to the public. Referring to the evidence of Dr. Peter Collins, she said that the women's emotional jeopardy was not of such an "extraordinary or compelling nature" to justify closing the courtroom.

Dawson told Debora Van Brenk of the *London Free Press* that he was pleased with what he called "a reasonable decision . . . it was based on solid research." Months later he commented, "Judge Livingstone was absolutely correct to open the court. The prosecution probably won't even seek it at the trial."

Livingstone took pleasure in the "solid research" to which Dawson referred. That opportunity doesn't occur often in the life of a lower court judge, she says. "Our court is a fast-paced, volume-laden, decide-off-the-top-of-your-head venue most of the time," she explains. "Ssenyonga and any case which takes as many days in court time as this one did is not that kind of a case, but that's the sort of mind-set that judges at our level are used to having. We listen and assess each witness and each argument as it is being presented. With this case, because of the length of it and the nature of it, I had time to reflect, I actually had time to write a judgement. In the General Division, trials take much longer, the pace is less intense, and judges have more time for reflection. Therefore, they have more written decisions. At our level, that's rare."

Nancy Gauthier was distraught at the ruling. That night she thought seriously about suicide. She called Debora Van Brenk at the *Free Press* and they talked for almost an hour. She had a number of things to say during the rambling discourse, the most striking of which was that she would testify anyway, although telling her story would put her "soul on the line."

"She speaks in great quotes," commented Debora admiringly, "but I didn't know how much I could use without being in contempt of court, since there was a publication ban and she was a protected witness."

Nancy was rebelling against what she saw as public apathy about her plight. Afterwards she explained her frustration. "People think this disease doesn't matter because it happens only to faggots and to people like me, who sleep with Africans," she said bitterly. "So their attitude is, who cares?"

Bruce Long was pained to see one of his star witnesses being chatty in a newspaper. He asked Terry Hall to rein Nancy in, a formidable task. Nancy already had phoned Debora back with a breezy "Nice job." Indeed, she became a regular caller, and Debora came to regard Nancy as a friend.

Joan Estrada wavered. The decision to open the courtroom rattled her. She announced she wasn't comfortable with involvement in any legal proceedings, and definitely would not participate, even as a Jane Doe, at the appeal. The pressure on all the women only increased when it developed that the preliminary trial would not resume for almost two months. Meanwhile, with Estrada out of it, Jane Doe 1 (Dalton) and Jane Doe 2 (Gauthier), faced appearances at the hearing called for January before the Ontario Health Protection Appeal Board. Since Charles and Connie planning to marry on January 1, 1992, Dawson intended to ask that the board amend the terms of the Section 22 restraint order to allow Ssenyonga to have sex providing his partner was informed of his HIV status, consented to have sex, and was counselled by a third party.

Richard Schabas, Ontario's chief medical officer, was opposed to lifting the ban. To his mind it was simpler to leave the celibacy order as it was. Otherwise, if Ssenyonga found other sex partners, the government would be obliged to prove that the person wasn't informed, or wasn't informed clearly enough, or wasn't counselled, or wasn't counselled sufficiently. Schabas thought too much quibbling would be required.

As the January 13 date for the appeal hearing approached, everyone on the Ministry of Health side of the arguments began to grow twitchy. With interest focused on strategy and the Charter challenge, it somehow had not been established that the hearing would be closed to the public. There was no assurance that the tribunal would protect the two remaining women who had agreed to participate.

To the relief of the government's lawyers, the appeal panel agreed to impose a publication ban. When the hearing opened on January 29, neither Francine nor Nancy was required to attend, but the room was packed with lawyers, doctors, media and constitutional experts. Dr. Peter Collins proved to be a compelling witness on the subject of the women's perilous emotional states. It would be detrimental in the extreme, he said, if they were obliged to appear at the hearing when they also faced the strain of testifying at criminal proceedings.

Government lawyers echoed his concern. They said the hearing could endanger Ssenyonga's trial because the women might be too traumatized to appear. Luba Kowal, speaking for the attorney general, was quoted in the *Free Press* as saying that the hearing could "seriously impair their ability to testify in the criminal proceedings."

John Judson, the lawyer representing the Middlesex-London health unit, concurred. "They may not be able to stand up to doing it more than once," he said. That was a pleasant surprise. When the women met with Judson they had the impression that London public health authorities were determined to ram the hearing through without regard for what was happening in the criminal courts.

Dawson protested at what he saw as a derailment of the public health issue. His client wished to marry, he said, and the sex ban affected his "normal human rights."

Then sanity descended. After two days of submissions, the Health Protection Appeal Board made a decision to back off until the criminal proceedings were completed. The matter was deferred until June 30 when it would be reviewed, and until then Ssenyonga was bound by Section 22 and the interim Section 101 order to remain celibate. That took some of the pressure off Dawson, who decided to postpone the appeal of the Section 101 interim order as well.

Ssenyonga, though presenting himself as a celibate man anxious to have the restraint orders lifted, was not in the least inhibited by Section 22 or the interim Section 101. He was having unprotected sex with Constance Neill and she was pregnant. Their plan to marry was on indefinite hold, however, because his brother John was unable to make the journey from Kampala in January.

Ssenyonga was ambivalent about his approaching fatherhood. He was uncomfortably aware that the baby would be proof that he had defied the restraint order, which would do his credibility no good at the trial, but at the same time he was pleased to contemplate a new role as teacher. He saw the function of fatherhood as essentially one of instruction, as his father had. In sentimental moments he spoke to Connie about this being his last chance to have a child he could train. At such times Ssenyonga seemed happy about the pregnancy, but Connie recalls him as mostly indifferent, as if he didn't expect to see the child. She was puzzled. For her, one of Ssenyonga's endearing traits was his love for children. She wondered why he wasn't more delighted to be having one.

Connie continued to pursue the theory that HIV does not cause AIDS, which the couple viewed as the strongest proof of Ssenyonga's innocence of the charges. If HIV didn't cause

AIDS, Ssenyonga was guilty of nothing more serious than passing along a pesky virus.

Fletcher Dawson was cool to their enthusiasm for that theory. Though he was tactful about expressing it, he thought a judge would find such evidence "too radical." He put them off repeatedly by promising to look into it.

12

THE PRELIMINARY HEARING finally reopened on February 24, 1992, before Judge Deborah Livingstone. Because the activities of a preliminary hearing cannot be reported until the trial ends, media coverage was severely restricted. The testimony of Dr. Iain Mackie, nurse Marylin McConnell, Dr. Janet Gilmour, and Dr. Henry Bendheim, who appeared on the first day, could be reported only in generalities. Debora Van Brenk, covering the hearing for the *London Free Press,* described them simply as "doctors and a public health nurse" without quotes.

Iain Mackie recounted his single meeting with Ssenyonga in December, 1987, at St. Joseph's Health Centre. Marylin McConnell, in her customary straightforward stiff-backed manner, gave her account of the frequent conversations she had with Ssenyonga, during which he assured her that he was practising safe sex. Gilmour, next in the stand, described her contacts with Joan Estrada, Nancy Gauthier, and Katie Newman.

Fletcher Dawson, with the intention of clouding the issue of causation, pounced on her testimony about Gauthier. He asked if Gauthier had been able to remember all her sexual contacts. Wasn't it true that she said to the doctor that she withheld a few from the police? Imbedded in his questions was the suggestion that Gauthier was unstable and someone else could have infected her.

Gilmour responded that the anxiety of having an indefinite result is sometimes even more traumatic than finding oneself positive. "I saw a woman under extreme stress, which was understandable," she said, but there were no signs of any mental or psychiatric illness.

Then Dr. Henry Bendheim testified that he had drawn Ssenyonga's blood, notified him that it tested positive, and counselled him to have safe sex.

It was a dramatic moment for spectators when Bruce Long called Francine Dalton, the first of the victims to testify. She retraced the events of her long relationship with Ssenyonga and acknowledged that in the year previous to meeting Ssenyonga she had relations with three other men.

Dawson rose for the cross-examination. Francine remained composed as he asked her intimate questions about her sex life, such as whether she practised oral sex. After that Dawson questioned every sexual experience she had had with Ssenyonga, and then had her retrace such activities as taking Ssenyonga's address book, the telephone calls to women in it, her long meetings with police and government lawyers, and discussions with the other women linked to Ssenyonga. Bruce Long, poker-faced as lawyers are supposed to be in court, could see what Dawson was doing. The defence attorney was trying to paint Francine Dalton as a jealous woman who schemed to discredit Ssenyonga.

Francine seemed not to notice the trap, but deftly avoided it anyway.

"I made this choice to warn other women about Ssenyonga," she explained, "because I knew he was not one to wear condoms. And I was really frightened for the number of women out there that he may well have come into contact with."

The questions went on all afternoon and resumed the next morning. When it was his turn to put final questions to Francine, Bruce confronted the unspoken accusation. He asked brusquely if she had acted out of vengeance.

"No," she replied, her eyebrows arching in surprise. "This was for justice. This was a very touchy ethical issue and a very strong moral one which I felt very strongly about ... These women deserved a chance to be able to have their own lives ... Somebody had to take responsibility for what was happening."

The next witness that morning was Joan Estrada, who had changed her mind once again, and counting on the publication ban to protect her, had decided to testify after all. She was trembling as she entered the courtroom. "I was feeling so sick that I didn't think I could testify," she says, "but I had so much hate for Charles that the power of it got me through."

Judge Livingstone was startled. She had seen Joan on jogging trails around London. "It was a shock," she confessed later.

The testimony followed the same line as Dalton's, a chronological recital of her meetings with Ssenyonga and then a list of her sexual contacts. Though she had promised herself not to look at Ssenyonga, Joan could not avoid glancing in his direction. He sat stone-faced, not an emotion showing, gazing calmly back at her. "I couldn't believe it. This man has affected so many lives," she says. She thought, "What is he feeling now? And yet he doesn't even blink." She had an urge to slap him.

Bruce asked Joan how the diagnosis had affected her.

"For a time I was suicidal. I used to be very outgoing, lots of friends, a very happy person. Now I tend to stay away from people. I'm afraid if they get close they will get hurt, because I am going to die."

She began to cry, and was angry at herself because she had hoped she wouldn't. "I am afraid of dying a lonely person. I am afraid of my little brother not having a big sister to take care of him. I am never going to be able to have children. I am never going to be able to love a man again."

She turned to Ssenyonga, who was bent over, head down. "Damn you," she flung out.

Ruth Rutherford had tears on her cheeks. She looked around the courtroom and saw that many people were wet-eyed. She couldn't be certain, but she thought the judge's eyes were shining too. Court was recessed.

Long after the trial, Judge Livingstone reflected on that moment. "It was the most emotional proceeding I had ever been in," she said thoughtfully. "I hadn't been a judge all that long but I had been a lawyer for thirteen years and I have never been in anything that was so heart-wrenching. And the clerk and the court reporter felt the same. When the complainants testified, all three of us were devastated by the sheer emotion of it all."

Bruce Long agrees. "Joan's evidence was the most chilling I have ever heard in almost twenty years in a courtroom." He found himself fighting to keep control, his fists clenched.

When court resumed after Estrada's outburst, Fletcher conducted a brief, subdued cross-examination. The next witness was Dr. Cheryl Wagner. She was feeling queasy because she was in the early stages of her second pregnancy. Cheryl was questioned by Geoff Beasley, the Crown's expert on medical evidence.

Cheryl described the appointments with Francine Dalton.

Asked about Francine's health status, she responded that Dalton was in Category Four, the most severe category of AIDS. A recent T-4 cell count registered only forty — "and this has a dismal prognosis." The average survival time for people with a T-4 count below fifty is between nine and twelve months, Cheryl said, adding that Francine, who was not in the courtroom, was at high risk for the development of lymph cancer, blindness and uncontrollable diarrhoea. Francine, in fact, developed full-blown AIDS at the very beginning of her infection.

On Thursday morning, Nancy Gauthier arrived to testify, taking long strides as she entered the courtroom, head up, looking as sassy as she could manage. She calls that her "hundred-dollar-whore walk." As Bruce Long asked questions, she told the story of her involvement with Ssenyonga up to the time of her three-month ordeal while waiting for her blood tests to be definite.

Bruce had warned his witnesses that he would be asking them to describe how the infection had changed their lives. He had in mind the case of Ottawa cheerleaders who received threatening letters that deeply unsettled them. Their testimony about the psychological havoc they suffered made legal history and established the principle that harm is not confined to the physical. Accordingly, he asked Nancy, "What is the effect of the news?"

Nancy stared at him. "How deeply do you want me to go into an answer?" she asked testily. "What it's like to be HIV-positive? What a question! I mean, how would anybody like to live with a death threat hanging over their head all the time, all the time. Like you're going to die, Mr. Long. And you're going to die, and you're going to die. Everybody here is going to die, and I know I'm going to die too."

"I have no further questions," said Long hastily.

"I'm not finished," Nancy said, eyes flashing.

"I'm sorry," Long said, making the best of it. "I didn't mean to interrupt you."

"I have a daughter to raise and she's six years old. And who is going to take care of her if I'm not here? I don't want to leave her in this wacky world ... She needs me. I am the only solid person she has in her life. I am more afraid of what will happen to her when I die than dying myself."

She took a ragged breath. "I think every woman in here has had dreams. When you're a little girl, you have dreams that you're going to grow up, and get married to a man, and have his baby, and live in a house. My life never fell into place, but I was sure it was going to happen. And I've been robbed of that."

She glared at Bruce. "I've been robbed of that. I've been robbed of a lot of precious things in life, even life itself. And the next time you have flu or a cold, just think of me. Just think about me. Just be glad for yourself that your body has the fighters because I'm losing mine.

"I know there's a lot of cruelties in this world, but I have to say that this is one of the top ten — to take a human being's fighters and leave their body open to anything, like cancer or anything. It's very scary to live your life in the unknown." She shook her head. "I'm losing perspective here."

The court recessed.

When court resumed, Fletcher Dawson registered a protest to the judge. Despite her decision that the courtroom be open to the public, he found a hand-written notice posted on the courtroom door: No Admittance While Court Is In Progress. Judge Livingstone demanded to know how this could happen against her express orders.

The Crown lawyers and police were in disarray, with contempt of court hanging over their collective heads. Livingstone curtly ordered that an explanation be provided her the next morning.

Fletcher then commenced cross-examination of Nancy, who watched him warily. At one point he said, "You'd agree with me, Nancy, that it was consensual sex that you had with Mr. Ssenyonga. The two of you agreed?"

Nancy replied coldly, "Your words went over my head. I wanted to have sex with the man, I had sex with the man."

"And times that you had sex with him without a condom, I mean, if you didn't want to have sex with him without a condom, you wouldn't have sex without a condom."

Confused, Nancy replied, "That's right. I choose to do what I want to do."

Fletcher was satisfied and prepared to shift the subject. He cautioned Nancy that the next line of questions he proposed to put to her might be embarrassing.

She smiled broadly. "It will probably be more embarrassing for you, Mr. Dawson, than me. Feel free to ask me anything you want."

"Thank you," Dawson said, his voice tight.

What followed were exhaustive questions about Nancy's previous sex life. Dawson's intention was to portray her as a promiscuous woman who could have picked up HIV in any number of other liaisons. Gauthier maintained a bemused attitude throughout and even gave Fletcher some cheery unsolicited information about condoms.

Dawson raised the matter of Nancy's telephone call to him following his statement that the Crown had not produced "a twit of evidence" to show that Ssenyonga was continuing to have sex.

"How am I for a twit of evidence, Mr. Dawson?" Nancy taunted him.

Dawson said evenly, "I'll ask the questions, okay?"

Nancy subsided with a triumphant, "Yes, sir."

"Do you remember saying on the telephone that you and the other women were team players? Do you remember saying that?"

"We are a team, but I stand alone," she retorted. "I was highly emotional, something I don't prefer to do."

Judge Livingstone intervened politely. "Did you say to Mr. Dawson that you and the other ladies are team players? That was the question."

Nancy replied, "I don't remember." Then she said, distractedly, "I am on my own. I take care of me and my girl."

When it came time for Katie Newman to testify, her father drove her to the London courthouse. She told him she was a secret witness in a trial, but did not reveal what the trial was about. They arranged to meet at the end of the day. He was worried as he watched her walk resolutely into the austere building. She seemed to be very ill, but always put him off when he asked about it.

Ruth Rutherford sat in the courtroom and was touched by the valour of the women. She noticed that none of them was able to avoid looking at Ssenyonga, who rarely raised his eyes to them. The women had promised themselves to ignore him, but every one of them ended up glaring at his bowed head.

"It was very moving in the prelim," Ruth says. "Everyone was very much touched. Joan Estrada had the hardest time with being in the same room with Ssenyonga. The women might have vented their feelings — anger just poured out of them — but everyone involved did their job properly."

She has a charitable appraisal of Fletcher Dawson's tough cross-examination. "The women felt that Dawson was hard on them, but I have seen him in other cases and he wasn't that hard, not to the degree that I have seen him cross-examine others."

Dawson took no pleasure in trying to find holes in the testimony of the victims, all of them young women with a fatal infection. "It's all part of doing criminal law," he says levelly. "It comes with the territory. You frequently deal with people who have been terribly hurt. It doesn't make the job any easier."

First thing on Friday morning, the Crown was ready to explain the sign barring entrance to the courtroom. Bruce

Long told the judge he was apprehensive about school-children visiting the courts on field trips. He feared for the disruption they would cause if they entered during testimony by the victims and he was also worried that they would be exposed to sexually-explicit statements. Simon Johnson, who cautioned a teacher escorting elementary students about the nature of the evidence in Courtroom Seven, told the judge it was not his intention to be contemptuous of her order. Tony Little, a lawyer retained by OPP officers Terry Hall and Chris Lewis, explained that Chris Lewis placed the notice on the door in response to a general sense that young children should be warned about the graphic nature of the evidence. In any case, the notice was on the door no longer than forty minutes.

"It was done with the intention of advising the teacher of the graphic sexual evidence," Long said. "It was not to preclude anyone from entering."

Dawson graciously said, "I am not interested in seeing anybody's head roll over this." Livingstone accepted the reasons and issued a stern caution against repeating the offence.

Dr. Rick Galli, head of the provincial government's HIV testing lab in Toronto, testified next. Geoff Beasley conducted the examination, in preparation for which he had spent a day in the Toronto lab to make himself familiar with the procedures.

"He was very, very good," Galli marvels. "For a layperson, he picked it up very rapidly. He wanted to see every stage so he could be certain of the integrity of the lab."

Galli's place in the Crown's case was to verify the dependability of test results and the unlikelihood that a switch of specimens could have occurred or that a mistake could be made about anyone's HIV status. For this purpose Galli identified the tubes in which samples were collected and the labels used to identify them. He explained that each kit containing a sample is assigned a number, on a sequential basis, which is entered on the label and on the accompanying document, as well as the name of the person whose blood it is. On receipt of the sample at the Toronto lab, technicians double-check the name and serial number before they begin the test process. If the identification on the tube doesn't match the information on the accompanying document, the test is aborted.

In February, 1989, when the sample of Charles Ssenyonga's blood was received from Dr. Henry Bendheim, the Toronto lab was processing several hundred HIV tests a day in a pocket-size lab and finding about three percent of them positive.

Rick identified the document that accompanied Ssenyonga's serum, noting the date it was received at the lab, 21/2/89, in red ink. The name and the number on the document matched those on the vial: Charles Ssenyonga, number A10784. Ssenyonga's virus, Rick said in the detached manner of a professional, tested in the highest range for concentration of the virus. Rick then produced arcane lab paraphernalia and records relating to Francine Dalton, Joan Estrada, and Nancy Gauthier, all of which were duly entered as exhibits.

Galli's engrossing lecture occupied most of the day. Fletcher Dawson's cross-examination demonstrated that the defence lawyer had done an impressive amount of homework himself on the subject, but it was brief. One matter he raised, in a respectful but sceptical manner, was Galli's testimony that Dalton and Gauthier were "textbook examples" of seroconversion, which indicated they were newly infected. Dawson's point was that the seroconversion process varies from one individual to another, the inference being that someone other than Ssenyonga could have infected them earlier than their affairs with him.

Galli replied that the variance was not that broad. The virus requires two to eight weeks to incubate in a new host, during which it is undetectable; the person will be infectious but test negative. Sometimes antibodies don't show up in a test for six months, but more commonly they can be detected in about six weeks. Dawson asked a few questions about quality control, suggesting that the testing process was fallible, but Galli, unflappable, responded that the system of double-checks and more double-checks made this impossible.

Dawson had anticipated that Galli's testimony would be difficult to shake, though he gave it his best shot. His real concern was the mysterious work being done in Ottawa by Dr. Michael Montpetit. Fletcher fumed that the Crown wasn't informing him how the testing was getting on.

He complained to the judge. "I have indicated to my friend [Beasley] that I know there is DNA testing going on now in Ottawa and it is going to be important at the trial. If there is some result in the not too distant future, I would really like to hear that."

Geoff Beasley quickly assured the judge that Dawson would be kept informed of the DNA analysis.

The hearing of the case continued on March 3. Linda Booker was the first in the witness box, her manner assured. She had been waiting almost four years to tell a judge that Ssenyonga had known since October, 1988, that he probably was infected with HIV.

Bruce Long, who examined her, asked the status of her T-4 cell count. She said that it had been fine, around seven hundred, but recently had deteriorated to less than four hundred.

"What effect has this [infection] had on your life?" asked Long.

She replied steadily, "I have been celibate since the diagnosis. I've gone through a dramatic weight gain, for me. I think that's out of some concern of wanting some extra physical padding in terms of what might lie ahead in terms of the wasting syndrome. It has had a very deep and profound effect on my life."

Though Linda Booker seemed self-possessed on the stand, she was in fact badly shaken. Using Ruth Rutherford's back route to the courtroom in order to avoid the media, she had encountered Charles Ssenyonga face to face on a narrow stairway. She had braced herself to see him in court, but this meeting caught her unprepared. For a frozen moment they were stiff with shock; then Linda brushed past him without speaking.

Watching from the witness stand, she saw only the top of Ssenyonga's bowed head. She felt contempt. "He doesn't feel guilty because he is too conceited," she thought. "He's tuning me out. A sensitive person would have killed himself."

Dawson's cross-examination drew from Linda Booker the acknowledgement that in February, 1986, when she was infected by Ssenyonga, most AIDS authorities believed that women were not likely to become infected with HIV through vaginal sex with an infected man. Dawson wanted the judge to be aware that Ssenyonga had reason to believe that Linda Booker was not at risk when he had sex with her.

The point made, Dawson left that line of questioning abruptly and moved to what the Crown lawyers had come to call derisively Fletcher's conspiracy theory. His tone by turns sarcastic and indignant, Dawson drew from Linda Booker admissions that she and other complainants discussed Ssenyonga on the telephone and at meetings, and that Dr. Cheryl Wagner contacted the women frequently. Linda could see his tactic was leading to a suggestion that women connived against Ssenyonga, but she was helpless to evade his questions.

Fletcher later said that the Crown's choice of the word *conspiracy* was too strong. "Let's put it this way," he says, a phrase he uses when he is marshalling his thoughts. "I asked some questions along that line but my thought was the existence of some degree of collusion." What he meant, he explains, was that people are suggestible. "People get ideas, people's memories and way of recounting events tend to vary over time as they retell their story and rethink things. If witnesses are talking to one another and they have a common interest, human nature being what it is, we would be fools to think there isn't a certain degree of accommodation that goes on. And a lawyer has to look for that. In a case like this where there was somewhat of an axe to grind, if you will, it's a factor. It is arguable that the women were faced with a government that wasn't taking action where they felt action should be taken. Dr. Wagner's legitimate concern was to have something done about this, so they naturally became involved in a process of advocacy. They were ultimately successful in getting the lawyers to move. There is nothing wrong with that, but that process may possibly have some effect on perspective and the way evidence was presented."

When Dawson was finished with Linda, having established that the witnesses frequently talked to one another, Geoff Beasley asked Judge Livingstone to adjourn the preliminary trial for a few weeks. The DNA testing in Ottawa wasn't yet completed, he explained, and the scientist conducting those tests, Dr. Michael Montpetit, would not be available to testify for three or four weeks.

In the meantime, Connie Neill realized that her pregnancy, then in its eleventh week, was not going well. Doctors confirmed that hers was an ectopic pregnancy, the foetus lodged in a fallopian tube where it could not survive. She was admitted in great pain to a hospital in Hamilton, where she remained for a week to recover from the miscarriage that followed. She did not request or receive a blood test for HIV.

Charles Ssenyonga took little interest in her situation. Her disapproving parents, who live in a small city near

London, paid a perfunctory visit to the hospital, but Ssenyonga did not appear for several days. When he finally came, it was late at night, long after visiting hours. "Rules didn't apply to Charles," Connie says with admiration in her tone. He explained he had been painting the bedroom.

It was not three or four weeks, as Geoff Beasley had suggested, but two months before Dr. Michael Montpetit was ready to testify. During the long adjournment, Bruce Long had numerous calls from Crown lawyers all over Canada who were floundering in the sea of AIDS non-law. Most of them sought his advice on what criminal charges were best to try. Inadvertently, Bruce had become an authority on the legal peculiarities of AIDS cases. The most startling of the calls came from Kathy Knox, a Crown lawyer in St. John's, Newfoundland. She told him of a man there, Raymond Mercer, in his late twenties, who had infected many women with HIV. Mercer was from Upper Island Cove on Conception Bay, and the women he infected, most of them young, lived in that area on the island's northeast coast.

As she described the man, Bruce was struck by how much Mercer resembled Ssenyonga. Like Ssenyonga, Mercer had been warned by public health authorities after testing positive for HIV but had continued to have unprotected sex with many women, insisting that he was HIV-negative. One of the women infected by him was a sixteen-year-old who became pregnant and had an abortion in order to avoid the chance of producing an HIV-infected baby. Another, Karen Thompson (her real name), twenty-two and the recently separated mother of a toddler, was infected by Mercer in 1991 only days after he learned he was HIV-positive and had been warned by Newfoundland public health authorities to practise safe sex.

When Mercer went to trial in July, 1992, on two charges of criminal negligence causing bodily harm, Karen Thompson was the only one of the women he had infected who appeared in court. The teenager who had the abortion refused to testify; she said she loved Mercer. Karen, however, not only took the stand but waived her right to a publicity ban.

She explained, with great dignity, that having her real name published would draw more attention to the case. She wanted other women to know that the same harm could come to them, that "somebody you trust can do it, can pass the virus on to you."

Karen, who lives in Toronto with her son, describes Mercer as a handsome, indulged, semi-illiterate scoundrel who drove motorcycles and cars at top speed and acquired the nickname Crazy in his teens. Like Charles Ssenyonga, he was regarded in his circle as "a Casanova," she says. On a visit home in July, 1991, soon after breaking up with her husband, Karen ran into Mercer at a dance. They renewed their longtime acquaintanceship, and Raymond pressed her to have sex with him. This was only days after his blood test proved positive and he had been counselled at length by someone from public health not to expose sex partners to risk. Karen asked him if he should wear a condom. He said there was no reason for it because he was healthy. Anyway, by that time the question was moot; he already was inside her.

Two weeks later she had classic symptoms of the onset of an HIV infection: a weight loss of fifteen pounds because of severe "flu", a rash all over her face, a sore throat, swollen glands. Karen returned to Toronto, where her mother reached her by telephone to say that Ray Mercer was HIV-positive. Karen went to her doctor and learned in October that she was HIV-positive. When the attorney-general's lawyers approached her, she agreed to testify against Mercer. It was not for revenge, she says, but because she wanted to protect other women. She believes that Mercer was angry about his imminent death and wanted to take as many people with him as he could.

Her testimony at Mercer's trial in the summer of 1992 was poignant. She said, "Right now, I just live each day, live my life day by day. Right now, I am going to stay in Ontario and like I just feel if I were to come home right now I would be giving up and I am not going to give up. I know I have to sit down one day with my family and make arrangements as to how I want to be buried. I have to plan for my own son, who is going to look after him and everything like that."

Ray Mercer was sentenced to two years and three months in prison, a term that took into consideration the fact that his plea of guilty spared the province the expense of a lengthy trial. The prosecution was disappointed: the sentence proposed by the Crown was four years. Although Mercer might not live to serve it, the reasoning was that a long sentence might act as a deterrent. The Crown therefore appealed, and in 1993 the Appeal Court of Newfoundland astounded the country by increasing the sentence to an unprecedented eleven years and three months.

The Mercer trial was quick and quiet, attracting little attention in the rest of Canada until his sentence was quadrupled. What Canadians did not know was that Mercer had infected many more women than court records show: a reliable source says at least nineteen women were infected by him. Like Ssenyonga, Mercer was a handsome, charming, and tireless sexual predator.

In good part because of Raymond Mercer, the incidence of HIV among women in Newfoundland is disproportionately high, especially in the Conception Bay area. While the rest of the province has an HIV-infection rate of eight pregnant women per ten thousand, in Conception Bay the HIV-infection rate is 26.6 per ten thousand. (Only pregnant women were tested.) Two women, among the many infected by Mercer, have died. As of the summer of 1994, health officials in the Conception Bay area knew of thirty-three HIV-positive cases, twenty-five of them young women.

In June, 1994, the startling news from Newfoundland was that the strain of HIV found in the Conception Bay area was particular to Uganda and Thailand and said to be more readily transmitted by heterosexual intercourse than North American strains. Scientists are comparing the Ssenyonga and Mercer HIV strains, but word is that they are unlikely to match.

Michael Montpetit took the stand on Thursday, April 23, 1992. The thirty-two-year-old scientist sat tranquilly in the witness box as Geoff Beasley advised the judge that Montpetit's evidence would be presented in a lecture form, complete with charts and diagrams. Livingstone asked Fletcher Dawson if he objected and Dawson, who had been forewarned of the format, replied that he did not.

In the lengthy exposition on DNA technology that followed, Montpetit was impressive as a witness, his material presented in an orderly and near-comprehensible form leavened by an unexpected flair for witty analogy. Geoff Beasley also gave an astounding performance. In the course of two days spent with Montpetit in the Ottawa lab, together with telephone calls and a lot of reading, he had made himself near-perfect in his grasp of biochemistry at the surreal level of the intricacies of molecular matching.

"It was the most difficult kind of evidence that I have ever had to put before the court," Beasley admits. "Difficult in that I had to understand it. I don't think you can lead evidence that you don't understand. That's a very dangerous proposition if you try it. I remember thinking to myself, 'This is insane.' Quite literally, I failed miserably first-year university biology. And here I am talking to a guy who has a PhD in biochemistry."

"For someone who has little scientific background, Geoff has done an extraordinary job of learning the science," Montpetit comments. "If I could learn law the way he learned science I might change careers. He has a very, very rapid ability to grasp the importance of specific points. He has a remarkable ability to apply what he has just heard directly to what he needs to know."

Geoff was in his element as he drew testimony from Michael Montpetit. The scientist began by explaining that DNA, the genetic material of most life, is an acronym for deoxyribonucleic acid. "Each of us has approximately four billion bases of DNA in each cell," he said. "They are arranged in a long string of bases. The DNA in each cell is very much like a large cookbook. It contains pictures, it contains beautiful formatting characteristics, but nonetheless it's just a very large cookbook with about a hundred thousand recipes, one for each of the proteins that we need in our bodies."

Later he described enzymes as "robots" that can't read the cookbook. An intermediary of the recipe does that, the RNA molecule, ribonucleic acid, containing a few thousand base pairs of information, which narrows the range to a single recipe for making a protein. HIV starts with RNA, then goes back and makes DNA, and then essentially hijacks the normal cellular system and proceeds on, multiplying in normal cells.

The blood samples Montpetit received from the women Ssenyonga infected were reduced to pellets of hardy white blood cells, which contain the blood's genetic material. To break the cells apart to gain access to the DNA, he lysed them in detergent. After that he exposed them to a protein-digesting enzyme that gobbled up unwanted material. After heating, no active enzymes were left to interfere with subsequent steps of the reactions.

"As you might imagine, we are rather paranoid about contamination at the best of times," Montpetit told the court, "but in this case [because of the importance of the evidence in the trial] I was even more paranoid."

The tubes containing what was left of the cells were frozen at a temperature of −70 degrees Celsius. What was left intact was the fragile genetic material of the cell, twenty-three pairs of chromosomes arranged in a long delicate strand of DNA. HIV infects only a small percentage of the cells found in the blood, often only one percent, "so it's like looking for a needle in a haystack in some ways."

DNA is two strands twisted together, so Montpetit's next step was to denature, or separate, the strands. Then he added primers, short pieces of DNA that matched specific areas of HIV genetic material. In the polymerase chain reaction, known as PCR, these primers seek their replicas on the long strand. The physico-chemical process of allowing two strands to come together in a stable structure is called annealing.

"One of the problems of working with HIV is that each infected individual carries slightly changed or slightly mutated versions in their body at one point in time," Montpetit said, with evident relish for difficult problems. Enzymes make mistakes, he explained, and reproduce their errors tirelessly, which is the cause of mutations. To focus on the consistencies within the virus, Montpetit concentrates on the HIV molecules.

"I isolate individual molecules which have been amplified and I look at them individually," he said, as if this was a piece of cake. In truth, he had to invent a computer program in order to simplify the part of the research that involves matching DNA sequences. Since Montpetit didn't know computer programming, he studied a manual, usually reading it in bed at night, and designed one. His program is now used worldwide to compare referenced DNA sequences with other sequences.

Then Montpetit described cloning the HIV DNA taken from the women infected by Ssenyonga, happily skipping through a biochemist's jungle verdant with laminar flow hoods, PCR amplification, cone-shaped bacterial colonies of DNA that glow with colour, and dideoxy chain termination sequencing. At the end of a long and exquisitely choreographed process, the scientist determined without a possibility of doubt that Francine Dalton, Nancy Gauthier, and Joan Estrada were infected by exactly the same virus.

The match was not perfect, Montpetit explained, nor could it be, given that HIV changes every time it replicates itself and the women were infected at different times, and, further, that each woman has personal differences that influence how the virus develops. The similarities, however, were compelling: more than ninety-two percent of the clones matched. The women indubitably had the same virus. "They were all infected from a single source," Montpetit declared.

Geoff Beasley was obliged to ask an obvious question, though he knew the answer was not good news for the prosecution. He inquired if Montpetit had tested Ssenyonga's virus. The scientist said he had tried but the effort was not successful. He did not elaborate on the reasons and Beasley didn't ask.

When Fletcher Dawson rose to cross-examine Montpetit, his frustration was showing. Dawson had spent dispiriting hours trying to learn enough about PCRs and reference molecules to cross-examine the witness. The few scientists who understood what Montpetit was doing had been uncooperative when the lawyer from Canada called. Their brush with lawyers during the sensational multimillion-dollar case involving the Florida dentist had been difficult for them. In some cases their research had been snapped up under the Freedom of Information Act before they could publish.

Despite the handicap, Fletcher had done extensive reading, and he mounted a tough challenge. His cross-examination fills 109 pages of transcript. In the course of the exchange, Dawson sought assistance from the young scientist himself.

He drew from Montpetit the name of the director at the Los Alamos data bank.

"Is there anyone closer to home?" Dawson asked hopefully.

"No, there isn't," Montpetit replied.

Dawson then probed for weaknesses in the prosecution. Picking up on Montpetit's admission that his one attempt to extract the virus from a Ssenyonga sample had failed, he asked how many more tests Montpetit could do before the Ssenyonga sample would be exhausted.

"Two, maybe three more," Montpetit admitted.

Dawson was intrigued. If Ssenyonga's sample couldn't be analysed, the prosecution would be significantly weakened. And there was always the chance that Ssenyonga's DNA would not match those of his victims. He made a mental note to advise Ssenyonga to beware of giving a fresh blood sample that the police could seize. His client would have to pay cash for all future blood tests, avoiding use of his traceable health insurance number.

Dawson asked the scientist an inspired question. "Since this is such a different strain, does that mean it is transmitted slightly differently?"

Montpetit honestly didn't know. "That's being studied right now."

It was time for both sides to present their closing arguments. The legal points were so dry that the courtroom all but emptied of spectators. Simon Johnson, giving the Crown's reasoning on the issue of legal consent, was nervous as he began. "It was the importance of the case, I suppose," he explains abashedly. He describes that case as being "like a murder trial, except the victims are still alive."

Simon meticulously covered the points involved in each of the four charges but the one of aggravated sexual assault was the trickiest for him. It was his responsibility to persuade the judge to widen the interpretation of consent in a sexual context. He had three carefully prepared arguments to make: one was that fraud occurred, since Ssenyonga presented himself as a man free of infection; another was the public policy argument, which holds that certain kinds of harm are so grave that consent to them flies against common sense; the third was that rules of consent should be stretched when such a catastrophe as HIV results from the activity.

Fletcher Dawson in rebuttal challenged each of the four charges, but he too dwelt longest on aggravated sexual assault. He stressed that all the witnesses had consented to sex with Ssenyonga. It was not relevant that Ssenyonga didn't tell them he was infected with HIV. Sex was a two-way street: surely the women bore some responsibility for the fact that they were infected.

With that, the preliminary trial of Charles Ssenyonga ended. It had occupied eleven court days sprawled over a five-month period from November 12, 1991, to April 24, 1992. The delays were caused by the need to accommodate the disparate calendars of the judge and four lawyers and the availability of twelve witnesses. Ssenyonga himself was silent throughout, an impassive, dignified figure.

Bruce Long had never seen Ssenyonga before the preliminary trial. He watched him with fascination. "I had difficulty understanding how he could be so cool and aloof," he comments. "I did not see any facial expressions over all the days we sat in court, even when the women were breaking up. He has to know that he is the cause of what they were describing up there."

13

MICHAEL MONTPETIT LEFT LONDON as the closing arguments were being made, troubled by Dawson's questions about Ssenyonga's blood sample. He was not sure that he would ever be able to analyse the DNA in Ssenyonga's virus. Everything about his work on matching the DNA in an AIDS virus had been more difficult than he had imagined when he volunteered for the project. For sixteen months he had tried to break out the DNA of the molecules in the HIV taken from the women, every attempt an abject failure, though he faithfully followed the PCR technique, using the same reagents that were developed to match the DNA of the virus found in the Florida dentist and his victims. When he consulted with the scientists at Los Alamos who had succeeded with the viruses in the dentist case, all were baffled. His technique was flawless.

"I modified, and modified, and it still wasn't working," Montpetit recalls. He never thought of giving up. "I'm too stubborn for my own good."

Ultimately, Montpetit decided on what he calls "the brute force approach." He barraged the virus with quantities of PCR well beyond levels he had been using. The virus suddenly yielded: the reason for the long string of failures was clear. The reagents used in Atlanta and, before that, in Edinburgh, where the work was pioneered, were applicable only to the North American strain of HIV-1, subtype B. Ssenyonga's virus was African, subtype A, much like a strain known in the international HIV data bank as SF170. It was so unlike the North American strain that it required different reagents.

Montpetit says he "bounced around the lab for an afternoon" after that development. Geoff Beasley solemnly requested an invitation to Montpetit's Nobel Prize investiture.

Over months of work, Montpetit capped off his effort by producing universal reagents that would work on all strains of the AIDS virus.

The world's scientific community recognized early in the AIDS epidemic that there were two major types of the virus. The most prevalent is HIV-1, found all over the world; HIV-2 is almost exclusive to west Africa. Within HIV-1, seven broad subtypes are found, among which HIV-1 B is most prevalent in North America, South America, Australia, and Europe, with some emergence in Asia; HIV-1 A is in Africa, Europe, and Asia, where other subtypes, C, D, and E, can also be found. The HIV subtype distinctions no longer are as sharp because of international travel, but the family traits of each are observable. To monitor the strains and mutants of HIV as they arise, a data base has been established in the National Laboratory HIV and Retrovirus DNA Sequence Database in Los Alamos New Mexico, to which scientists from all over the world forward samples for classification.

The virus sequences received from Montpetit astonished the scientists at Los Alamos. Dr. Gerald Myers, director of the data base, informed Montpetit that computer searches established that the virus that infected Ssenyonga's sexual partners was not in the data base: it was something new in the known world of HIV. Though it correlated strongly with a virus sent from Rwanda to San Francisco for analysis, a virus known in the data bank as SF170, it was dissimilar in significant ways. Although many others in North America may carry the same HIV-1 virus, the Canadians infected by Ssenyonga are the only people on the continent whose DNA has been examined and identified as this African subtype-A virus. Montpetit testified that it was "the first time anyone has seen anything like it."

"There probably are more subtype A viruses in the United States and North America," Gerald Myers told Henry Hess of the *Globe and Mail,* but the cluster in Ontario was the first the data bank had seen.

By a piece of luck, Montpetit had acquired a sample of Ssenyonga's blood. In a telephone conversation between Montpetit and Cheryl Wagner one day in the months leading up to the preliminary hearing, she had observed that it was regrettable that Michael could not obtain a sample of Ssenyonga's blood for a matching, since blood cannot be taken against a person's will.

"Ssenyonga certainly won't provide you with a sample," she said, "and you need fresh blood for this work, don't you?"

Montpetit said, "Maybe not. Is there an old sample somewhere?"

Cheryl perked up. "I think the Toronto lab keeps all HIV-positive samples. I'll talk to Rick Galli."

She called the Toronto testing lab, and Galli confirmed her guess. The lab keeps all serum, negative and positive, for a year. After that, negative samples are discarded, but samples that react positive are kept forever. "We retain all our positives because we want to see if we have a diminished response or an increased response when the next sample from that person arrives," he explains. "By comparing the samples we can trace the progress of the infection."

The Ssenyonga sample was available for the investigation, but Galli said he couldn't yield it up. "We're bound by a lot of rules about confidentiality," he explained to Cheryl. "Regardless of the circumstances, we cannot release information to third parties." The only way the sample could be obtained would be with a subpoena.

Cheryl phoned Terry Hall to tell him that Ssenyonga's sample was available: it was somewhere among some quarter million serum samples stored in fourteen freezers in Galli's lab.

"We can get a search warrant, but we'll never find it," Terry groaned. "Maybe we can pin it down by the date. When was he tested?"

"End of February or early March, 1989," she said.

Terry narrowed it down further. Checking Henry Bendheim's medical records, he found the number on Ssenyonga's sample and served a subpoena on the central lab for A10784. Galli yielded a small amount of Ssenyonga's serum: "what we could spare," he explains. This scrap, too tiny to be useful to anyone working above the molecular level, was prepared for shipment to the federal lab in Ottawa.

To guarantee for purposes of the trial that this indeed was Ssenyonga's sample, Terry Hall took the tube in a freezer box to Ottawa and personally handed it to Montpetit. Michael received the bit of Ssenyonga's plasma sample, serum with no blood cells, in January, 1992, soon after the preliminary trial began. He had time to make only one attempt to extract the DNA before going to London to testify. To his dismay that effort was a failure. He dared not risk a second disaster. The biochemist had received only nine hundred microlitres of Ssenyonga serum from Rick Galli. The disappointing attempt to extract HIV used four hundred microlitres. He had sufficient for only two more tries.

Montpetit was able to be profligate with the samples taken from the women. Each had provided him with two to four full tubes of blood and willingly would give more. The scrap of Ssenyonga's serum from the Toronto lab, however, was all he was likely to get.

Extracting HIV from serum was new technology. Some success had been reported at a medical conference attended by a colleague of Michael Montpetit. She brought back to Ottawa a book of abstracts from that conference, one of which was from an Australian group using an elegantly simple method. The Australians stuck HIV antibodies on the side of a tube and let them find the virus. Since it was a single-step, one-container procedure, none of the precious serum was lost, as occurred in the many decantings required by Montpetit's method.

The problem was that Montpetit couldn't find the Australians to ask how they did it and what equipment they used. He tried phone calls and letters to the address listed in the abstract, but the group had scattered and no one seemed to know where to find any of them. He had come to a dead end, unwilling to risk any more of his precious sample. He set it aside in a freezer until he could figure out what to do.

On May 28, 1992, Judge Deborah Livingstone was ready with a fourteen-page decision. As Dawson expected, the charge she found most applicable in the circumstances was criminal negligence causing bodily harm. In the formal language required for such decisions, Livingstone bound Ssenyonga over to appear "at the next court of competent jurisdiction" on charges of causing bodily harm to Francine Dalton, Nancy Gauthier, and Joan Estrada, whom she named by their initials alone.

"The issues remaining, then," she continued, reading her decision, "are whether I have heard sufficient evidence upon which a reasonable jury, properly instructed, could convict Mr. Ssenyonga of three counts of aggravated sexual assault, three counts of administering a noxious thing, and three counts of common nuisance."

She turned first to the most contentious one, the aggra-vated sexual assault charge. "Since consent has been admit-ted," Livingstone said, "counsel for the accused argues there is no sexual assault. The Crown argues that the com-plainants' consent has been vitiated in one of three ways: by fraud, through public policy, or because the risk inherent in any sexual activity with the accused is so grave it lies out-side the ambit of consent to sex *per se*."

She reviewed the Crown's argument that a new defini-tion of consent was established by the high court ruling on the hockey injury case where a player was seriously injured in a brawl. In a landmark decision, the court had declared that hockey players consent in a legal sense to whatever in-juries occur while playing their rugged sport, but they do not consent to being grievously injured in a fight. Simon Johnson had drawn a parallel with Ssenyonga: the women consented to sex but not to AIDS.

"Should policy-based limits on the freedom of adults to engage in sexual activity be more restrictive than those placed on willing participants in a game of hockey?" Livingstone asked. She quoted from the decision on the hockey player: "The sanctity of the human body should militate against validity of consent to bodily harm."

She said, "Having listened to the emotionally searing evidence of all three complainants, one of whom is a single parent of a young child, this argument holds some attrac-tion." As the tense, expressionless lawyers waited, she ended the suspense. She said, "I am satisfied that the argu-ments as presented by the Crown with respect to the vitia-tion of consent to unprotected sex with the accused are sufficiently persuasive for me to conclude that there is some evidence upon which a jury, properly instructed, could convict Mr. Ssenyonga of aggravated sexual assault."

Connie Neill, sitting at the back of the courtroom, began to cry.

It was a significant victory for the Crown. Fletcher Dawson comments, "If the sexual assault charges had been dismissed at the preliminary hearing stage, the prosecution would not have had the right to an automatic ban on publishing the victims' names."

When asked later if her decision was influenced in any degree by this, Livingstone replied carefully, "That was a consideration, but that was not the reason the aggravated sex charge was kept in." She hesitated, then sat back and spread her hands eloquently. "Oh, sure," she admitted, "it was on my mind."

The young judge made another significant ruling when she threw out the charges of common nuisance, even though it had been accepted by the Ontario Court of Appeal in the case of the Ottawa man who gave contaminated blood to the Red Cross. In order for a common nuisance charge to stand, Livingstone said, she would need evidence that Ssenyonga was endangering the health of the public. No such evidence had been produced. "The accused did not offer himself to the general public," she observed dryly. His sexual relations were with specific individuals, and "attachments" had developed, demonstrating that these were serious liaisons rather than casual ones.

This was as close to a comment about Ssenyonga's character as the decision was to come, but in truth Judge Livingstone had noticed that each woman who testified against Ssenyonga spoke of having respect, admiration, and even love for him. None of the women lacked intelligence and discernment. In an interview in her spacious, handsome courthouse office after the hearing, Deborah Livingstone commented, "The testimony of all the complainants showed how sincerely and intensely they cared for him. It was an impressive person they cared about when they had their relationships. While the prelim was something like being at a murder trial, it wasn't fuelled with the same hatred and anger. It was more intense than that." She concluded sadly, "I was struck by all of them in different ways because they are all such different ladies. All bright, all vital."

Judge Livingstone also dismissed the charges of administering a noxious thing. Semen, she declared, was not a "poison, or noxious medicine, or substance" as the law generally requires, nor did she find any evidence to suggest that Ssenyonga intended to harm the women when he ejaculated in their bodies.

"There is no evidence that the accused could have foreseen the certainty or substantial certainty of infecting the complainants with HIV by having unprotected sex with them," she commented, dismissing the Crown's contention that Ssenyonga's "recklessness" in exposing the women to HIV was synonymous with an intention to infect them.

Although judges at preliminary hearings cannot expect that their decisions will have a far-reaching influence on what happens in other courtrooms, observers of the Ssenyonga case believe that the scarcity of precedents in AIDS-related criminal trials will give much weight to Judge Livingstone's well-pondered decision and her rejection of the charges of common nuisance and noxious substance. Crown prosecutors across Canada are obliged to study her reasons when considering those charges in future AIDS cases.

Others, and Judge Livingstone frankly is among them, are hopeful that the difficulty in finding charges to fit Ssenyonga will move legislators to write new law. "My overriding concern throughout the prelim was that there isn't a charge out there that's correct. Why isn't something being done to create the proper section? With the prevalence of this disease and the concern about blood and the concern about hospitalization and the concern for the social aspect of it, why is the criminal system not addressing it?"

She was struck by a comment of one of the complainants that she was unsure whether the trial was about a moral

issue or a legal one. Livingstone comments, "She was absolutely correct. All of us were troubled by the fact we
weren't sure at any time whether this was a legal issue. The
moral side of it cut to our very roots."

In the media scrum following Judge Livingstone's decision, Fletcher Dawson was asked to comment. He confined
himself to a statement that it was "interesting." Some time
later he elaborated. "Judge Livingstone is a bright, conscientious, hard-working judge with a good reputation," he
observed. "At that time [of the preliminary hearing] she
was only recently appointed to Provincial Division bench in
London but she listened to all the arguments with great patience, and I think she worked hard on it. I may disagree
with her judgement but it is something to be reckoned with.
It was a studiously prepared legal decision."

Though they differed with some of Judge Livingstone's
observations, Crown lawyers were pleased overall. The sex
charges were in: the women would be able to testify anonymously. Furthermore, clinching evidence for the criminal
negligence charge was on the way if Michael Montpetit
could extract the DNA in Ssenyonga's virus and match it to
that of the victims.

Montpetit, however, was not risking any more of his tiny
sample. It remained in his freezer while he set about working on the blood of other women infected by Ssenyonga.
Geoff Beasley called him almost daily, but Montpetit was
not willing to proceed until he found the Australians.

Beasley had an inspiration. "I'll ask Terry Hall," he told
Montpetit. "He knows people everywhere."

The biochemist gave Terry the names and the address, a
teaching centre where the scientists once worked. Hall
called a friend of his in Australia, a former OPP colleague,
and the man tracked down the scientists within hours.

"Mike is as impressed with Terry as we are with
Montpetit," Geoff comments.

Montpetit excitedly called Australia from his lab at nine o'clock on a Sunday night, Monday morning on the sub-continent. The scientists were enthusiastic about helping and sent instructions and descriptions of the necessary equipment. Michael followed to the letter the directions, no longer concerned if a test failed. The Australians had shared with him a trick of the trade: diluting samples to make them stretch to near infinity. Under their guidance, Montpetit diluted one microlitre of Ssenyonga's serum a hundredfold and got "phenomenal results" immediately. He now had sufficient serum to run all the tests he liked, with ample in reserve.

Fletcher Dawson had to admit that the defence was in trouble. The women complainants were credible, reinforcing and fortifying each other's testimony by sheer weight of numbers. It looked as though Montpetit's work on the DNA matches was unassailable, which meant all the complainants were infected by the same person. Further, numerous witnesses had established that Ssenyonga knew he was infected.

In view of the Crown's strong case, Fletcher wondered if his client would like to change his plea to guilty and bargain for a short sentence. He asked Ssenyonga's permission to inquire what reduced sentence the Crown would ask if Ssenyonga changed his plea.

Fletcher explains that this was routine in the circumstances.

"It is my obligation as a lawyer to raise that possibility with every client when there is any evidence that might warrant it," he explains. It was not the first time Fletcher had raised the possibility but Ssenyonga always rejected it flatly. Dawson reflects, "He didn't know if he was guilty. He wanted the court to make that determination."

It is an interesting comment, and others close to Charles Ssenyonga have said much the same. It wasn't that Ssenyonga doubted that he had infected the women. He *knew* he had infected them, but he wasn't sure he had broken any law. He was curious, in the way of a lawyer, to hear what a judge had to say.

A man of Ssenyonga's legal training certainly could not escape the realization that the prosecution was in good shape. When Fletcher asked him a second time about changing his plea to guilty, he gave his lawyer permission to approach the Crown. Accordingly, Dawson made a telephone call to Beasley and asked, "If there were to be a guilty plea in regard to criminal negligence, what sentence would the Crown be seeking?"

The answer was, "Five to eight years."

Dawson was disgusted. "My immediate reaction to that was, *My client's going to be dead by then.* It certainly wasn't any kind of an inducement to change the plea."

Cheryl Wagner heard rumours that Fletcher was making inquiries about a plea bargain. She was horrified. "Francine and Nancy and Joan need to have their day in court," she commented. "They deserve it and there will never be a stronger HIV-infection case than this one. If they plea bargain it, Francine and Nancy will fall apart."

Dawson's main hope was to discredit the charges themselves; he didn't think either applied to his client. "There really was a legal issue here whether those acts, which we know he did commit, constituted criminal negligence," the defence lawyer comments. "And certainly the element of consent ruled out the appropriateness of the aggravated sexual assault charge."

Connie Neill and Charles Ssenyonga were still pushing Dawson to bring in expert witnesses to testify that HIV was not the cause of AIDS. Dawson stalled, concerned that such a defence was open to ridicule. International AIDS conferences do not include such theorists among their main presenters and the HIV/AIDS community in general regards them as a lunatic fringe. The more promising avenue, Fletcher thought, was to examine the riddle at the heart of the case, which was Ssenyonga's state of mind when he had unprotected sex. Whatever way he turned, Dawson could see no alternative to psychological testing.

Ssenyonga, angry and insulted, refused. Fletcher waited an interval for Ssenyonga to calm down, and then put the request again. He suggested that there might be something in Ssenyonga's psychological makeup that would render him unable to control his sexual behaviour. "The basic thought I was having," Dawson later explained, "was that if someone were to deliberately do this, if someone were that callous, there's got to be a screw loose. You wouldn't expect a normal person to engage in that kind of activity for so long, after so many warnings. There had to be some illness, or some problem that was distorting his perceptions. Or even that he might be a psychopath, a completely uncaring individual."

When Ssenyonga continued to refuse Dawson's urging, insisting he wasn't crazy, the lawyer embarked on what he delicately referred to as "a process of education" about Section 16 of the Criminal Code. As Connie describes this period of meetings, Dawson patiently explained to Ssenyonga that the word *insane* is no longer used; the new terminology is "not criminally responsible," often known by its initials, NCR. Fletcher told Ssenyonga that if the NCR defence held up, he would seek a conditional discharge with no incarceration in a psychiatric facility. It was new territory, but he thought the argument would have a good chance.

Ssenyonga was still repelled by a defence that would call his sanity into question. Connie Neill disagreed with him. They argued so often and heatedly that they eventually decided to avoid the volatile subject. "He just wouldn't listen to reason," Connie says, in an amused tone. Fletcher was less amused. "Ssenyonga was pretty strong willed," he says, his expression neutral. "He didn't always want to listen to my advice."

After hours of discussions with his client and Connie Neill, Fletcher finally won him over by assuring Ssenyonga that the results would not be used in the trial without his agreement. The examination, he promised, was purely exploratory. Fletcher selected an expert on sexual disorders and male violence, Dr. Ronald Langevin, a senior research psychologist in Toronto.

Charles Ssenyonga's first of three appointments with Langevin was in May, 1992. Connie Neill drove him, though she was still recovering from her miscarriage, and waited outside. During a break in the testing, he walked around the block with her to calm himself. He was horrified by the pictures shown him during the phallometric testing, which involves presenting the subject with a variety of images to determine what brings him to erection. "It was very difficult for an African to learn that some people are aroused by children or by very old people," Connie recalls. "For some time he was so upset he didn't talk."

Langevin, a big, heavily bearded, greying man with a calm, steady manner, found nothing in Ssenyonga's tests to indicate that the man was a psychopath, a sociopath, violent, sadistic, or sexually disturbed. What he did find, almost accidentally, was post-traumatic stress disorder, a condition known in World War I as shell shock. Langevin believed that two events, Ssenyonga's experiences in Uganda and his subsequent discovery that he was HIV-infected, were so disturbing that he had blocked the knowledge of his infection from his conscious mind.

When Fletcher Dawson read Langevin's report, he was surprised that there was no evidence that Ssenyonga was in any way mentally unbalanced. That meant Dawson could not use a Section 16 NCR argument — unless he based it on post-traumatic stress disorder, or PTSD. The problem was that PTSD had never been advanced in any trial in Canada as a reason for being not criminally responsible. Dawson put law students to work on the problem and read everything they unearthed, together with some research of his own. When he learned that PTSD is a defence successfully used many times in the United States, he decided it had a chance. In strictest confidence, he consulted with a few colleagues who agreed with him that it was worth a try.

Fletcher was plunged into a dilemma. The consequences of pleading that Ssenyonga was not guilty under the provisions of Section 16 could be dramatic: his client might be confined to a mental institution for the rest of his life. He had assured Ssenyonga that he would ask the judge for a conditional discharge but he could not be sure of success. Over the next few months Dawson continued to research the disorder and mull over his choices.

"Section 16 is really one of the last resorts of a criminal lawyer," Dawson says. With the Crown's case almost impregnable, he came to the conclusion that he had to pursue this slim hope. Dawson was strongly influenced in his decision by Ssenyonga's deteriorating health. If the choices for his client were dying in prison or dying in a mental hospital, the latter was preferable.

Dawson had still to convince Ssenyonga. There had been little direct communication about Langevin's report. Charles was sick in bed when Fletcher called, so Connie took the message and passed it along. Ssenyonga hit the roof. Under no circumstances, he said, would he agree to such a defence.

"Fletcher really had a hurdle there," Connie says.

Fletcher had another hurdle on his mind. Langevin, his star witness, was not an expert in post-traumatic stress disorder. This was a serious disadvantage. The prosecution certainly would find someone more qualified in that field to challenge what Langevin had to say. On the other hand, one distinct benefit in using Langevin was his unquestionable expertise in sexual disorders. Langevin's testimony that Ssenyonga was not a pervert who gained sexual pleasure from controlling or hurting others would be respected.

Dawson says, "I thought it was very important to show that Ssenyonga didn't fit into those categories and there was no one better than Langevin to do that." His plan, if he could get Ssenyonga's cooperation, was to have a second expert witness with a solid background in interpretations of Section 16, who would testify that PTSD fit under the categories. He mulled over his choices. To his mind, the best person was a prominent psychiatrist, Dr. Robert Wood Hill, the Clarke Institute of Psychiatry director of the forensic intake service, which deals in criminal behaviour. Wood Hill had testified on Section 16 cases many times and knew the provisions backwards.

Ssenyonga remained obdurate: he would not put in a defence that to his mind equated with an admission he was insane. Connie Neill argued in vain. Despite the nurturing role she played in Ssenyonga's life, or perhaps because of it, Ssenyonga had periods when everything she did seemed to irritate him. He would fly into a rage if she watched certain television shows, berating her for a lack of intelligence. When she was pregnant, he had often shouted that she was too ignorant to raise a child. He hated her friends; to keep the peace she gradually lost contact with most of them.

Charles would say contemptuously, "Who do you think you are? You're no saint." Sometimes they went days without speaking. Once he said that he should have stayed with Francine Dalton because "at least she had something in her head."

When moods of wrath were on him, Connie would retreat. One night he was so angry after a friend of hers came for a visit that he raged for hours. Around three in the morning, Connie slipped out of the house while he was in the bathroom and spent the rest of the night shivering in her jeep in a parking lot. It was not the only night she slept in her car. More than once she considered seeking shelter in a women's hostel.

The other side of Ssenyonga, however, was a joy. When he was feeling fine he would tell her that she was the first soul mate he had known since John Webster, and that she alone of all the women in his life was his intellectual equal. "Finally," he said to her one time, "I have someone in my life who doesn't judge me. I can think what I want, say what I want."

She says earnestly, "John Webster was the ultimate relationship for him, though it wasn't sexual, of course. It was as though they shared the same soul. He kept looking in women for what he shared with John and he wouldn't settle for second best. With me he had the intellectual, spiritual, emotional quality he sought."

She readily forgave the times when Ssenyonga turned on her. A Ugandan couple close to them told her that Ssenyonga confided in them that he was ashamed of his behaviour and that he deeply appreciated Connie's loyalty and tender care of him. They quoted him saying, "How can I treat her this way when she is so good to me? I don't know how I can talk to her like that. Thank God for her." She wished he would say the same to her, but even second-hand it gave her comfort.

Soon after the preliminary hearing ended, Ssenyonga and Connie Neill moved to a remote farmhouse near the charming town of Listowel, an hour's drive northeast of London and deep in Mennonite country where families still travel in horse-drawn buggies. Connie found it, following Charles's instructions that he wanted "a lot of open space in the country."

Though the tiny house looks bleak, standing alone at a crossroads with fields of corn stretching in every direction and a sagging red barn beside it, Connie's nesting skills transformed the storey-and-a-half building into a cosy place full of white wicker furniture, African artifacts on the walls, pretty rugs, and a wood-burning stove for warmth in winter.

For income they depended on his medical disability allowance and some part-time work she found as a nurse. Isolated as they were, with few visitors, they were almost inseparable. "I think the only time we were apart was when I went to do the laundry," she says. In September, 1992, they bought a frisky dog, a mixture of shepherd and collie they named Simba, the Swahili word for lion. With a friendly goat, Sammy, two ducks to feed, and the landlord's horses to tend, they filled their days taking long walks and caring for the animals.

Ssenyonga often spoke of home. He told Connie he feared he would never again "look into the eyes of my mother." He spoke little of his father but missed his mother acutely. Of his large family, only his brother John, a law professor in Kampala, knew that he had AIDS and was facing criminal charges.

His father wrote him a tender letter to come home. "You have plenty of cows," he said, referring to Ssenyonga's bride-purchase herd. Ssenyonga put him off. There was no point in telling him the wretched truth.

In good weather he and Connie enjoyed camping trips. She planned their days with his health in mind. In the hope of restoring his collapsed immune system, she fed him a diet of her own construction: foods such as shiitake mushrooms, and potions and nutritional supplements she bought at health food stores.

They used her battered jeep for transportation. Connie drove; Ssenyonga had amassed so many minor traffic tickets that eventually he lost his driver's licence.

Connie was aware that much of the public saw her as either a fool or a dupe. When she yields to rhapsodic flights about being Ssenyonga's "soul mate," she does appear stunningly gullible. Her appearance, a small, soft-bodied woman with huge dark eyes and rich loose dark hair, heightens that impression of childishness, but Connie also is dependable, hard-working, and loyal. She loved Charles Ssenyonga with her whole being: it shone from her whenever she looked at him across the courtroom, even while women were testifying that he was a consummate liar. "That's not my Charles," she told friends.

14

MEANWHILE, SSENYONGA'S SIBILANT NAME had become known across the country. The Ugandan communities in Ontario, wincing every time Charles was described in the media as a countryman, did not know what to make of him. Ugandans who knew Charles Ssenyonga were baffled. To them he seemed to be two people, one of them charming and the other detestable. Despite their ambivalence, some wanted to offer Ssenyonga friendship and support out of a sense of national solidarity. To their dismay, he kept them at a distance. Ugandans were scandalized to hear that Charles Ssenyonga was almost always the only black person in the courtroom. That was shameful, they said, but Ssenyonga seemed to want it that way. In truth, most Ugandans were happy to keep their distance from the case, which they felt reflected badly on all Ugandans in Canada. They brooded about the publicity he was receiving and wondered if it didn't owe something to racism.

In August, 1992, Dr. Cheryl Wagner gave birth to a second daughter, Alexandra. Cheryl was forty-two years old and anxious to spend time with her children, but the Ssenyonga trial still gripped her. She left the Sherbourne Street partnership, transferring most of her patients to other physicians, and restricted her practice to two days a week in a basement suite on Bloor Street West. Among the patients she retained were all the women infected by Ssenyonga.

Later that year, on November 5, Geoff Beasley and Fletcher Dawson appeared before Mr. Justice Roland Haines, who happened to be the husband of the preliminary hearing judge, Deborah Livingstone. (Such coincidences are not uncommon in professional communities the size of London.) The lawyers were there to set court dates for Charles Ssenyonga's trial on the charges of aggravated sexual assault and criminal negligence causing bodily harm.

Beasley appeared nonchalant but he was growing concerned. Dr. Michael Montpetit still had not isolated the DNA from Ssenyonga's virus, which would be the prosecution's linchpin. Beasley asked for a delay to give the biochemist some room. "As recently as within the last month, I understood that he [Montpetit] hadn't started that work because he was trying to obtain some new technology or information, perhaps from Australia, and it is recognized that there is some fragility to this work he is doing. It is very sensitive work. We don't know if it's going to be successful or unsuccessful."

Fletcher Dawson was incensed. A postponement would inconvenience him greatly, as he explained to the judge, because he had a month-long murder case scheduled for January, and another murder trial was set for February and March in Windsor. Besides, he went on, he didn't believe he was being informed by the Crown about Montpetit's activities.

The fact was that Fletcher was still unable to find anyone willing to help him challenge the evidence that Montpetit would be presenting. As he described it to Judge Haines, an assistant had spent the previous day talking to people in

Maryland, California, New Mexico, Vancouver, Montreal, and various other places. The assistant confirmed what Dawson had discovered earlier: there really was almost no one in Montpetit's class.

"What people are telling us is that there are just a couple of people perhaps in the world who are really qualified to look at this," Fletcher observed. Most vexatious for the defence lawyer was that none of them would agree to come to Canada to testify. "People are saying that DNA cases in this area could keep them literally in court every day of their lives."

Montpetit got wind of Dawson's frustrated efforts to find the experts he needed. "The small group that worked on the dentist's virus got burned," he explains. "They weren't prepared for the adversarial approach in courtrooms. They were jarred to be asked belittling questions and distressed to be in the eye of media who hadn't the faintest idea what they did but wanted thirty-second summaries for news clips."

Beasley explained to the judge that Montpetit was "expanding the test, making it bigger." At the preliminary hearing Montpetit reported on a two hundred-base pair analysis, Beasley said, comfortable with the terminology, and now he was working on a six-hundred-base pair.

Pushing for a January date, Beasley added, "These victims are in a unique position, one which the courts in the past have not had to deal with on a regular basis and one which I suppose unfortunately courts will have to cope with in the future." He refrained from elaborating on what was the "unique position," namely, that the witnesses could be dead or too sick to testify if the trial was delayed too long.

Judge Haines asked how long the trial was expected to last. Lawyers are pathologically optimistic when asked how much time they will require. Beasley guessed about three weeks; Dawson thought the range of probability was between two and six weeks. The actual length of the Ssenyonga trial was four months.

Bruce Long says that the prosecution was ready to go to trial only weeks after the decision from the preliminary. "Apparently, Dawson's schedule was a problem," he says dryly. "The tests were held up only because Montpetit wanted to repeat them over and over to get mathematical certainty. That wasn't a hold-up for us."

Appreciating Dawson's predicament that the biomedical data would need to be critiqued, Judge Haines first set the trial date for March 29, 1993, and then moved it back another week, to April 6.

The delay of five months before the commencement of the trial came as a shock to the edgy women infected by Ssenyonga. The irrepressible Nancy Gauthier shot off angry letters to Bruce Long that the postponement was intolerable. She warned that she was thinking of withdrawing as a witness and observed, "In many ways I have put my life on hold and I am becoming resentful of living my life under the Charles Ssenyonga case...I would like my life to be my own again...All that I am asking and pleading is that the trial date for the Ssenyonga case be set as soon as possible."

Her sense of urgency did not seem misplaced. Soon after Judge Haines made his ruling to wait five months, Katie Newman, the Brantford woman who was planning to be a witness at the trial, became very ill. In February she sank into a coma and died. She was twenty-nine years old and left a small son a friend is raising. Her father says, "Some mornings you wake up and it seems like a nightmare. Then you realize it isn't. It happened."

Dawson's long search for someone to scrutinize Montpetit's work ended with Dr. James Mullens, director of microbiology and immunology at Stanford University in California, an expert on HIV cloning and genetic matching. Mullens agreed to assess what Montpetit was doing, and the Ontario Legal Aid Plan gave its approval. Some of Montpetit's work was rerun on Stanford's own computer programs, which required extensive use of computer time and the assistance of a graduate student. Though Mullens's review eventually cost legal aid thousands of dollars, it was crucial to Ssenyonga's right to a fair trial. Geoff Beasley obtained data from Michael Montpetit and gave it to Dawson to relay to Mullens, whose name the Crown did not know. Eventually, Montpetit and Mullens cut out the legal middlemen and communicated directly by computer, their admiration for one another growing. The two continue to work together.

Fletcher Dawson's criticism of the Crown, particularly his complaint that he wasn't being informed as rules of court require, was galling to the prosecution, who felt the allegations were unfair. Bruce Long made a tactical decision not to argue the point in court. He felt that kind of dispute — "No I didn't," "Yes you did," — would only distract from the real issues of the trial. "That is so silly," Long sighs. "Disclosure began on June 20, 1991, the time of Ssenyonga's arrest. The next day Dawson had the statements of three victims and their names. That was two days after arrest, four days before the show-cause. How in the world could you do it faster than that?" Dawson received 1,935 pages of disclosure, he says. "By October 21 of 1991 he had full disclosure of the Crown brief," Long says. "The same one I had. Exactly the same."

Further, Long continues, in February, 1992, he gave Dawson all the evidence in the police files, six banker's boxes of it, which Dawson was at liberty to copy as he pleased. "We even gave him the Crown argument that we were going to make at the preliminary, and we don't have to give our argument." Long contends that the findings of Michael Montpetit, about which Dawson was particularly suspicious, were provided to the defence lawyer as soon as they became known. "We told him everything as soon as we physically could. I had one secretary working almost full time on disclosure."

Dawson has a different view. He says disclosure improved once he started complaining in court. "Eventually, the prosecution got the message," he says sardonically. "As they say, the squeaky wheel gets the grease." He hunches his shoulders. "Let's put it this way, the prosecution and defence did not always operate on a completely harmonious plain."

Fletcher Dawson, faced with three major trials bunched together, relied on junior lawyers for support. The one he chose to assist with the Ssenyonga trial was a bright young woman, Jeanine LeRoy, who had not yet been called to the bar. She had just begun the bar admission course in London and had decided on criminal law.

"Can you give me some time?" Dawson asked her.

Jeanine, thrilled to be asked by a lawyer of Fletcher's calibre, promised to find the time. He instructed her to concentrate on two areas, the Supreme Court of Canada's recent interpretations of criminal negligence, and what consent means in sexual assault cases. She began with a basic primer, *Stuart on Common Law,* to find the major cases in English common law that best fit the Ssenyonga situation. She worked on the Ssenyonga research steadily for three months, simultaneously taking bar-ad courses, a prodigious feat.

Jeanine LeRoy is a compact, well-groomed, crisp woman in her twenties with silky reddish-blond hair stylishly cut. Her father is a conservative Wesleyan Methodist minister, and she was raised in parsonages, first in Canada and then in Michigan. An ardent reader and high-achiever in school, she found her niche when she took part in a student mock trial. She grins, "I got the bug."

She married her high school sweetheart, journalist Christopher Clark, in the middle of law school at the

University of British Columbia, then articled in a tax firm on Bay Street in Toronto. She joined Dawson's firm in February, 1993, after her call to the bar. She counts working on the Ssenyonga case as a privileged time in her life.

"I got very lucky. Fletcher is a wonderful lawyer and a very good teacher," she says.

One of her early assignments was to prepare summaries of the bulky transcripts of the preliminary trial for Fletcher's convenience. Then he asked her to take a detailed statement from Ssenyonga. A meticulous woman, Jeanine spent six days questioning Charles; "a long and harried process," she recalls. The transcript of those sessions runs two hundred pages. Ssenyonga felt more comfortable with Jeanine than he had with Fletcher, and a friendship developed. A close and trusting relationship also grew between Connie Neill and Jeanine LeRoy, with the result that telephone communication between Dawson and Ssenyonga flowed through the women.

"Jeanine was so compassionate," Connie explains.

Jeanine says, "I admired Connie as a woman who would stick by this man, and face the ridicule. She cared for him physically and emotionally. I don't think too many people understood her and knew what moved her. And I liked Charles very much. He was a pleasure to spend time with."

At the same time, LeRoy has great sympathy for the women Ssenyonga infected. "I had a hard time sometimes compartmentalizing my mind so I could play the game," she comments quietly. "And it is a game."

Connie's understanding from Fletcher was that Jeanine would be responsible for gathering evidence on the theory that HIV doesn't cause AIDS. Connie turned over to Jeanine the formidable amount of material she had gathered and gave Jeanine some names to contact. Connie and Charles were delighted that Fletcher at last was paying attention.

The documents assembled for the defence occupied many boxes. One contained binders and notes, another transcripts and summaries of the preliminary, two boxes held law references, one box was filled with the Crown's disclosure, and another with the defence's case. Similarly in the Crown's office, one bookcase was devoted entirely to Ssenyonga documents. Long counted fifteen loose-leaf notebooks containing Ssenyonga material.

Fletcher waited expectantly for Mullens to provide him with a review of Montpetit's work on the DNA. When the report finally came, he was disappointed. Mullens had minor reservations about parts of Montpetit's methodology, but on the whole the young Canadian scientist had done superb work. The match of the women's DNA was valid.

In January, with the trial less than three months away, the defence lawyer was rocked with a new blow. Geoff Beasley notified him that Montpetit had just succeeded in matching the DNA of Ssenyonga's virus with the DNA found in the virus of all the witnesses. Dawson, much shaken, sent this data to Mullens at Stanford, who responded a few weeks later. Montpetit's newest finding was unassailable. Without question, all the women were infected by Ssenyonga.

Fletcher Dawson had lunch with Geoff Beasley to discuss what this meant to the conduct of the trial. They struck an agreement. Since the match was indisputable, there was no reason for Dawson to insist that the twenty previous sexual contacts of the women be compelled to testify.

"It's to Fletcher's credit that we didn't have to call all the contacts," Geoff Beasley says. "He agreed to that, and it was a considerable concession by him. We could have had a parade. First of all, it would have been a monumental task to get one, no two, of them. He could have insisted we bring them all into the court."

Dawson says he was never comfortable about calling the twenty contacts, though he was prepared to do it. "My concern was not in any way to embarrass or denigrate the complainants," he explains, "but it could have been relevant to the causation issue, so I was very interested in it. But as the DNA evidence came along, that evidence became less important."

Bruce Long was vastly relieved by Dawson's decision. The financial cost of bringing the twenty contacts to London would have been horrendous, not to mention how long the trial would have been prolonged. The twenty men, unaware of the behind-scenes negotiations, never knew how close they came to being subpoenaed into open court, their identities possibly unprotected.

Long grins. "And all because Terry Hall knew a policeman in Australia."

As the winter of 1992 curved into the spring of 1993, Fletcher Dawson considered asking the judge for yet another delay. Charles Ssenyonga was not at all well. The lawyer rarely saw him. Connie Neill reported that Charles was withdrawn. He was sleepless until almost dawn and then collapsed in bed for most of the day. Ulcers had erupted on one arm and he was losing weight. Dawson wondered if the man could survive a long trial.

Fletcher himself wasn't feeling too well. He was exhausted from the demands of the two other major trials on his agenda. Although he had backup assistance from his firm, it is his style to do the court work alone and he was feeling harried and unprepared, something he hates. It was depressing news from Geoff Beasley that Michael Montpetit was still working on Ssenyonga's DNA. "Who knows what we're going to find in the midst of this trial," Fletcher grumbled irritably.

The prosecution wasn't without its own problems. The health of the women infected by Ssenyonga was vulnerable to sudden disintegration, as the death of Katie Newman had tragically demonstrated. Francine Dalton, the only one of the three witnesses with full-blown AIDS, was subject to severe symptoms, such as night sweats and headaches, and her T-4 cell count was dropping.

In the year that separated the preliminary hearing from the criminal trial, the women kept bumping into one another. Linda Booker went to an HIV-positive women's support group in Toronto and found another woman infected by Ssenyonga. Shrinking from the note-comparing that might lie ahead, she never returned.

It was not surprising that Ssenyonga-infected women were meeting; many of them existed in southern Ontario and services for HIV-infected women were few. Ssenyonga's former lovers stood out in HIV/AIDS groups because they were almost always the only ones who were infected by someone who knew he had HIV. Mostly, women contract the virus from men who aren't aware of their HIV status.

Joan Estrada, always protective of her privacy, also avoided support groups. She saw a psychiatrist instead and depended on Cheryl Wagner's regular telephone calls. A former lover moved in with her. Though the couple used condoms to protect him, she lived in horror that he might become infected.

Francine Dalton heard of Voices of Positive Women, a Toronto support group composed of women with HIV or AIDS. She went to workshops, one on public speaking and another on public relations, running into Jennifer Anderson at the latter. Of the ten women in Francine's group, three were infected by Charles Ssenyonga. She also tried a support group at the AIDS Committee of Toronto (ACT). She says, "About twenty women were there, and we went around the circle, each telling how we were infected. A sort of social thing. I dropped out because I didn't want to go on hearing other people's troubles. And I couldn't talk much about my own because we were all forbidden to discuss the court stuff."

That encounter at a Voices of Positive Women meeting was Jennifer Anderson's only visit. "It didn't work for me," she explains. "As the new one in the group you are expected to tell your story. I'm just not comfortable with that." She checked on the support groups at ACT and learned that other Ssenyonga-infected women were attending there. "I don't know who they are and I don't want to," she explains. "I just don't want to be part of that story-sharing."

Danielle Fitzgerald went to the AIDS Committee of London the week after her diagnosis. She says the medical information she received was useful but she wanted no part of the support group. "I have a hard enough time trying to deal with this," she told the counsellor bluntly. "I don't know if I could sit through all that negative stuff. I'm going to sort this out myself. I'll call you." Instead she found a psychiatrist.

Nancy Gauthier, still relying on telephone calls to get her through each day, also decided to go to the AIDS Committee of London. At first she was disgusted. "They seemed to see Charles Ssenyonga as just another HIV-infected person, just as worthy of support as I was. That pissed me off."

There was no danger that she would encounter Charles Ssenyonga there. His friendship with Michael Sauer ended abruptly in December, 1991: Connie Neill will not explain why the breach happened, and Michael is bound by rules of client confidentiality. Estranged as he was from most Ugandans, Ssenyonga then was left with few resources except for Connie. At least once, it seems he turned to his family's faith. One Sunday morning, Paula Adamick, London stringer for the *Toronto Star*, saw him sitting by himself at the back of the city's largest Roman Catholic church, a sad expression on his face.

Gauthier, temporarily at outs with the AIDS Committee of London, hooked up instead with Voices of Positive Women. Her first meeting in Toronto included women who had come from Guelph and from Ottawa. "The room was packed," she recalls. "I thought I was going to cry on the spot. It was packed with women, all HIV-positive, and they were from all walks of life. That just blew me away, so many women."

Ssenyonga-infected women were among the earliest to join support groups of HIV-infected women that sprang up across Ontario, the first one in Toronto in 1987. HIV women's groups resembled the first HIV men's support group in Canada, which was formed in January, 1985. The facilitator for both was Theresa Dobko, a pioneer in AIDS counselling.

Theresa is a solid-bodied woman with fine dark hair cut short and a calm, empathetic manner. She chose social work as her field when she was a teenager. In 1984 she was the first counsellor hired by ACT. In those days the cramped offices were over a fast-food outlet at the intersection of Church and Wellesley Streets, just around the corner from the Hassle Free Clinic.

"All the infected people then were men," Theresa recalls, "either bisexual or gay. They died rapidly. The average life expectancy after diagnosis was nine months." In 1986 she stopped counting the losses. She had been to a hundred funerals.

"There was a sense of real sadness when the first woman with AIDS came to us in 1985," Theresa says. "Yvette Pereault, the other counsellor, and I realized she represented the next wave of the disease."

As more women arrived, some of them from great distances who sought the anonymity that Toronto provided, the counsellors noted some similarities with early men's groups. All the women feared to have their HIV status known, just as men once did.

"Men stopped worrying years ago about others finding out that they are HIV-positive," Theresa says, "but in 1994 women aren't there yet. They seem to see the world as a tough place where they will be harassed if anyone knows — anyone at work, especially. Often even family and friends don't know."

In contrast to the men's groups, though, the women had little in common beyond the virus. Lacking the cohesiveness that gay men had developed over a lifetime of being marginalized, many women come to the group only once or twice because they feel no bond with the others.

One electrifying evening in Theresa Dobko's group at ACT, two newcomers told about the man who infected them. Each said she was infected by a man from Uganda who ran an African store. They looked at one another in horror. "Ssenyonga?" one of them gasped. "My god," said the other. "Yes. You too?"

Theresa thinks they were somewhat relieved to meet one another, that there was comfort for them in finding themselves in the same boat. "Ssenyonga infected so many it was bound to happen," she observes laconically.

Infected women in the late eighties and early nineties kept such a low profile that the country was slow to discover they existed. At a time in 1991 when Dobko was counselling sixty HIV-positive women from Toronto, public health statistics claimed that the total in Toronto was thirty. She grins. "That meant I knew two hundred percent of the HIV-positive women in Toronto."

Otherwise the groups were much like the ones Theresa had conducted for men. Six or eight women gather in a room with comfortable furniture, someone puts on the coffee, and then they talk: about how they were infected, about their emotional disarray, about the treatments they are trying; sometimes, about death.

In almost all cases, they tell of doctors who thought their symptoms were nothing serious. A major issue for HIV-infected women is that doctors, even in 1994, still don't expect a woman to have the AIDS virus and, accordingly, don't suggest a blood test. Says Dr. Iain Mackie, one of the country's experts, "Women's symptoms are ignored by physicians who simply don't know any better."

"Women get sick differently than men," Dr. Cheryl Wagner explains. "The symptoms often are in the gynaecological area." Frequently, in as many as one-third of cases, the infection manifests itself first in a common disorder such as a vaginal yeast infection that does not respond to usual treatments, or in hard-to-treat cancer of the cervix, which is five times more prevalent in HIV-infected women than in women who don't have the virus. Genital warts are another manifestation, as well as severe pelvic inflammatory disease.

"Physicians still don't suspect HIV when these not uncommon conditions occur," Cheryl comments. "This is a real problem because the only way to treat AIDS is to do early intervention. Doctors still think a women can't get HIV, certainly not this professional woman sitting opposite me. There is still that stereotype. Perhaps the Ssenyonga case will change that."

In recent years Voices of Positive Women has become a major resource for HIV-positive women in southern Ontario. Founded by Darien Taylor, an HIV-positive activist, it functions as a support and education service but also has become a powerful advocate, particularly in pushing doctors to provide early treatment for HIV-infected women. The most controversial position taken by Voices of Positive Women is its view that infected women have no obligation to inform sex partners. This stems from the premise that people are responsible for for their own protection.

In a brochure, "Positive Sexuality," Voices of Positive Women declares, "It is up to you whether you say that you are HIV-positive, *as long as you use safer sex* [emphasis added]. Figure out beforehand how you are going to introduce the topic of safer sex. Clearly think your strategy through before you are in the heat of passion and might make a decision you regret."

Theresa Dobko, a committed feminist, believes all women in the nineties are responsible for their own protection and should buy condoms themselves rather than relying on the good will of men. "On the other hand," Theresa observes, "not many women are capable of fighting for safer sex. You have to be assertive to insist that your sex partner wear a condom. Few women are strong enough for that. In our society we teach women to trust men, and we teach men to con women. Both are acting out what they are told to be."

Dr. Iain Mackie makes the same point. "In terms of power politics women have difficulty negotiating safe sex," he notes. "Unfortunately, heterosexual women still do not perceive themselves as being at great risk of contacting HIV. That's a process of education. It's the old story: 'He looks clean, he looks well, he doesn't have any diseases,'" He once had a patient who protested that she couldn't possibly have HIV. Her boyfriend, she explained, drove a BMW and his father was a stockbroker. "In the past," Iain continues, "women were seen as a low-risk group and therefore educational efforts have not been aimed at heterosexual women."

Nancy Gauthier later changed her mind about the AIDS Committee of London. She decided they had something to offer her after all. She was the only woman in the first support group she joined, but eventually the numbers of HIV-positive women increased sufficiently and they formed a support group of their own. It consisted of six women, half of them infected by Ssenyonga. Though they had nothing else in common, the Ssenyonga-infected women felt a bond: they considered taking vacations together, or sharing Christmas dinner.

Barbara Williams was in that support group, one of the Ssenyonga-infected women Crown prosecutors never met. She followed the preliminary trial by reading newspapers and watching television news, her stomach twisting when Ssenyonga's face was shown. Her HIV-infection was two years old, and she had full-blown AIDS. A small, chubby woman, blond and freckled, Barbara met Ssenyonga in London in August of 1990, when she was twenty-two years old. Her family, middle-class people, were at their cottage, and she was on her own and working in a department store. That summer was an emotional low for her. She was depressed about her weight: more than fifty pounds too many on a small frame. Her mother nagged about it; Barbara was discouraged that she couldn't be the thin person her mother wanted.

Charles Ssenyonga lived nearby. In the evening she used to see him sitting outside with a book. Lonely as she was, it was easy to fall into the habit of chatting with the congenial Ssenyonga. He told her she was beautiful. In Uganda, he said, plump women were much desired, a sign of a man's wealth. They went to a movie or two and then began sleeping together. Ssenyonga, knowing he was HIV-positive, wore a condom sometimes, but two or three times he didn't.

"He was very complimentary," Barbara says. "He was fun to be with. He wasn't a monster. I wouldn't have slept with a monster."

The affair lasted a month. When she left in September to begin a psychology major at university in Ottawa, she gave him her address. She never heard from him. In November she developed a painful vaginal yeast infection, dermatitis so severe that her hands cracked and bled, and some strange purple lumps on her arm and leg. A doctor thought her ailments were odd but nothing serious.

Working nights and weekends in a restaurant and attending classes, Barbara had no time for newspapers or television, so she missed the uproar about Charles Ssenyonga that began the following spring. In the summer of 1992 she had a fulltime summer job in an Ottawa restaurant. She was baffled by her fatigue. Walking to the bus stop became almost too much for her. For a while she put it down to strain from a new diet she was trying, but finally she went to a doctor. In two minutes the doctor had a diagnosis. "You've got pneumonia," she said.

"Look," Barbara replied, "I'd like to have an AIDS test. I've been reading that there is a lot of AIDS in Uganda and I had an affair with a Ugandan two years ago."

The doctor said, "One thing at a time. We'll treat the pneumonia first." The pneumonia, in fact, was a parasitical type known as pneumocystis carinii pneumonia, or PCP, which is associated with AIDS. Hospitalized for six weeks, at one point near death, Barbara was informed that she had AIDS. She was twenty-four.

Crying, she called home. "It's not pneumonia," she said. "It's worse. It's AIDS."

"Was it that bastard who is in the news?" her father asked.

She didn't know what he was talking about. She had forgotten Ssenyonga's last name; she couldn't even remember very well what he looked like. Her father gave her more information. "Yes," she told him. "It was Charles."

She moved back to London to live with her parents, too exhausted to care for herself. Barbara dragged herself to a meeting of the support group at the AIDS Committee of London. She was urged to talk about her illness. When she mentioned Ssenyonga's name, another woman burst into tears.

"He infected me too," she sobbed.

The other woman pressed Barbara to testify at Ssenyonga's trial, since Barbara too was infected after the celibacy order. She refused firmly. "What's done is done," she said. "Nothing will change it. It would be me that would get all upset, not him. My infection makes no difference to him."

The woman did not press her, knowing how traumatic it was to agree to testify. The embarrassment of telling strangers about sexual relations was only part of it. There was also the burning risk that relatives, employers, and friends would find out and rejection would follow. Worst was the real possibility that witnesses were shortening their lives. Immune systems are sensitive to stress: HIV-positive people make conscious decisions every day to avoid putting strain on their fragile health. The women who testified were all aware that their immune systems could be weakened by the pressures of being witnesses, perhaps hastening the onset of AIDS and their deaths.

The Ssenyonga-infected women often talk of their blasted lives. Jennifer Anderson has not had a sexual relationship since learning of her HIV status in 1988. "I can't imagine putting somebody else at risk," she says bleakly. She keeps relationships at arm's length. "Having children is out," she says, "for sure."

Danielle Fitzgerald echoes this. "A lot of people have asked me out," she says, "but I can't get involved. If they wore fourteen condoms I still would worry for them. I figure I will live maybe five more years. I once thought I would marry and have a child, but I had to let that go. I still can't believe what has happened to me."

Barbara Williams agreed. "I'm really lucky I'm not married and I don't have kids," she said one afternoon in the spring of 1993. She was stretched out on a sofa where she spent her days, often too weak to care for herself. "I would feel really badly if I gave this to children." She said she didn't plan ahead. Her goals were short-range: her hope was merely to live through the summer. It was the season she loved.

She got her wish, but 1993 was her last summer. In March, 1994, she died of AIDS, aged twenty-five. She was the second women infected by Ssenyonga who is known to have died of his virus.

A year before her death, Barbara Williams had brusque advice: "Always insist on a condom. Always, always, always, no matter what colour the man is, no matter how important he is. There is no way to tell."

Fletcher Dawson spent much of the months before the trial working on the evidence he would elicit from Dr. Ronald Langevin, the research psychologist who would present the Section 16 defence that Ssenyonga suffered from post-traumatic stress disorder.

It was time to call in Dr. Robert Wood Hill, a forensic psychiatrist familiar with Section 16, who might testify that Ssenyonga's disorder fit under the provisions. On a blustery day in March, Wood Hill drove to the farmhouse near Listowel where Ssenyonga and Connie Neill were living. In preparation for his visit, Charles Ssenyonga was thrown into a frenzy of tidying. When vacuuming failed to remove dog hairs from the living-room carpet, he got down on hands and knees and picked them off one by one.

Connie chuckled when she overheard Wood Hill asking Charles if he had compulsive habits. Ssenyonga replied that his father was an obsessive man, but he wasn't.

"Charles," she chided him, "you are a neatness freak like your father. How about you spending about two hours getting Simba's hair off the rug?"

She was appalled a few minutes later when Wood Hill broke the news that Katie Newman had just died. He asked Charles how he felt about it.

Ssenyonga replied stolidly, "I would have to see proof. I don't believe she died."

"Well," Wood Hill said, "I can assure you that she has died."

Connie says that Charles still did not react. Instead he changed the subject. Wood Hill tried to draw some response from him but Charles would not discuss the death or his feelings. Connie decided that Charles didn't want to break down in front of her, so she left the room to give him privacy to cry. She later learned that it made no difference. He would not talk about it.

"I think it was so devastating that he couldn't absorb it," she explains charitably. "He didn't know how to deal with it."

In the nearly two years that Connie and Charles had been together, she did not once raise the subject of the women he had infected. "I never asked him to talk about what he had done," she said in a reflective mood long after the trial was over. "I knew that he had slept with those women, knew that he slept with three different women on the same day, but he didn't want to talk about it. Maybe I didn't press him because I was afraid I would maybe lose my loyalty to him. Maybe that's part of my guilt. I gave him the opportunity to hide behind me. I gave him the research that supported one set of ideas that he could hide behind. I handled the lawyers for him, so he could hide behind that. I faced the doctors for him, he could hide behind that. I think I was dangerous for him. I think I was bad for him. Because then he could hide away from the problem. He couldn't face it, so it was comfortable and convenient that he had me."

Connie Neill's mixture of astute insight and plain foolishness makes her an engaging though sometimes exasperating person. She builds for herself an imaginary world of sweetness that can be cloying but then, a moment later, she says something that demonstrates a wealth of common sense. Charles Ssenyonga's bursts of irritation at her were understandable but his cruelty was not: her support of him in the worst time of his life was unconditional and touching.

On the eve of the Ssenyonga trial, Ruth Rutherford called Bruce Long from her office in the victim-witness assistance program. She wondered if he would help her with a practice session to make the witnesses comfortable. Bruce was agreeable, although the only other time he had performed such a simulation was with child witnesses. He met with her and the women in the austere courtroom that had been reserved for the trial. He showed them where he would be standing and where Fletcher Dawson would be. At Ruth's request, he even played the role of Fletcher Dawson so they would know what to expect in cross-examination.

He had his own preparations to make, reviewing with each witness the areas he intended to explore and providing them with copies of the preliminary transcripts to refresh their memories about such easy-to-confuse matters as dates. He spent nearly an hour with each, Jennifer Anderson, Linda Booker, Francine Dalton, Joan Estrada, and Nancy Gauthier, reminding them not to talk about the case to anyone except personal counsellors such as a psychiatrist or family doctor. He added a final warning: they should expect to hear the clatter of a keyboard while they were giving evidence. The judge was one of a handful in Canadian courtrooms who uses a laptop computer instead of a notebook.

Jennifer Anderson was feeling coerced and rebellious when her turn came with Long. She had planned to avoid testifying but at the last minute she learned that her name was part of the evidence seized at the Middlesex-London public health office and might emerge at the trial. The only way to be certain that her identity was protected was to be a witness.

"I'm profoundly disenchanted with the justice system," she comments bitterly. "I knew in my gut that I should testify. If I have information that will help convict Ssenyonga, then I should be a witness. But if the Crown is going to subpoena me anyway my moral dilemma was irrelevant."

Bruce Long was finding the situation equally trying. "Murder cases are easier." He sighed. "You don't have to worry about the victims. They can't change their minds."

15

DAY ONE: *Monday, April 5, 1993*

THE LONG-AWAITED TRIAL of Charles Ssenyonga opened in Courtroom 18 on the eleventh floor of the fortress-like London courthouse. There was no jury. Like most modern courtrooms, number 18 is windowless, high-ceilinged, and panelled in wood stained the colour of peaches. Jeanine LeRoy, wearing a black court gown, was the first lawyer to arrive, tugging behind her a baggage cart piled with legal boxes. Fletcher Dawson came next, tested the chair set out for him and switched it for another. His back hurt.

Reporters and sketch artists chatted in the aisle behind the defence table, their seats staked out by overcoats piled on the front row of wooden pews whose cushions were upholstered in an electric shade of purple. Debora Van Brenk of the *London Free Press* took compliments on her story in the morning's paper: "AIDS and sex are scheduled to enter a London courtroom this week ... Only a few Canadians have ever gone to court accused of knowingly spreading the virus ... likely to break ground ... "

The court staff moved about languidly, checking on the ice water in thermos jugs available to the judge and lawyers, stepping over an extension cord connected to the laptop computer the judge would use. They seemed already bored. Rumour was that the trial would be postponed.

Geoff Beasley arrived next with Simon Johnson, fresh from a conference in vacant offices on the second floor where the Crown had established a field base. They were expecting a delay. A week or two before the trial date, Fletcher notified Geoff Beasley that he would be requesting a medical examination to determine if Ssenyonga was well enough to stand trial. The prosecution had been dreading this move. To offset a possible motion that the trial should not proceed because Ssenyonga was too ill, Bruce Long sent someone with a videocamera to catch Ssenyonga moving briskly around town on his errands. Long was even prepared to show the judge tape of Ssenyonga hauling lumber.

All the lawyers left as ten o'clock approached, a sure sign that they were conferring with the judge. Seventeen minutes later they returned. Harvey Bailie, the urbane court clerk, commanded everyone to rise, and the judge entered, his black gown emblazoned with the diagonal red sash of the Ontario Court, General Division. Dougald McDermid, eighteen years on the bench and regarded as one of the finest judges in the country, is a tall, spare man with a long, severe face and a cap of silver hair clipped close at the sides. He seated himself and booted up his compact computer. McDermid is a touch-typist and likes computer technology because it eases the chore of writing judgements: the search device in his software can instantly summon the reference he needs.

He peered over his reading glasses at the defence table. Fletcher Dawson rose to commence, "My client has been ill of late and I have conferred with my friend..." Geoff Beasley concurred that "Mr. Dawson should have an opportunity to assess his client's condition."

Ssenyonga, bearded and wearing a grey-patterned jacket with a black collarless shirt and black trousers, a worried and meek expression on his face, indeed appeared to have lost much weight since his last appearance in a courtroom. Dawson explained that the medical examination had taken place early that morning but the report was not yet available. He asked for one day's adjournment. Beasley said he agreed with that, and the judge, forewarned in his office about the motion, promptly declared that the trial would resume at ten the next day.

Later, copies of the doctor's report were made available. Dr. Dan Gregson stated that Ssenyonga was well enough to withstand the rigours of a trial. The stress on him would not be life-threatening or life-shortening. The trial could commence.

DAY TWO: *Tuesday, April 6, 1993*

The hands of the courtroom clock showed exactly ten, to the second, when Judge McDermid entered the courtroom. He is a renowned stickler for punctuality, his fearsome reputation gained in his first week on the bench when he threatened badly shaken Crown lawyers with contempt of court for being late. No one has been late for McDermid since. But on this morning Charles Ssenyonga still had not arrived.

Fletcher Dawson was nervously apologizing to the judge when Ssenyonga hurried in. The judge said dryly, "You should advise your client that court starts at ten o'clock." Dawson fervently gave assurances that he would.

The next order of business was crucial. On a motion by Bruce Long, unopposed by Fletcher Dawson, the judge imposed a publication ban on the real names of Jennifer Anderson, Linda Booker, Francine Dalton, Joan Estrada,

Nancy Gauthier, and John Webster. (He later extended this to include the deceased witness, Katie Newman.)

Then Ssenyonga and Dawson stood as clerk Harvey Bailie read the charges in a sonorous voice: three charges of aggravated sexual assault and three charges of criminal negligence causing bodily harm. Ssenyonga, dressed as on the previous day, his hands loosely clasped behind his back, responded firmly to each, "Not guilty."

Bruce Long rose to give a lengthy, detailed chronology of Charles Ssenyonga's activities and the case the prosecution would be presenting to the court. Then he called John Webster, an unwilling witness who was cornered with a subpoena. As Long asked his first question, he allowed himself to feel pleasure and vast satisfaction. At last, after two years of legal fighting and stalling, after all the fears that the accused might be found too ill to face the justice system, the trial of Charles Ssenyonga was truly under way.

John Webster was a necessary witness to link Ssenyonga to Anderson and Booker, the first women known to have been infected by him. Webster appeared unhappy and uneasy as he testified that he had introduced both women to Ssenyonga. Asked to characterize his relationship with Ssenyonga, he said they were "quite good friends." At this point, dry-mouthed, the witness asked for a glass of water. As he sipped, the courtroom fell silent, the dry rattle of the judge's computer momentarily stilled.

Chris Karuhanga came next. He also was an unwilling witness. A handsome, straightforward man, he traced his long association with Ssenyonga, beginning when they were children in Uganda. The relationship ended in August, 1991, he said. Long didn't ask him the reason for the abrupt termination of their friendship, but Dawson did.

"He stole two girlfriends from you," Dawson said bluntly. "That hasn't bothered you at all?"

Karuhanga replied evenly, "Absolutely not."

During the recess, reporters sat over coffee, chuckling about Ssenyonga's tardiness. Debora Van Brenk said, "Charles was always late at the preliminary trial with one excuse after another. His car broke down, or he couldn't find the courthouse. And then he gets McDermid, a punctuality freak."

When court resumed, Dawson continued to question Karuhanga, this time about Marian Clark.

"Did you know she was angry at Ssenyonga?" he asked. "Yes," Karuhanga answered tersely. He was volunteering nothing.

Linda Booker followed him to the witness box. Dressed in a schoolgirl blazer, long loose skirt, silk shirt and a string of pearls, she answered Bruce Long's questions impassively, looking more at ease than she felt. Ruth Rutherford watched with pride as Linda did everything a well-prepared witness knows to do: the straightforward answers, the level gaze, the voice projected. Linda was flustered, her face pink, only when speaking about being tested for HIV.

"Jennifer Anderson is HIV-positive and I am HIV-positive," she said unsteadily, "and the only thing we have in common is one boyfriend."

Fletcher Dawson's cross-examination was courteous. Often he prefaced a question with "I mean no criticism, but..." or said "If you don't know, that's a fair answer" as he inquired about her relationship with Ssenyonga.

Jennifer Anderson next took the stand. She looked the picture of a dressed-for-success executive in a well-tailored suit and buttoned-up blouse. Despite the polished appearance, she was visibly upset to be there. As she responded to Bruce Long's questions, her sentences were jerky and abrupt. She found it difficult to look into anyone's face; her gaze kept sliding away to inspect the walls. Only once she glanced in Ssenyonga's direction; he was staring into space. By the end of the seventeen-minute recital of her long affair with Ssenyonga, she seemed close to tears.

Dawson probed as he had with Linda Booker. Imbedded in the cross-examination was a key question: "Was the sex consensual?"

"Yes."

"In every respect?"

"Yes."

Dawson finished in fifteen minutes. Witnesses were moving along at a much faster clip than in the preliminary.

Bruce Long summoned Joan Estrada from the dreary adjoining room where she had been waiting. She was the first of the three complainants, the women infected after Ssenyonga officially knew he was HIV-positive. She entered with long, coltish strides, wearing a sophisticated dress and a nervous, twisted smile.

Towards the end of her testimony Bruce Long picked up a piece of paper. He would read a list of names, he said. He asked Joan to tell the court which men had been her sexual partners. Though Joan was ready for this, her face was a mask of misery as she identified six of them.

Reporters by unspoken agreement did not note the men's names, deciding mutually that it was unfair to publish them. But they kept count: twenty.

Bruce Long gently asked how the infection had affected her emotionally. Joan began to fall apart.

"Virtually my entire life is a mess," she began, struggling against tears. "To this day I don't make any new friends. They might get close to me and I don't want to hurt them when I die..." She began to sob. "I always wanted to have children, now I can't...I'm twenty-five years old and this should be the prime of my life. And what do I have to face? *Death*."

She turned to face Ssenyonga, who sat with his head down. "Look at me, *damn you*," she cried. "Are you proud of yourself? How do you feel, damn you. I'll be buried next to Katie."

In the agonized silence that fell, Justice McDermid said quietly, "I understand why you would make an outburst like that. I appreciate your feelings, but please answer the question."

Joan took a ragged breath. "How has it affected me emotionally? Irreversibly. Irreparably. I'll never be the same person, ever."

Charles Ssenyonga might have been crying. He was bent over with a blue handkerchief at his face.

Jeanine LeRoy was shaken. "Joan's testimony was very hard," she says. "For me it was the most poignant moment in the trial. But you can't let your face react." Her voice bleak, she said, "Sometimes it was difficult being a woman sitting at that counsel table. I felt there were women in the audience who despised my role."

When the cross-examination began, Fletcher Dawson's calm, matter-of-fact tone helped restore normalcy. His questions were meant to make Joan seem a young, naive woman who was so infatuated she was heedless of risk. He also went to pains to establish that Joan had many meetings with the other two complainants, Francine Dalton and Nancy Gauthier.

When her testimony was done, Bruce Long said his next witness was "quite ill" and someone was administering to her.

"I take it you're telling me she's too ill to testify?" the judge asked.

Long didn't think so. She probably would be able to testify the next day. The trial therefore adjourned.

Connie Neill says, "Charles was appalled to hear the stories the women told in court. In the evenings, he was crushed to contemplate the grief he had caused women he genuinely cared about. He was hurt. He would cry." He had listened to the same stories at the preliminary hearing, but

Connie maintains he was deeply moved when he heard them again.

DAY THREE: *Wednesday, April 7, 1993*

London was waking from the tyranny of a long winter. The sky was a sparkling blue and the streets full of people jubilantly walking to work with their coats open. Courtroom 18, airless and stale-smelling, already seemed familiar, a timeless cocoon enveloping lawyers and journalists and court staff who had become a family.

Charles Ssenyonga arrived with one minute to spare. He wore a loose sweater and dark trousers, with a fringed scarf around his neck. Judge McDermid entered on the dot of ten to the cry of "All rise."

Francine Dalton was summoned and walked steadily to the witness box, impeccably turned out in a sleek navy suit. Despite the advances of AIDS, she looked well. Bruce Long steered her through details about her background and how she met Charles Ssenyonga, and what happened after that. She had reached the point of describing her "bad flu" symptoms when Fletcher Dawson interrupted.

"My client is feeling quite ill and dizzy, Your Honour," he said. "Could we have a short recess?"

Ssenyonga, hunched over, pulled his fringed scarf over his head. The recess was granted.

When court resumed, so did Francine Dalton's account of her dates with Ssenyonga. At one point she said, "I paid for the dinner."

Dawson, who had been restless in his chair, stood up.

"I don't know what that's got to do with anything, frankly, Your Honour."

"Neither do I," the judge agreed amiably.

The story of their relationship resumed. When Francine reached the end of it, Bruce Long read the names of the twenty men. She identified five. In all but one case, she said, condoms were used.

"Would you have had unprotected sex with Charles Ssenyonga if you had known he was HIV-positive?" Long asked.

She gasped. "Definitely not."

Fletcher Dawson's questions were smooth. He said "No criticism is intended at all by these questions, but in any given year you had several sexual contacts?"

Judge McDermid said coldly, "I am uneasy that this is getting at sexual history." It is an area of witness examination that is now forbidden in sexual assault cases except in unusual circumstances. Dawson proceeded, but more cautiously.

Francine conceded that she had a "serious emotional attachment" to the accused. She glanced at him. Ssenyonga had pulled his scarf forward like a visor to shield his face.

"This was a completely consensual sexual experience?"

She nodded. "Completely consensual, so far as using a condom."

"But the next morning you didn't object to unprotected sex?"

Her face suddenly pinched and sad, she said, "No."

"There were drugstores in your neighbourhood but you didn't get a supply?"

Francine made a lame reply.

At the recess reporters grumbled, "What's Dawson getting at? That she's responsible?"

During the cross-examination, a middle-aged man slipped into the courtroom and quietly took a seat. It was Katie Newman's father. Someone pointed him out to Buzz Girden, the court constable positioned at the door. Buzz is a veteran of World War II and years of court duty, and a man whose habitual expression indicates that he has seen every disgusting thing the human race can devise. Buzz was concerned that a recently-bereaved father was so close to Ssenyonga, who had infected his daughter. The grieving parent just might have brought a gun. He checked with Terry Hall, who told him not to worry. The OPP inspector was right; Katie's father was not there for revenge. "I just want to see what happens to him," he explained. "I wonder why all the parents aren't here."

Dawson continued to hammer at his theme. "You assumed the risk of a sexually transmitted disease," he declared. "There was no discussion about his health?"

Flailing against the tide, Francine said weakly, "I was going on faith." She had tears on her cheeks and frequently blew her nose. Sometimes she closed her eyes and took deep breaths, as Ruth Rutherford had recommended for relaxation. By the time Francine's testimony ended, she was wrung out and weeping. Ruth, sitting in the courtroom, watched stolidly though she ached with pity. Judges can be stern about displays of partisan emotion so Ruth could not make a gesture of sympathy; this judge, for sure, would tolerate none of it.

Nancy Gauthier had announced the night before that she was going to walk into the courtroom "like a million-dollar whore." She explained, "You have to walk in like you're worth a lot. I'll pretend I'm doing a trick."

Summoned next, wearing tailored walking shorts and matching shirt purchased for the occasion, she bathed the room with a beatific smile. On the stand, though, her gestures gave her away. As she described her brief affair with Ssenyonga, her hands fluttered anxiously; she kept pushing back her hair and shifting her weight from one foot to another.

"He was intelligent and in my estimation he was safe," she said breathlessly. "I asked him to his face if he was safe and he said he was."

Lunch recess arrived. Len Michaels of radio station CFPL, a grizzled, wheezing veteran of more than thirty years in newsrooms, ordered his usual hamburg at Billie's, a cheerful diner a block from the courthouse where court reporters like to gather. Len told his colleagues that Joan Estrada had called the station the night before, threatening legal action if she was described as "a twenty-five-year-old woman from Hamilton" again. In her precarious emotional state, she imagined that people would guess her identity from that clue. He shook his head.

After lunch Ssenyonga took his place at the defence table beside Jeanine LeRoy and pulled four pill bottles out of a soft satchel. He arranged them in front of him and set a glass of water at the end of the row. Then he arranged the scarf over his head and did not look up as Nancy Gauthier continued her testimony. A few times she glared at Ssenyonga's bent head.

When Bruce Long read the names of the twenty sexual contacts, she identified nine of them as hers. Long ended as he had with the other two complainants by asking if she would have had unprotected sex with Ssenyonga if she had known of his infection. She misunderstood.

"Well...I might have come around."

Aghast, he rephrased it.

Straightening to ramrod stiffness, she replied indignantly, "Of course not!"

Fletcher Dawson suavely asked when she was a prostitute. She didn't mind talking about it. "In 1985. Toronto women were very sweet. They taught me the business," she told him. She likes Dawson. She has said if she ever needs a defence lawyer, she'll hire him.

"You initiated this sexual activity with Ssenyonga?"

"Yes."

"You decided to check him out sexually?"

She studied him warily, no longer charmed. "Yes."

"You agree the sex was with your consent and your agreement?"

"Yes."

"You made a judgment based on your experience that he was okay?"

Her face was growing hostile. "Yes."

Dawson consulted his notes. Nancy, head down, paced the confines of the witness box and took a sip of water.

Dawson returned to his portrait of Nancy as a promiscuous, careless woman, but she was under control. She remained dignified and touchingly candid.

"Is it fair to say you've tried hard to remember people you've had sex with but you could have forgotten? Is that true?"

"No, definitely not."

"It was a difficult task for you to remember your sex partners going back for eighteen months or so."

She denied it.

"Many are black gentlemen?"

"Yes."

This led to a discussion between lawyers and the judge, with Nancy excluded from the room. Dawson wanted to establish that she might have had other lovers from Africa, but Long was opposed to questions beyond the time Gauthier was tested.

When Nancy returned to the stand the issue was quickly resolved. Dawson asked, "Prior to May, 1991, did you have sex with anyone from Africa?"

She replied flatly, "No."

People who have watched Fletcher Dawson's cross-examination style, which has been described as "blistering," maintain that he was not particularly hard on the five infected women. He says he made a decision not to go after the inconsistencies in their stories. "This is not a case that lends itself to fancy cross-examination," he comments. "I didn't accept everything the women said but I didn't think the differences were all that relevant. There was a tactical decision not to put the case on that kind of a basis. By the end of the day there may not be much contest about the facts, so there was no point in trying to shake their testimony."

The medical evidence began with Dr. Henry Bendheim, who had taken Ssenyonga's blood in March, 1989, and informed him that he was HIV-positive.

A chilling moment for the prosecution occurred when it was established that Ssenyonga's blood sample was left untended for some time in a cooler on the doctor's front porch, where anyone passing by could have tampered with it. For the remainder of the trial, Geoff Beasley was expecting Dawson to attack that weak point, but he never did.

Dawson didn't think it worth pursuing. "We didn't have any basis to go after that."

Next in the chronology the prosecution was laying down, public health nurse Marylin McConnell told of counselling Ssenyonga for a year to have safe sex and then serving him with the Section 22 order to abstain from sex entirely. Her glasses perched on top of her hair, her gestures controlled, every inch of her taut posture signalled her resentment at being taken for a fool.

She conceded that the Middlesex-London health unit continued to receive reports that Ssenyonga was infecting women, despite his assurances to her that he was celibate. Her superior told her, "Marylin, I believe he needs more counselling. I don't think he's listening to what you're saying."

Dawson, in cross-examination, drew from her the admission that information at that time about heterosexual transmission of the virus to women was sketchy at best and frequently wrong.

Nancy Gauthier was gratified to read that part of the testimony in the next day's paper. "I run into people who say I'm responsible for being infected with HIV. They drive me crazy," she snapped. "Gay men have known for a long time about the risks, but who was telling women?"

The court adjourned. Debora Van Brenk caught Geoff Beasley in the corridor waiting for the elevator. He was ebullient. The trial might be over in less than the three weeks that had been set aside. The agreement not to call the twenty sexual contacts made a world of difference.

DAY FOUR: *Thursday, April 8, 1993*

This was a day of medical testimony, led off by Dr. Iain Mackie, head of the HIV/AIDS clinic at St. Joseph's Health Centre, and Dr. Janet Gilmour, who also works in the clinic. Mackie told the story of his two-hour discussion with Ssenyonga during which he was impressed that Ssenyonga was not the kind of man to put sexual partners at risk. "He assured me he was wearing a condom at all times," Mackie told the court.

Janet Gilmour testified about the two complainants she had treated, Nancy Gauthier and Joan Estrada. She spoke in such a rush of words that the court reporter, Gail McGilvray, a sardonic, much-respected veteran of the courts, was exasperated. Afterwards, passing Geoff Beasley on her way out of the room, she said out of the corner of her mouth, "Pu-lease, control your witnesses."

DAY FIVE: *Tuesday, April 13, 1993*

Following the Easter weekend, Geoff Beasley picked up the chain of medical evidence by calling Ssenyonga's family doctor, Nancy Reid. She said Ssenyonga told her in 1987 that he always wore condoms. Next was Jessica Msamba Lewycky, the Ottawa woman who was a partner in The African Store. She told the court that a woman who was the former girlfriend of both Ssenyonga and Chris Karuhanga (this could be Marian Clark) phoned her to say that Ssenyonga had infected her with HIV.

Ssenyonga's response, Jessica said, was that "the woman was just trying to tarnish his name." And then, a year later, a second woman called with the same accusation.

The next six witnesses, laboratory technicians, traced the testing procedure for Ssenyonga's blood sample. The point Geoff Beasley was making was that the sample with Ssenyonga's name on it that went from the London laboratory to Rick Galli in Toronto could not possibly have been mixed up with someone else's.

Fletcher Dawson poked hopefully for flaws in the method. At the end, he could glean only one, a long shot. In his summation he would attempt to make something of the fact that there was one stage in the London lab when vials being moved on a tray are uncapped.

"Often what you do as a criminal lawyer is you make the Crown prove certain aspects of the case," Dawson explains. "And when I looked at it, it seemed to me an awful lot of people had handled Ssenyonga's blood and these were not legally trained people, not investigators, and they didn't know about continuity of evidence. We just happened on the uncapped vials. That sort of thing happens a lot."

Jeanine LeRoy, only three months a lawyer, made a cameo appearance in the Ssenyonga trial by cross-examining two of the technicians. She didn't resent her minor role: "I was completely content to watch the master at work," she comments. Her contribution as note-taker was not insignificant. In breaks, at lunch, and after each day's trial, she and Fletcher would go over her notes, paying particular attention to parts she circled. "Fletcher was very good about asking my opinion," she says appreciatively.

When Ssenyonga and Connie Neill drove into the underground parking garage of the courthouse that morning, photographer Susan Bradnam of the *London Free Press* caught an overhead shot of him crouched in the passenger seat, the top of his head gleaming through his thinning hair and the dog Simba beside him. The cut lines read, "On previous mornings Ssenyonga has hidden behind the German shepherd on his left to avoid being photographed." Ssenyonga was barely recognizable in the rushed photograph, but it offered some relief from the one picture of him that the *Free Press* had been using for more than two years.

Ssenyonga, however, was annoyed. In the corridor outside the courtroom he complained to reporter Debora Van Brenk that he not been hiding. If she wanted to line up a photo session with him, he would be pleased to cooperate. She suggested the next lunch break. Ssenyonga eyed her coldly.

"I will tell you when I want it done," he said.

She was struck by his need to be in command. "Despite the fact he was on trial," she comments, "despite the fact he was showing increasing symptoms of AIDS, despite the fact the Crown was forming a really indicting case against him and the crimes were serious, he still needed some sense of control. It was a telling few minutes."

In the next break, Ssenyonga told her the photo op was off. Dawson disapproved.

That afternoon Geoff Beasley reported bad news to his boss, Bruce Long. One of the twenty sexual contacts had not been tested. Geoff discovered the omission when he checked the results of the the blood tests in order to show them to Dawson as part of the agreement not to call the twenty men. Somehow, the tempestuous, difficult twentieth man had been overlooked.

"Dawson just went ballistic," Beasley says. Fletcher doesn't say the Crown or police hoped to slip that by him, but he comes close. "I had been advised by the Crown attorney's office that that fellow had been tested and was negative," he says stiffly. "The Crown was Geoff Beasley and I have a great deal of respect for him. I am not suggesting it was deliberate by him. I knew at the prelim that this fellow had not been tested and was refusing to be tested. And later I was told he had cooperated. Then I was told there had been a slip-up."

Bruce Long says, "That was a low point. We misunderstood the police and thought all the contacts were tested." Judge McDermid was advised that a problem had arisen. The Crown would need a day's adjournment to work it out.

Bruce, Simon Johnson, and Geoff Beasley had "a bad night" in their barren makeshift office in the courthouse. Terry Hall, dismayed by the oversight, called in Beth Pimm and the group discussed what to do. In the United States, courts commonly order blood tests, but Canada does not grant that statutory power to judges. Without a negative test from the twentieth man, a sexual contact of Francine Dalton's, Dawson might maintain that Francine could have been infected by him instead of Ssenyonga.

Bruce telephoned the twentieth man, who called him a pig and hung up. Bruce then phoned the man's lawyer to tell him that he had a subpoena for the man but didn't want to resort to using it. Next he talked to the man's psychiatrist, finding the name in reports of earlier conversations. Professional decorum required respectful comment about the man's obdurance, but everyone was exasperated despite their sympathy for the confusion his head injury had caused him.

Early the next morning Beth Pimm sweet-talked her way into the man's apartment in Toronto. Somehow she persuaded him to drive with her and Terry Hall to Cheryl Wagner's office. The man, screaming curses, would not have his blood drawn there. Hours passed. Finally, late in the day, he agreed to go to his own doctor, where he gave a sample. To Hall's vast relief, he even signed a consent form to allow the test result to be given to the police.

Rick Galli and technicians at the provincial lab were waiting to receive the sample and in three hours whipped it through: negative. "Someone worked overtime," Rick says. "You don't see that every day in a lab." He adds hastily that no one's place in the testing order was usurped. "This was an extra."

"That was a real touchy time," Bruce recalls, looking ill at the thought of it. "Not that it would have ruined our case, but it would have put a question mark as far as Francine was concerned."

DAY SIX: *Thursday, April 15, 1993*

The startling news that morning in court was that Charles Ssenyonga was in hospital. Fletcher Dawson explained to the judge that his office received a call that morning to say that his client after a sleepless night was going to hospital "in considerable pain ... possibly related to his liver. There's some suggestion it could be hepatitis."

Dr. Rick Galli was standing by to testify, with Dr. Michael Montpetit scheduled to arrive in London that night. Geoff Beasley called Ottawa to tell Montpetit not to come. He advised Galli gloomily that the delay could be indefinite. Dawson, looking distressed, murmured, "I knew this would happen eventually in this case."

Bruce Long was less sympathetic. He called around to nearby hospitals but none had a patient named Charles Ssenyonga. Long asked the judge to issue a discretionary warrant so that Ssenyonga could be arrested. It was a technicality in order to maintain jurisdiction and not out of the ordinary in such situations, but Long's fear was that Ssenyonga was running.

Courtroom spectators emerged on Oxford Street to unexpected sunshine as waiters set out sidewalk tables for the season's first really warm day. Simon, Bruce, and Geoff stayed in their bunker, drinking coffee out of plastic cups with Terry Hall and Chris Lewis and going over their notes. The mood was loose and punctuated with laughter. The men like one another and the post-mortem sessions were proving helpful.

"We never had an argument," Bruce Long marvels, "which is incredible because none of us is a wallflower. We sometimes had to convince each other about something, but we always accommodated one another's views. There was never a harsh word."

DAY SEVEN: *Friday, April 16, 1993*

Arriving on the eleventh floor on a soft, drizzling morning, Bruce Long was in a perky mood. "Surprise," he said to a knot of reporters in the corridor. "He may show up."

Fletcher Dawson and Jeanine LeRoy emerged from the elevator. Long could not resist a needle. "Your client was seen walking around on the streets yesterday, doing his banking," he said to Fletcher.

The defence lawyer stiffened but replied evenly. "He is taking heavy pain medication. We have to go by what the doctor said, and the doctor said that my client is pretty sick."

A draw.

Jeanine LeRoy greeted the court reporter, Gail McGilvray. "Get out your dictionary, Gail," she said with a grin. "There're going to be some medical terms today."

Charles Ssenyonga entered the courtroom, a grey scarf over his head. Dawson informed the judge that his client was prepared to continue but there might be "further interruptions." Ssenyonga, he said, was waiting for certain lab tests.

Geoff Beasley asked the judge to cancel the bench warrant issued for Ssenyonga. He then began a résumé of the events surrounding the testing of the twentieth man, leaving out the drama.

With that out of the way, three women from the Toronto HIV laboratory testified about the handling of blood samples as they arrive from other labs around the province. The first steps, it appeared, are done by all three in rotation, with multiple checks of requisition forms and labels to eliminate error.

Then Rick Galli took the stand for the rest of the day.

Galli's absence of pedantry was helpful and occasionally his good humour crackled through, but the dissertation on the Western Blot test made for slow going. Geoff Beasley, his brow furrowed in a perpetual expression of mild surprise and his gown often awry on his lanky frame, made sure that no detail was left unexamined.

Nancy Gauthier, heavily perfumed, slipped into the courtroom to watch. Casting a withering glance at Ssenyonga, hunched over with the scarf over his head, she commented sourly, "I wonder if that scarf helps his liver."

"We tested all samples in duplicate," Galli was saying, "and then the microplates are incubated at thirty-seven degrees Celsius...Now we are doing seven hundred samples a day...Confirmatory tests are done by a senior technologist double-checking everything...We put the HIV lysate on top and pass a current through it which drives the proteins into the gel...molecular strips...twenty-five milled troughs ...enzyme conjugated globulin...GP41 band... P24 antigen test..."

Tapping away on his laptop keyboard, the judge got it all down. So did Simon Johnson, head bent so that his nose almost touched the paper. So did Jeanine LeRoy, a bank of sharpened pencils beside her. And so did the official court reporter, Gail McGilvray, efficiently taking Pitman shorthand.

In mid-afternoon, when Galli began to deal with testing samples from people involved in the trial, a sense of doom entered the room. Spectators were still as Galli said that Ssenyonga's sample tested a dense yellow, indicating the strong presence of HIV; a second, confirmatory test was "strongly reactive." Ssenyonga didn't move a muscle.

DAY EIGHT: *Monday, April 19, 1993*

It was Dr. Michael Montpetit's turn to testify about the astonishing technology that matched the DNA of the HIV virus found in Ssenyonga and the three complainants. Rick Galli was among the spectators, having remained in London for a display of his science at its best. Francine Dalton and Nancy Gauthier arrived together, Francine to take notes and Nancy to glare at Ssenyonga. Connie Neill, excluded from the courtroom during the early part of the trial because Fletcher Dawson thought he might want her to testify, was allowed entrance for the first time. Unaware that the women sitting together were Gauthier and Dalton, she took a seat near them.

Geoff Beasley draped himself on the lectern where his notes rested and let Montpetit run the show. The scientist's lecture, a dance through the outer reaches of biochemistry, lasted the day. At one point Francine Dalton was jolted: Montpetit said he detected in her blood sample not only the Ssenyonga virus but also the "daughter of the virus." What he meant was that her infection was so established that the initial virus had mutated to form a different, but recognizably related, strain.

Unsure what that indicated for her health, Francine began to cry softly. Nancy, furious to see her friend in pain, looked around and spotted Connie Neill. She scribbled a note, "You must be one dumb cunt," and passed it to her during the next recess.

Connie gasped in shock and managed to sputter, "I don't think this is any of your business."

Nancy explains, only slightly apologetically, "I felt so bad for Francine, this 'daughter of the virus' thing. I just had to do something."

Montpetit had thoughtfully prepared for the court a five-page glossary of the terms he used and nine pages of diagrams. Ssenyonga followed the testimony with a copy of it before him.

Fletcher Dawson scored an interesting point in his cross-examination. Montpetit had said that Ssenyonga's Rwandan strain was "extremely rare" in North America. The defence lawyer wanted to know if Montpetit had tested the DNA in a control group to determine if it really was rare or maybe a rather common strain that as yet had escaped analysis.

Montpetit conceded it was possible the strain could be found in others but said the uniqueness of the virus was almost irrelevant. The fact was that the match was certain. At the end of the process he had an elegant chart of the DNA of Charles Ssenyonga's virus that matched irrefutably with the DNA in the virus that had infected the three complainants, ninety-two percent of the clones corresponding beautifully.

Dawson asked a provocative question about HIV not being the cause of AIDS. Wasn't it true that no one really knows the cause of AIDS?

Montpetit considered this and rejected it. "It's a long way to go from not knowing [the cause of AIDS] to say that we don't know that HIV causes AIDS," he said.

In one of the breaks, Michael asked Geoff Beasley to approach Fletcher Dawson with a request. He wanted Ssenyonga to donate a blood sample to him after the trial, whatever the outcome, on condition that it would never be used as evidence in any proceedings. It was of enormous importance from a purely scientific point of view, he said, to follow the strain's changes.

Later that day, Dawson took Montpetit aside. Ssenyonga had agreed to it. "I think Ssenyonga appreciated what it means to science," Montpetit says gratefully.

Dawson said admiringly to the scientist, "What you do is so sophisticated, Dr. Montpetit."

Montpetit smoothly replied, "Oh no, Mr. Dawson. What *you* do is sophisticated."

DAY NINE: *Tuesday, April 20, 1993*

In the morning cluster outside the courtroom door, Debora Van Brenk overheard Connie and Charles talking to Fletcher Dawson. Dawson said, "You're not feeling all that well." Ssenyonga nodded, saying that he had "a rough night". Dawson, showing concern, suggested, "If you like we can put it over for another day." Ssenyonga replied, "No. Let's go."

After the judge was seated, Dawson rose to say that his client had been ill in the night but nonetheless was willing to proceed.

Connie Neill no longer sat in the general body of the courtroom where Nancy could have access to her. Instead, she nestled among the media people seated directly behind Ssenyonga.

The spectator seats were sparsely filled. Reporters scanned the room, trying to guess which of the solitary women who occasionally dropped in on the proceedings might be one of those infected by Ssenyonga. The solitary women would stare hard at Ssenyonga's back as he sat, very still, beside his lawyer. One passed a note to Nancy Gauthier; it read, "I am a victim too." One woman broke into tears and left the room with hands over her face.

Danielle Fitzgerald, the woman Ssenyonga infected when he raped her, decided to stay away. "Reading about the trial in the papers, I longed to go down and look at him," she says. "Then I decided I had better not. I might try to kill him."

The main witness of the day was Dr. Cheryl Wagner, who described her activities to stop Ssenyonga from infecting others and provided medical information about her three patients who had been Crown witnesses. Francine Dalton, cautioned in advance that this would happen, sat quietly as Cheryl commented that she was the sickest of the three, her immune system all but wiped out and her life expectancy less than a year.

Reporters were startled when Cheryl offhandedly described her coding system. The original designation of patients X, Y, and Z, she said, became "patients A, B, C, D, E, F, G, H." That made *eight* women infected by Ssenyonga. Though the names of two or three other women had emerged during testimony, there had been no intimation until then that there were so many.

The same day, most poignantly, the preliminary-hearing testimony of Katie Newman about her affair with Ssenyonga was read into the record. Debora Van Brenk noted the next day in the *London Free Press* that Katie, unidentified by court order, had died recently and "she leaves her young child motherless."

That concluded the prosecution's case, sweeping away all doubt that Ssenyonga knew he was infected with HIV when he had unprotected sex with the complainants, and establishing that the virus that was killing them could have come only from him. Observers wondered what Fletcher Dawson could possibly do to keep his client out of prison.

Fletcher and Jeanine LeRoy had been working long hours on the Section 16 argument, which was the pillar of the case for the defence. Dr. Robert Wood Hill had confirmed the diagnosis of post-traumatic stress disorder and was willing to testify that PTSD properly belonged under Section 16 of the Criminal Code. Even though the trauma had not yet been cited in a Canadian trial, Wood Hill believed it suited Ssenyonga's situation and he was "not criminally responsible" when he infected the women.

Fletcher met with Charles Ssenyonga and Connie Neill to tell them of his progress. To his dismay, his client was still vehemently opposed to the use of Section 16. Instead, Ssenyonga asked angrily what Fletcher was doing about the material Connie had given to Jeanine to show that HIV was not the cause of AIDS. He was shocked to learn that Jeanine had not followed up as expected.

Connie was furious. "All along we had been spending money and time doing research, calling Europe, California, all over," she says, "and Fletcher and Jeanine hadn't been giving it that much weight."

As Connie reconstructs the discussion, Dawson expressed his concern that the two lines of defence, post-traumatic stress disorder and the minor role of HIV in AIDS, would be difficult to combine. "It would just make things too complicated," he explained to his client.

"Fine," said Ssenyonga, "then we'll drop post-traumatic stress disorder."

That ended the argument. Dawson offered a deal. He said he would present the medical evidence in return for Ssenyonga's agreement to go along with the Section 16 defence. Together they studied the list of authorities Connie had compiled. Ssenyonga's preference was Dr. Peter Duesberg, a professor of cell and molecular biology at the University of California at Berkeley. Duesberg is one of the world's leading retrovirologists and the most extreme of the scientists who hold the view that HIV is not the direct cause of AIDS. He maintains that HIV is an essentially harmless virus that doesn't cause AIDS. AIDS, he says, is not transmissible or infectious. Ssenyonga was particularly taken by

Duesberg's opinion that condoms are not necessary in order to avoid AIDS.

It was not a view that Fletcher found particularly tenable, but he agreed to rethink. "You have to be especially broad and open-minded," he says. However, Duesberg seemed to Fletcher "too radical."

Dawson explained later, "It is important that as a litigator the evidence you bring to court is credible. Duesberg's ideas didn't seem to be very well accepted." Besides, Dawson said, it would be expensive to transport Duesberg from California and pay his witness fee; he wasn't sure that legal aid would agree to it.

At Ssenyonga's insistence, Dawson pored over his collection of newspaper and magazine clippings about the relationship of HIV to AIDS. He screened videos of the 1992 VII International Conference on AIDS in Amsterdam. "All the sceptics at the AIDS conference in Amsterdam were at a symposium on alternative AIDS research," Dawson says. "All the leaders in that theory. I started to see there was a diverse range of people out there with different views."

Law students were put to work on computer searches of medical journals to find articles dealing with the controversial topic. As they uncovered material, they fed Dawson summaries. Fletcher became intrigued with one name, Dr. Robert Root-Bernstein, an associate professor of physiology at Michigan State University and author of two controversial books, *Rethinking AIDS: The Tragic Cost of Premature Consensus* and *The AIDS Myth*.

"I read the first seventy-five pages of *Rethinking AIDS*," Dawson says, "and I thought this was the guy we needed. The lights came on for me, but I didn't know if he would be a good witness." Connie Neill provided him with a transcript of Root-Bernstein on the CBC radio show "Ideas". Dawson hunted through videotapes of the Amsterdam alternative conference on AIDS and studied Root-Bernstein closely. "He didn't look too radical, he didn't sound too radical. I checked him out and got good reports."

Besides, Michigan State was close by, which would reduce the travel costs. What helped even more was that Root-Bernstein when approached said he was so fascinated with the Ssenyonga case that he would testify without a fee.

16

BUZZ GIRDEN was in a reflective mood as reporters and lawyers gathered on the tenth day of the Ssenyonga trial. The weathered court constable was saying, "This is the most meticulous trial we've ever had here. It's probably the most meticulous trial ever held in Canada."

He predicted what was going to happen that day. Court officials usually have the best scuttlebutt. Buzz said, "Fletcher's going to put in a motion to drop the charge and the judge will recess until May 4 to consider his decision."

Nancy Gauthier and Francine Dalton, now regulars in the courtroom, arrived together and sat on the opposite side of the room from Connie Neill. As Buzz foretold, Fletcher Dawson opened his defence with a motion for a directed verdict of acquittal on the three charges of aggravated sexual assault. The sexual acts were consensual, therefore no assault occurred, he said.

What followed was a display of legal argument at its best. Fletcher Dawson's presentation occupied two hours and was a model of dry analysis laced with moral indignation. "You would have to torture the law of assault to make it apply in this case," he told Mr. Justice Dougald McDermid.

Aware that the judge had never shown enthusiasm for courts making law, Dawson was virtuous about the authority of Parliament. "This isn't a case where criminal law should apply," he declared. "This is a case for legislation... It is the kind of thing that should be dealt with by Parliament and be open to public debate." He returned again and again to the "legislative proportions" of the Ssenyonga case.

He also stressed that the women should have protected themselves instead of relying on Ssenyonga. "When a woman agrees to the physical contact involved in a sexual activity," he declared, "she must be aware that there is a whole gamut of risks that are associated with that activity."

Fletcher's oratorical style tends to be flat and almost monotonal, but he holds attention with the intensity of his conviction. As he presented each of his arguments, his manner was grave and logical and his reasoning was clear.

Simon Johnson, whose job it was to defeat Dawson's argument, suffered initially in contrast. Because Johnson normally speaks in a rush of words, he feared that the judge would not be able to keep up with him on the computer. To facilitate note-taking, he therefore decided on long pauses between sentences to allow the judge to catch up.

"It is not an easy situation to argue in, but after a while you get used to it," Johnson observed. However, his consideration cost him. Though his delivery was scholarly and thoughtful, the long gaps made him appear hesitant and uncertain.

Simon made the same three-pronged case for a broad interpretation of consent that had succeeded at the preliminary hearing. This time around his arguments were embellished with even more citations drawn from all over the world. Simon had been burrowing in law books. It was an academic triumph, but the sheer number of his references seemed to the uninitiated to clog his points and in some instances introduce confusion.

Ssenyonga listened for a few minutes and then tuned him out. He took a book out of his satchel and began to read.

Consternation rippled through the cluster of journalists in the front pews. Was the Crown blowing it? Around one o'clock, the judge called a lunch break.

By the afternoon session, Simon Johnson had recovered his aplomb. With the benefit of the quarterback huddle in the Crown's temporary offices, he retraced some of his steps from the morning and painstakingly simplified some points.

"Simon understates," Bruce Long says with admiration. "A lot of us are more blunt than Simon. He has a very polished manner of speech."

As he had with Fletcher Dawson, the judge frequently probed Simon Johnson's arguments. Often his interventions were Socratic. "Even though people may be aware of those risks [of AIDS], will the law allow them to assume those risks?" he asked in a ruminating tone. Another time he wondered, "Is it a socially acceptable act to engage in unprotected sex when you know you are infected with the AIDS virus?"

Simon Johnson pondered his replies and framed them with care, his manner serious and reflective. It was evident that the certainty of his presentation came from a belief, as he put it outside the courtroom, that Ssenyonga "went out and did harm — and what he did is no less harmful because of the way he did it than if he had gone out and murdered these women."

Simon's learned presentation lasted almost four hours, twice as long as Dawson's. When he was finished, the judge looked inquiringly at Fletcher Dawson. Dawson said he had nothing more to say.

Spectators couldn't guess which way McDermid was leaning. His impartiality had been perfect — he had peppered both lawyers with challenging questions — and his guarded eyes gave nothing away. He said he would adjourn the trial to consider his decision. "Obviously," he commented dryly, "this is a matter of some complexity." The trial would resume, he said, Friday, April 30, at ten in the morning.

Buzz Girden's prophecy was off by a mere two court days.

DAY ELEVEN: *Friday, April 30, 1993*

Mr. Justice Dougald McDermid acquitted Charles Ssenyonga of three charges of aggravated sexual assault.

His written analysis of the sexual assault law as it applies to consent filled four typewritten pages, and his views on the fraud charge filled three more. At the end of a learned document that included an appendix of thirty-five authorities, the judge said, "In my opinion, the law of assault is too blunt an instrument to be used to excise AIDS from the body politic... As the old adage states, 'Hard cases make bad law.'

"If no other section of the Criminal Code catches the conduct complained of, which remains to be seen, then it is a matter for Parliament to address through legislation."

McDermid concluded starkly, "Although as a citizen I am also concerned about the devastating effect of AIDS, as a judge I feel bound in law to grant the motion and to acquit Mr. Ssenyonga on the three counts of aggravated sexual assault, which I do." Court would resume in ten days to hear Ssenyonga's defence on the three charges of criminal negligence causing bodily harm.

"All rise," cried the clerk. When the judge's spare frame had disappeared through a door, Connie Neill threw herself in Charles Ssenyonga's arms.

Fletcher Dawson had the smallest of satisfied smiles. One charge down, one to go. He was not disheartened by the Crown's air-tight case. "The Crown's allegation in essence is 'We can prove he's got the virus, we can prove he knew he had the virus, and we can prove that he infected them. And he didn't take precautions,'" he said. "But I've got a surprise for the prosecution."

His normally sombre expression was lit by a smile. "This is the fun part of defence work," he said.

Geoff Beasley has great respect for Fletcher Dawson. He says, "Fletcher is extremely good. There is no doubt Fletcher is one of the brightest lawyers in London. He is maybe the only lawyer in the criminal bar in this city who could have conducted this case in this way, frankly."

The week before May 10, Fletcher Dawson and Geoff Beasley had two or three telephone conversations about scheduling. These exchanges are normal between opposing lawyers in lengthy trials. In one of them early in the week Dawson mentioned that he would be calling Robert Root-Bernstein.

"What's that about?" Geoff inquired, alarm bells ringing.

"Read the book," Dawson advised him.

Geoff could not find a copy of *The AIDS Myth* in London. He called Dr. Cheryl Wagner in Toronto. Wagner knew about Root-Bernstein. "He's not a stupid guy," she warned Geoff. "He's the least crazy of the people who say that HIV doesn't cause AIDS." She called around to bookstores and finally found a copy in Toronto's This Ain't the Rosedale Library bookstore, the last one in stock.

Geoff Beasley settled down to read, taking extensive notes. He smiled when he came to a passage near the end of the book: "The chances that a healthy drug-free heterosexual will contract AIDS from another heterosexual are so small they are hardly worth worrying about," Root-Bernstein wrote. "One statistician has compared them to the probability of winning a state lottery game or being struck by lightning."

Bruce Long says the prosecution wasn't rattled by the news that Dawson was bringing in Root-Bernstein. The three Crown lawyers sat around over coffee deciding whether to call another expert to refute what they expected Root-Bernstein to say and decided against it.

"What Bernstein puts forward is so purely theoretical that we didn't feel like bringing in another theoretician to present another theory," Bruce explains. "We're concerned with proof beyond a reasonable doubt, and we thought we had the best proof when Dr. Mackie went up. He's a clinician, he's a treating doctor. Root-Bernstein only reads other people's works. We did not want to dignify that argument by calling a counter-argument."

Late on the Friday afternoon before the trial resumed, Geoff called Fletcher again to ask how long Root-Bernstein would be testifying and when he might expect the defence to finish its case. Root-Bernstein was not available, Dawson told him. He was recovering from pneumonia.

"On Monday I'll be calling Ronald Langevin and maybe Robert Wood Hill," he said smoothly. "They will be giving evidence about state of mind."

Beasley was stunned. "Do you mean a Section 16 defence?"

That's just what he meant, Dawson assured him, no hint of triumph in his voice.

Geoff walked to the office occupied by Simon Johnson, leaned his long, loose frame against the door-jamb, and said wearily, "You're not going to believe this." When Simon heard about the Section 16 defence, he groaned. There went the weekend. He would be spending it with law books.

Then Geoff phoned Bruce Long, who was driving home. "Bruce," he said genially, "I know you are sitting down but

I want you to put both hands on the wheel. Fletcher is going to plead Section 16, not criminally responsible."

The news came as a "complete and total shock," Geoff recalls. "It was totally out of left field. I didn't know the mechanics of a post-traumatic stress disorder defence. And we had two days, over a weekend, to prepare."

Bruce Long calls it a piece of luck that Geoff Beasley was already on the Ssenyonga case when Dawson pulled post-traumatic stress disorder out of the hat. "Say 'mental disorder' to Geoff and immediately he thinks DSM IIIr," Bruce says admiringly. DSM IIIr is the American Psychiatric Association's *Diagnostic Statistical Manual,* third edition revised, the diagnostic bible of the profession. Revised again in 1994, it is usually part of psychiatric evidence in legal actions.

The Crown's preparations were twofold: Simon would research Section 16 and Geoff would find someone with sufficient authority to examine Ssenyonga and perhaps dispute Langevin's testimony. The plan was to ask the judge to order Ssenyonga to cooperate with the Crown's designated psychiatrist.

Geoff called Dr. Cheryl Wagner and told her what had happened. It sounded to her like a tactic born of desperation. "Insanity is the defence you use when you have no defence," she commented.

"Any ideas?" Geoff asked. She said she would talk it over with her friend psychiatrist Peter Collins. Meanwhile, Geoff polled other psychiatrists he knew from his long experience of trials involving mental illnesses. Finally he gleaned the names of two experts on the phenomenon of PTSD. One was a psychologist, so he was ruled out. The judge would not order Ssenyonga to be examined by someone who was not a medical doctor. That left the Crown with one candidate, Dr. Klaus Kuch, a psychiatrist who had studied PTSD in Holocaust survivors and Vietnam veterans.

The big worry in the Crown's office was that this meant more delay. If the case dragged into fall, perhaps Ssenyonga would be too sick to attend.

Dawson had a major problem of his own. The hitch in hurling the thunderbolt that he was aiming at the prosecution was that his client hated the Section 16 defence and was adamant that he would have none of it. Ssenyonga seemed to have forgotten his deal that he would accept the Section 16 defence if Dawson presented testimony that HIV didn't cause AIDS. On the day before the trial was due to resume, Dawson discovered that Ssenyonga had reverted to his former position that he would not abide any slur on his sanity.

On Sunday evening, Dawson called a desperate last-minute meeting in his office. Present with him were Jeanine LeRoy, Connie Neill, and Ssenyonga.

Connie describes what happened: "Charles went into a speech that lasted about an hour and a half and Fletcher was very patient. Fletcher said he had to have an answer by the morning or otherwise we don't have a defence. He said he didn't know where we're going to go if we didn't go with the Section 16."

When the meeting ended inconclusively, Jeanine rode down the elevator with Connie and Charles. Connie recalls that Jeanine said, "Fletcher won't lead you astray. He's not going to make you do something you really don't believe in. But, Charles, if you go to prison you are likely to die there. Fletcher has a solid case with this and he's trying to do his best for you."

Charles said, "Ultimately it is up to Connie."

Connie promptly said, "Okay, we're doing it."

Jeanine was cautious. "Think it over," she advised them. "Tell me in the morning."

"No, Jeanine," Connie said firmly. "I think we should go with it. I have always believed that finding out you have HIV is a traumatic life event." The notion that Ssenyonga was in some kind of shocked state when he infected the women had appeal for her: it was unthinkable that he might have been aware of what he was doing.

DAY TWELVE: *Monday, May 10, 1993*

Dr. Ronald Langevin's testimony astounded the legal profession. The psychologist asserted that Ssenyonga was not responsible for what he did because he suffered post-traumatic stress disorder as the result of two terrible events, the student uprising in Kampala and the discovery that he was HIV-positive. As a result, Langevin said, Ssenyonga experienced "a lot of active denial" about his status. The knowledge of his infection was buried somewhere in his mind and not available to him when he had intercourse with the women he infected. "At the time he had sexual relations with the complainants," the research psychologist said, "he was not aware he could harm them." Having sex "served as a confirmation that he was normal."

Langevin, an expert on male sexual disorders, also said that in his three examinations of Ssenyonga, using standard psychological tests, he found him free of sadistic tendencies. Ssenyonga's sexuality was "conventionally heterosexual," he said.

Dawson, having one of his best days of the entire trial, declared that Ssenyonga fell under Section 16 provisions and was not criminally responsible for what he had done.

Bruce Long informed the judge with an edge of annoyance in his voice that he had learned of Ronald Langevin only late Friday afternoon. He asked for an adjournment to give the Crown time to prepare its cross-examination.

George Seremba, the Ugandan who was tortured and shot six times, was indignant when he read that Ssenyonga was claiming PTSD. "I felt insulted. Not that I have a monopoly on suffering, but I felt cheated. What are people going to say about me if *Ssenyonga* has PTSD?"

DAY THIRTEEN: *Wednesday, May 12, 1993*

Dougald McDermid ordered Ssenyonga to undergo testing by a psychiatrist, Dr. Klaus Kuch, designated by the Crown. Bruce Long requested a delay in the trial of a month to allow the examination.

"I wish I hadn't done that," he said much later. "A month would have made such a difference. But we needed time to prepare for the psychiatric defence. Geoff learned of it Friday afternoon at four or four-thirty, but what could you do on a weekend?"

The judge adjourned the case until June 14.

The change in schedule put the prosecution in a bind. Bruce Long intended to appeal Judge McDermid's decision to acquit Ssenyonga on the aggravated sexual assault charges. He explains, "Although the judge considered all the arguments that were put forward by Simon, I think the judge was wrong on the public policy issue and wrong on consent. I don't believe that you consent to everything if you consent to go to bed with someone."

The motion to the Ontario Court of Appeal had to be filed within thirty days of McDermid's decision, which Bruce had expected would fall well after the completion of the trial. The delay for expert witnesses meant that he would have to submit the motion while the trial was continuing. His concern was not that the judge would be miffed — McDermid is too professional and too interested in the development of the law for that — but that Fletcher Dawson might claim that the appeal put added stress on his client, making it impossible for him to continue with the trial.

As Simon Johnson polished his submission citing the reasons the Ontario Court of Appeal should study McDermid's decision, Bruce hit on a wild plan to file the motion without Ssenyonga learning of it. He arranged to serve a substitution notice of the appeal to Fletcher Dawson instead of to Ssenyonga and he asked the Ontario Court of Appeal for a closed courtroom and an unnamed accused. Madam Justice Rosalie Abella would have no part of secrecy. To Long's surprise, neither would Dawson. Bruce was obliged to file the motion in the usual way and hope that Ssenyonga would not become ill because of it.

Klaus Kuch arranged an appointment with Charles Ssenyonga in his office in Toronto's Clarke Institute of Psychiatry. Connie Neill drove him there on a hot summer day when Charles was feeling especially unwell. He was feverish, with pain in the region of his liver and nausea that resulted in frequent vomiting. The pain medication he was taking left him somewhat dazed.

She scoffs at what happened in the interview. "What a joke, a big farce," she says dismissively. "I waited outside and Charles was finished in what seemed an hour and a half, most of which was a written exam. I walked around the block with him during the break. He said the thirty-minute interview was contrived. Kuch spent it mostly going over Charles's answers on the written test."

Kuch was in touch with Geoff Beasley to report his findings. He was absolutely certain, he said, that Ssenyonga did not suffer from post-traumatic stress disorder. He had seen the man only once and was prepared to see him again, but there was no question in his mind. Ssenyonga was suffering depression, but not PTSD.

Beasley decided one examination was good enough in view of Kuch's expertise and his emphatic opinion. "Don't bother seeing him again," he said. "There's no reason to pad a second interview. If you are satisfied, so are we."

Connie and Charles used the month-long break for camping trips, which both of them loved. Ssenyonga was taking a great deal of medication, and his mood was depressed and testy. "He would blow up over small things, things he blew out of proportion," she says. "I realized he was just venting anger. I understood that, but sometimes it would get out of hand and I would feel threatened. Mostly it just hurt my feelings."

She noticed that his bouts of anger usually signalled the onset of illness. "I would revert to my role as his nurse and take care of him and then he would be fine," she says.

Ssenyonga was still unhappy that his mental clarity was being questioned. He told his lawyer that it wasn't fair that two witnesses would testify on the Section 16 but only one witness, Root-Bernstein, spoke for the medical side. Dawson said legal aid would not accept two such experts; Ssenyonga countered by pointing out that Root-Bernstein wasn't charging a fee.

Connie made several telephone calls to locate an additional retrovirus expert. Everyone she contacted said Root-Bernstein was outstanding, Ssenyonga didn't need anyone else. Finally, Ssenyonga conceded that Root-Bernstein would suffice.

DAY FOURTEEN: *Monday, June 14, 1994*

Ssenyonga wore a flowered purple and white shirt loose outside his pants. He was noticeably thinner than he had been a month before, the angle of his neck and shoulder sharp where once it had been muscular. It was his thirty-sixth birthday. An air conditioner fought the muggy heat of the summer day, spreading a clammy chill in the room.

The trial resumed with some initial awkwardness. Geoff Beasley wanted to challenge Dr. Ronald Langevin by showing him Dr. Klaus Kuch's report, but the report could not be entered into evidence until Kuch himself testified to its authenticity.

With that nicety sorted out to the judge's satisfaction, Fletcher Dawson returned to the interrupted examination of his star witness.

Langevin was calm and unruffled in the witness box. He stuck to his appraisal that Ssenyonga's reasoning was seriously impaired by post-traumatic stress disorder, a symptom of which is described in the American Psychiatric Association's diagnostic handbook as "transient dissociative episodes."

Dawson asked smoothly, "Is dissociation a huge break with reality?"

Langevin nodded. "It can be very great, a trigger to push someone into unreality."

"What does it mean?"

"It means that unpleasant reality is shut out of the conscious mind."

In his cross-examination, Geoff Beasley attacked Langevin's weakest point, his lack of experience with post-traumatic stress disorder. Establishing that Langevin had written 127 articles in the field of sexual disorders, Geoff observed — his brows arched in astonishment — that "not one single item in the 127 deals with post-traumatic stress disorder."

Langevin agreed that his experience was "not that broad" but he maintained stoutly that he was familiar enough with the disorder.

"How many cases have you treated?"

"Not a lot," Langevin admitted.

After lunch, Beasley continued to hammer at Langevin's credibility. Langevin remained unperturbed. Ssenyonga's denial of his HIV status, he said, was a classic symptom of the disorder. Langevin added, "I don't think he is a callous person. He cares for other people. If he were a callous person, I would see certain behaviour, and he doesn't have that. I think he can't cope with the stress."

Beasley suggested, "The other explanation might be that he simply is lying and doesn't care."

Ssenyonga was taking rapid, shallow breaths. His body was rigid, arms folded tightly, but his face remained impassive.

Beasley wanted to know if Ssenyonga could have lied in the tests. Langevin didn't think so. The results were measured on a validity scale and found to be genuine.

"It is on that basis that everything you say of the results is based?" Beasley said.

Langevin shrugged. For instance, he said, no one can fool a phallometric arousal test.

Just before the afternoon break, Dawson asked the judge to set aside a day for his client to see a doctor. Ssenyonga had a swelling on his leg, he said, that needed attention.

Geoff spotted Dr. Robert Wood Hill in the corridor outside, waiting his turn to testify. They have been through many trials together. Though they were on opposite sides this time, they greeted one another warmly.

After the break, as Dawson commenced the customary establishing of his witness's credentials, Geoff graciously said that would not be necessary. The Crown accepted that Wood Hill "is a very qualified psychiatrist."

Indeed he is. A lean, handsome man with a shock of silver hair and thick moustache, he is an assistant professor in psychiatry at the University of Toronto medical school and a consultant to prisons and jails. He testified that he saw Charles Ssenyonga twice in March, once for three hours and again for two hours, to assess him for mental illness and for post-traumatic stress disorder. He found evidence of PTSD, a disorder so new to psychiatry that it was not yet fixed in a category. Perhaps it belonged in the category of anxiety states, or perhaps in the category of dissociative states, or "maybe it is an entity in its own right."

The onset of PTSD varies, he continued in a relaxed, authoritative style. "Sometimes it presents itself years later."

When Ssenyonga learned of his HIV infection, Wood Hill said, "he distanced himself from the information...he distorted the information as being of any danger to himself or others...he did not address the fact that he might be a dangerous person to other people." It certainly seemed to describe the way Ssenyonga had behaved.

Late in the day, Wood Hill made a statement that stuck in people's minds. He said, "I think Mr. Ssenyonga, in spades, has abnormal fears of death."

As for post-traumatic stress disorder fitting under Section 16, Wood Hill was certain that it did. Although it had not yet been used as a defence it Canada, it frequently was part of insanity defences in the United States.

It had been a long, wearying day. Court adjourned at almost five o'clock. People were subdued and thoughtful as they waited quietly for the elevator. Connie took Ssenyonga's hand. It had not been much of a birthday, but she had a surprise waiting for him at home: she had baked a cheesecake.

DAY FIFTEEN: *Tuesday, June 15, 1993*

London was at its prettiest on a soft, breezy summer day, the lawns and gardens around its huge houses refreshed by an overnight rain. The court constable, Buzz Girden said, "Ssenyonga will testify this afternoon."

Jeanine LeRoy, asked about the abscess on Ssenyonga's leg, said she had seen it. "It looks like it will explode," she commented with a worried frown.

Ssenyonga wore a patterned cotton sweater, a Christmas gift from Connie Neill, and he appeared tired. Connie reported that he wasn't sleeping well.

Fletcher Dawson finished with Wood Hill in about a half hour. Geoff Beasley then sauntered to the Crown's lectern and leaned on it. What he wanted to know, it seemed, was whether Ssenyonga could have fooled Wood Hill. Also, he intended to establish, politely, that the Crown's witness, Klaus Kuch, was an expert on anxiety states and post-traumatic stress disorder, while the two defence experts were not.

On the first point, Wood Hill conceded that "it is fair to say that self-interest is present" in the testing situation, and Ssenyonga could have read up on the symptoms of post-traumatic stress disorder. Wood Hill appeared to be conceding that it was possible that Ssenyonga had fooled him, as he had so many others. But Wood Hill would not accept that Kuch knew more about PTSD than he did. He had examined Vietnam veterans in Montreal who suffered from PTSD, he said, and he "wouldn't give up the field" to Kuch.

Beasley, his manner affable, pointed out that Ssenyonga's behaviour often demonstrated inconsistencies. What did Wood Hill think about that? Wood Hill, looking discomfited for the first time, mused, "Is he psychopath? Is he narcissistic personality? Or is it PTSD? A lot of variables go with it, one of which could be psychopath."

Later, as Dawson was winding up the testimony, Judge McDermid apologized for intruding and advised the defence lawyer that he was free to object to what he was about to do. He then asked Wood Hill a series of biting questions.

The first was, "Is post-traumatic stress disorder a disease of the mind?"

Wood Hill replied, "I believe it is, sir."

"Was Ssenyonga suffering a disease of the mind while having sex with the complainants?"

"I believe he was."

"In your opinion, was the disease he was suffering a permanent one?"

"It need not be. A person may show degrees of remission...He may have another illness now, depression."

"Would that state of PTSD continue unabated and uninterrupted?"

Wood Hill replied that it could, "more or less."

The judge wanted to know if there was some way of knowing at any given moment whether Ssenyonga was in a state of repressed memory or whether he was conscious of reality.

"Not that I know of," replied the psychiatrist.

Martha Allen, a tall, composed, grey-haired woman, slipped into the courtroom. When Connie saw the retired schoolteacher who had befriended her and Charles, she sprang from her seat and went to greet her.

Geoff Beasley asked Wood Hill if Ssenyonga's repressions were linked to sex.

Wood Hill thought not. "The tragedy is that sex was not a fear for him. Death was a fear for him."

Simon Johnson, taking down every word, decided Wood Hill was a good witness for the defence, a man who came across as very fair. Even so, he didn't think that he had done the Crown's case any damage. "The bottom line for Hill and Langevin was that everything they said stood or fell on Ssenyonga's credibility," Johnson says. "They had only his self-report on what he had gone through and what the effects on him were." And there was plenty of testimony to establish that Ssenyonga was an adroit liar who could fool experts.

Court adjourned for lunch. When Ssenyonga saw Martha Allen, his face broke into a wide grin. She went to him and put her arms around him comfortingly, ignoring the stares of amazed spectators.

Martha recalls that meeting vividly. "We ate in that dismal witness waiting room. Connie had prepared a bag lunch for us. After that I didn't go back, I didn't want to.

Charles had become an old man. His hand felt like a dry leaf."

After lunch Buzz Girden was found staring reflectively out the window at strollers far below. He hadn't been feeling well but the case had a grip on him. He said it was because he has daughters the age of the complainants. On his days off he could be seen, out of his uniform of navy blazer and grey flannels, sitting in the court.

"Dawson's no dummy," Buzz said gloomily. "He'll keep Ssenyonga on the stand until he collapses and they take him away on a stretcher. I'll bet on it." And that would end the trial.

As soon as the judge was seated, Charles Ssenyonga was called to testify. He opened with an apology to the judge. "English is my second language," he explained. "Sometimes I am misunderstood."

Nancy Gauthier and Francine Dalton did not move a muscle, both of them mindful of stern instructions from Bruce Long that they should not react to anything that happened, but they had never heard Ssenyonga speak with such a thick African accent. "Distance" came out "distawns", "reserves" was "resairves", and "size" came out unintelligibly "sayze". Bruce Long was not surprised. He had been preparing his cross-examination "from day one" in the expectation that Ssenyonga would play a simple country boy who had trouble understanding English.

Fletcher Dawson, his voice soothing, took his client patiently through the story of his life in Uganda up to the point of the unrest at Makerere University in Kampala.

News that Ssenyonga was testifying had spread. That afternoon several young women not previously seen in the courtroom appeared, each one alone. One began to weep. Francine Dalton passed her a tissue and they looked at one another for a long moment.

In the break, Dawson was heard to ask Ssenyonga, "How are you holding up, stamina-wise?"

Ssenyonga nodded. "I'm all right."

That day it was evident to spectators why so many people loved Charles Ssenyonga. Projecting a magnetism that filled the room, he was eloquent, graceful, and passionate. His blackness in a room peopled only with whites, as it had been almost every day of the trial, emphasized his exotic isolation.

Bruce Long studied Ssenyonga closely. He was changing his mind about the accused. He decided, "This man has a massive ego. Now I know why he didn't tell anybody he was infected. It was not that he didn't understand, it is that he didn't care." Long made some notes. When it came time for the cross-examination, he would try to show Ssenyonga's manipulative side.

The most compelling part of Ssenyonga's testimony that day was his description of the carnage he witnessed in Uganda. During the shelling of Kampala in 1979, he said, his voice low and musical, "you could go anywhere and turn any corner and you would see a dead body." He described a mortuary so full of bodies that the overflow was dumped on the ground outside and "you couldn't get rid of the smell."

The judge called a halt at almost five o'clock. Outside the courtroom, Nancy Gauthier had a bitter comment. "He can remember every tree on the campus of the university, but he can't remember he has AIDS."

DAY SIXTEEN: *Wednesday, June 16, 1993*

The thick African accent of the previous day was less noticeable as Ssenyonga continued his testimony. He appeared relaxed as he picked up the account of the student uprising at Makerere University from the point he had left it. His hand gestures, fan-like motions with fingers closed, were more frequent and his voice stronger.

His description of his escape from the campus, surrounded by troops, was hair-raising. He exchanged clothing with a friend, he said, and fled down a fire escape. With secret police looking for him he departed Kampala in the back of a coffee trailer. In Kenya, penniless and lacking papers, he lived in a refugee camp in Nairobi before enrolling in law school. When he came to Canada, he said he was "ecstatic." He finally had a chance to put his "troubled life" in order.

Dawson asked about his relations with women in Africa and Canada. Ssenyonga replied that it was difficult to make comparisons. "A Ugandan woman never says yes to a sex proposition. They say no, and it is up to you to judge at what point they mean yes." The court gathered that Ssenyonga was sexually active at an early age, despite being in a seminary. He acknowledged he had his first of many bouts with a venereal disease when he was in high school. "Most of the males I know have had sexually transmitted diseases," he added.

His answers began to be uncertain when Dawson asked him about the women who had testified against him. He was also vague when asked what he knew about AIDS. "It was very remote from my mind and my reality." Only in 1985, he said, did he realize that people from Africa might be at risk. Even that was "pretty hazy," and "one of the things spread about Africans." Mostly, he felt, Canadians were ignorant about Africa, and had "almost a racist kind of attitude." He thought stories about the high incidence of HIV in Africa were part of that prejudice.

He could not say where or when he contracted HIV. When Dr. Iain Mackie and Dr. Nancy Reid told him he had HIV symptoms, he thought they were making a presumption based on his being African, that they had "a derogatory attitude...based on a stereotypical kind of information."

He said, "I did not see myself as developing AIDS...The categories I had heard about were gay men and Haitians...I had never eaten monkeys. I had never seen them eaten anywhere in my area, and those who did eat monkeys I didn't see they were dying of any different ailments than anyone else."

He said he hated waiting for his appointment with Mackie, sitting for an hour among gay men, some of whom looked very ill. It made him "uncomfortable." When he saw Mackie, he understood that he had nothing to worry about. Ssenyonga, testifying under oath, had trouble remembering any discussion about safe sex. His impression was that Mackie told him he should "use caution and protect myself...it's out there."

When asked about the telephone call from Jennifer Anderson to say she was HIV-positive and he should be tested, Ssenyonga's voice slowed. He pulled at his nose and stared at the floor. "I was shocked by this information...I was sad...I was stunned, I was stunned, I was incredulous. I couldn't believe it."

"What about yourself?" Fletcher asked.

"It took me a while to internalize it...It was very emotionally upsetting. For a number of days I went through a period of shock."

In halting style, Ssenyonga struggled to explain why he subsequently put Katie Newman at risk for AIDS. "If I could explain it more fully I would not be sitting here," he said tearfully. "I have had many opportunities since to examine that...I have not come up with an answer. I had these relations with Katie. I don't think I could injure her at all."

Just before one o'clock, Ssenyonga's answers were more laboured and he asked for a break. After lunch, with Dawson pointing the way, he stumbled through an outline of his relations with the women who had testified. He spoke of his resentment at Linda Booker's threatening attitude. "I told her I am upset enough as it is...This information is going to spread like wildfire."

He said that after he was tested in February, 1989, and found positive, "I can only describe my thinking as very confused." He couldn't recall Dr. Henry Bendheim discussing safe sex with him. "I was upset very much, very deeply upset...He may or may not have given me that advice."

His eyes down, he said, "It's like someone shooting you dead but you are not dead. Like being a ghost."

"Why did you engage in acts of sexual intercourse with Joan Estrada without a condom?" Fletcher asked.

"Why?" Ssenyonga echoed.

"Yes, why?"

The accused man pondered on this. He said, "I do not have a satisfactory answer why I had unprotected sex with her, or any of these other ladies. I couldn't offer any satisfactory explanation why."

A curious aspect of Ssenyonga's replies was an almost complete lack of concern for the women he infected. It was odd that such an intelligent man would not appreciate that a show of remorse would be to his advantage. Instead he spoke of his own distress and was not only perplexed but indignant that women he had infected would yell at him. Describing the scene in Francine Dalton's kitchen the morning she told him he had infected her, he did not speak of her anguish but of his. "I was trying to deal with her outburst," he explained. When Linda Booker telephoned him, discussing her infection, he recalled only that he "felt harassed."

A few times he disputed what witnesses had said. He denied, for instance, that he told Francine Dalton he was HIV negative; he took exception to testimony from nurse Marylin McConnell; he had almost no recollection of ever being counselled to wear condoms by anyone. Of the nurse, he said she "may or may not have mentioned condoms, but I don't remember."

Bruce Long decided Ssenyonga was making "a tactical mistake" by calling McConnell a liar. "You don't call a dear old nurse a liar," he said. "That's not the way to make points with a judge."

In some of Ssenyonga's replies to questions about his awareness of his infection, his language was lifted intact from the testimony of Dr. Ronald Langevin. "On some occasions this information would be available to my mind," Ssenyonga said at one point. "At other times, no."

He said with a sigh, "I was not thinking of HIV with respect to myself when I was with these women. If I had thought I was a threat to them, I never would have done it. I really do regret that my paths and theirs ever crossed each other."

Bruce Long wondered about that. Did Ssenyonga mean that he was sorry for what he did, or did he mean he wished the women hadn't caused him all this grief? It struck him as a comment that was more than slightly ambiguous.

Dawson boldly asked Ssenyonga why he had lied to him about being celibate. Ssenyonga spoke of his confusion at the time. "I was really struggling to understand, to get a grip on reality...I have to admit now that my thinking was way off. I was going through a muddled state."

"Do you accept that you have HIV and it is a fatal condition?"

The courtroom was very still while Ssenyonga considered his answer. Gail McGilvray, court stenographer, put down her pencil and flexed her cramped hand. Ssenyonga's head was down, his face concealed. He cleared his throat. "The information I have is that I have HIV...but death might not necessarily be the result of having the virus." Ssenyonga, in truth, knew that he had passed into a state of full-blown AIDS.

"If you have been misleading people, been untruthful, before," Dawson asked, "what is different now?"

"I think I'm in better touch with the reality of my situation now than I was before. I am facing the demons that have been in the background about this whole situation. And I'm still alive. My conduct is more in harmony with what I am." He blew his nose. "If indeed, as science says, I am dying and I'm dying soon, it is right to finish this stage of my existence in truthfulness."

Court adjourned a few minutes later.

DAY SEVENTEEN: *Thursday, June 17, 1993*

The shock of the day came when Bruce Long asked Ssenyonga if he had had sexual relations with women other than those who had testified.

After a long delay, Ssenyonga answered, "Yes."

Fletcher Dawson objected. The Crown was attempting to imply that Ssenyonga was "of bad character." Long, deadpan, denied this. He meant to show only Ssenyonga's "desire to have sexual intercourse with any and all female contacts."

Judge McDermid upheld the defence's objection.

As he proceeded with the cross-examination, Bruce Long found himself revising the strategy he had plotted months earlier. Because Ssenyonga had chosen to wear a shirt with an African pattern and a scarf wrapped around his head, Bruce expected that he would present himself as an unsophisticated immigrant. He was surprised, therefore, that Ssenyonga not only dispensed with the heavy African accent but even began to show off his erudition.

"That threw me for a bit," Long recalls. "I almost wanted to ask for a recess so I could get my thoughts together. My direction for cross-examination turned around totally. When I started hearing the vocabulary, I couldn't believe it. Words that I don't use. And he started coming across as really wanting to impress with his intelligence and sophistication. Maybe his ego took over. His brain must have gone into neutral because surely he should have realized that wasn't . . . the way he should have been portraying himself."

When Bruce asked Ssenyonga why he had not obeyed the Section 22 order to be celibate, Ssenyonga said evasively that he didn't understand it. Long, his voice heavy with sarcasm, read the order one sentence at a time, pausing after each to ask, "What word is it that you don't understand?"

Ssenyonga, the pauses growing longer, coolly maintained that he was confused.

At the end of the day Dawson asked the judge for an adjournment until Monday. Ssenyonga needed to see his doctor on Friday, he said, to have the infection on his leg examined.

Nancy Gauthier watched Ssenyonga intently from a seat in the courtroom that confronted the witness box. Everything about his testimony annoyed her. "He thoroughly enjoyed himself on the stand," she complained afterwards. "He got more and more natural. I was upset that he wore a turban because it made it look like we were dumb chickies who fell for a man just off the boat. Ssenyonga has more intelligence and class than most Canadian men. He was definitely not just off the boat."

She would have preferred to see Ssenyonga squirm. She hoped for a sign of his suffering. "I don't want him to die for a long time," she says. "My daughter will be tormented all her life because her mother will have died when she was young, so I want Ssenyonga to be mentally tormented a very long time."

What would she want the law to do to Ssenyonga? Her answer was quick. "Cut off his dick. He would never feel like a human being without his dick."

17

RAIN SQUALLS sent Londoners scurrying under umbrellas as a small knot of people gathered in the London courtroom for another day of Ssenyonga's testimony. Dr. Cheryl Wagner had taken a day off her Toronto practice to watch Ssenyonga, her first opportunity to get a sense of him. Geoff Beasley greeted her outside the courtroom with a cheerful account of how the cross-examination was going. The prosecution was delighted, he said; Ssenyonga was emerging as a far from credible person.

Simon Johnson arrived, looking pale and drawn. He had spent the weekend working on legal arguments that Bruce Long might use to persuade the judge to allow him to ask Ssenyonga about sexual partners other than those who had testified. The search had not been fruitful.

Bruce Long had also toiled over the weekend analysing Ssenyonga's testimony. He made a list of reminders for himself:

> 1. Go through opening point by point. Get Ss to agree with it. Use exhibits.

2. Keep chronology (use one Simon drew up).
3. Keep the date of March 6 1989 in mind (Bendheim told him he was positive) etc. Stress that Ss never showed or expressed any concern about the people that he infected. Show his lack of concern for others before and after he infected them.

On legal foolscap paper, Bruce wrote prompts. "Map of Uganda." He would show Ssenyonga a map of Uganda and have him point out where the fighting was and where he was. "He went in the other direction from the fighting," Long explained afterwards. "He wasn't arrested, no one shot at him." If he could establish those points, it might help to cast doubt on the post-traumatic stress disorder theory.

Long circled the place in Ssenyonga's testimony when he said that his mind went in and out, that sometimes he remembered he was infected and sometimes he didn't. "I don't think Fletcher expected him to say that," Long said, pleased. He planned to put the question plainly to Ssenyonga: "You *never* remembered you were infected when you were with the women?"

With Ssenyonga in the stand wearing a neat grey-and-black striped shirt, Long settled behind a lectern holding a thick loose-leaf binder. He started with the callousness issue.

"Have you tried to contact your sex partners?"
"No."
"Why?"
Ssenyonga stared at him a long time. "I have tried my best to locate them as best I could."
Long asked, "Do you know how they are?"
"No."
Connie says Ssenyonga was annoyed that Fletcher Dawson didn't object more often. Some of Long's questions

were repetitious, he thought. Also, Ssenyonga felt orphaned because his lawyer would not discuss his testimony with him during the breaks. He was looking for some guidance about how he was handling Long's thrusts, but Dawson, observing the prohibitions against coaching of any kind during a cross-examination, offered his client no assistance.

Connie performed that service instead. Her advice to Charles was, "Don't go on. Keep it short. These people can never understand." She adds, "Fletcher and Jeanine LeRoy were very ethical. Fletcher wouldn't speak about anything but personal things, nothing about the trial. That was very hard on Charles because he didn't know whether he was saying the right thing. He was afraid he damaged Fletcher's case."

As the morning of testimony wore on, Ssenyonga often took pains with his replies, concentrating at length before speaking. It seemed that he saw himself in a battle of wits with Long. "Hell," said Long afterwards, "he had more law school than I did."

Ssenyonga's answers emerged as vague, evasive and rambling. A typical exchange occurred when Long put some questions about why he didn't wear a condom after Dr. Iain Mackie advised him he should.

Ssenyonga: "The message was to be careful for your own sake."

Long: "Why did you not follow the doctor's advice to protect even yourself?"

Ssenyonga: "I don't know what time we're talking about here."

Long patiently repeated the question.

Ssenyonga: "Was I supposed to walk out wearing a condom? I'm sure he didn't mean anything like that."

Long: "The next time you had sexual intercourse after you left the doctor's office, did you use a condom?"

Ssenyonga: "Can you help me with my memory here?"

Long: "Do you recall who your first sexual partner was after you left the office?"

Ssenyonga: (considering a long time) "No, I can't remember."

Long: "Were you seeing Francine Dalton at that time?"

Ssenyonga: "I'm confused in my memory. Perhaps you could help me with that."

For the first time, all three complainants were sitting in the courtroom, side by side. Bruce Long, happening to look around at the spectators, saw Joan Estrada. He was disconcerted. His next line of questions would be about Ssenyonga's sexual relations with Joan and he didn't want her to be embarrassed. He sent Terry Hall to warn her in a whisper what was about to happen. Joan considered and decided to stay.

She blushed scarlet as Bruce asked Ssenyonga about the seduction in his apartment and subsequent sexual acts. Once, she dabbed at her eyes with a handkerchief. Afterwards, she thanked Bruce for his thoughtfulness in forewarning her.

Long then asked Ssenyonga about Katie Newman and if Ssenyonga had remembered that he was HIV-positive when he saw her in Brantford. Ssenyonga began to cough and asked for his inhaler. The judge suggested a five-minute recess.

Late that morning Long pulled out from the exhibits the letter from Linda Booker that Ssenyonga had described as threatening. He said, his tone civil and cold, "Indicate where the letter is threatening."

Ssenyonga read it slowly, twice, as Long leaned on the lectern, having a fine time.

"First of all," Ssenyonga said at last, "it is the tone."

"Where does it show that tone?"

Ssenyonga couldn't find anything specific. He said lamely, "I got a sense of threat..."

Eventually he had to agree that the letter now looked "less malevolent than it did at the time." He embellished this observation. "She [Linda] was depriving me of the calmness that I got, for example, from Jennifer...it simply added to my sense of upheaval, of being overwhelmed," he said, his eyes flashing with indignation.

Another time Long asked him if he ever thought about the feelings of Jennifer Anderson and Linda Booker.

"Not really," Ssenyonga replied, "because I would be thinking of death."

"Your death?"

"Yes."

"Why would you not be thinking of the deaths of others?"

"I don't know...I cannot give reasons why this would not come into my mind."

"Maybe you didn't care," Long suggested in a chilly tone.

"No," Ssenyonga said sincerely. "I know for sure, I never felt callous about these complainants."

Connie believes that Charles hadn't prepared himself for such questions, even though Fletcher Dawson had cautioned him before his testimony began that they would likely be asked. "He is going to say that you slept with these women when you knew you were infected," Dawson said. "What are you going to answer?" Ssenyonga shrugged and looked to Connie to reply. Fletcher, exasperated, snapped, "You can't consult with Connie when you are on the stand."

That afternoon Long confronted Ssenyonga with his earlier admission that sometimes his memory of his HIV status improved. Ssenyonga had trouble remembering he had ever said such a thing. Long asked him to read the relevant passage from the transcript. Ssenyonga did so impassively, but his body language expressed dismay. He said stiffly, "At times I remember things clearer than at other times."

After that his replies tended to be terse and irritable. He regarded Long balefully. The Crown attorney, his voice laden with contempt, started down a line of questions concerning the period when Ssenyonga lied to Fletcher Dawson about being celibate.

"Would you characterize that as manipulation?" Long asked.

Ssenyonga said carefully, "I would more characterize it as deceit...I do not think I had the will required for manipulation...In hindsight it was part of the whole feeling that this can't be true."

"How do you find that to be different from manipulation?" Long asked, his tone innocent.

"Manipulation takes a lot more mental presence than I had," Ssenyonga replied evenly.

"In spite of the confusion in your mind, you were able to devise a lie. Am I correct?" Long asked.

Ssenyonga stared at the ceiling a long time. Finally he said, "You are incorrect. Your terms imply some kind of constructive manipulation...I just couldn't believe that this was happening."

When Charles was asked about using condoms, Connie took a deep breath.

Charles said, "There were times when I would use them and times when I would not."

Bruce Long called the accused man's attention to the incident when he slept with Joan Estrada a final time, long after learning he was HIV-positive. Ssenyonga removed a condom before having intercourse with her. Bruce Long asked why.

"I think because it was uncomfortable," Ssenyonga explained. Then he thought better of what he had said. "Actually," he said hastily, "I don't remember very well. Maybe she was the one who was uncomfortable."

In the recess that afternoon, Fletcher Dawson asked Bruce Long if he thought he would finish the cross-examination in time for Dawson to get his next witness on that day. This would be Robert Root-Bernstein, newly arrived from Michigan.

"Not likely," Long replied curtly.

Joan Estrada and Nancy Gauthier discussed Ssenyonga's evasions. Joan said, "It is sickening to hear these lies."

Nancy agreed. She felt besmirched when Long reviewed her sexual history with Ssenyonga. "I feel I'm being revictimized," she said to Joan. Nancy wasn't looking her chirpy self. On the day Ssenyonga began to testify she developed sores in her mouth and then swelling of her feet and hands. Though she was miserable with the discomfort, she tossed the infection off as "just one of those things that HIV-positive people are passing around."

When court reconvened, Bruce Long returned to the attack.

"Why did you put Francine Dalton at risk?" he asked bluntly.

Ssenyonga, angry and frustrated, replied, "I was not in my right mind."

The exchange went on in that vein for an hour. Fletcher Dawson then objected. "Your Honour, this is about the thirty-fifth time my friend has asked these questions."

"Sustained," said the judge dryly.

When Judge Dougald McDermid called a halt around five, Long said firmly, "Your Honour, I anticipate being some time further."

DAY NINETEEN: *Tuesday, June 22, 1993*

Early in the morning, Bruce Long ended his cross-examination with a flourish of stinging questions. When Ssenyonga said something about how thoughts of his impending death sometimes crossed his mind, Long asked if he had ever thought about the impending deaths of the six people he had infected with HIV.

"No," Ssenyonga replied.

Long named each woman in turn, asking if Ssenyonga thought of her death. The answer, six times, was no.

"Did you ever tell them you were sorry for what you'd done to them?"

"No."

"So, really, Mr. Ssenyonga, you just thought about yourself, didn't you?"

Ssenyonga, thoroughly fed up with the way the testimony was going, responded with a ramble about his "mental processes" and his inability to think organized thoughts.

Long, satisfied, said he was finished.

Bruce actually had four more pages of questions for Ssenyonga, enough to keep him on the stand for at least another day, maybe two. He had changed his mind. Though Dawson's comment about repetitious questions had made him smart a little, Long's decision was based on other considerations. He feared he might seem overbearing if he continued. "I thought best to stop," he explains. "I thought I might overdo it and lose the judge. Besides, I didn't see any more purpose in it."

The decision to curtail the cross-examination had been reached jointly in the Crown's courthouse office. Simon Johnson and Geoff Beasley agreed that Ssenyonga had been hammered enough. Simon observes, "On the first day of Ssenyonga's testimony you could see he was a magnetic person, even have some sympathy for him, but by time Bruce finished the cross there was not much sympathy."

When Long finished with Ssenyonga, Fletcher Dawson was free to call Robert Root-Bernstein. Connie Neill was beside herself with delight. "Where is the Globe and Mail reporter?" she asked Debora Van Brenk of the *London Free Press* anxiously. "This is the most important day of the trial and the Globe goes coast to coast." Debora tactfully did not say that *Globe* reporter Henry Hess had announced when the trial adjourned on Monday that he saw no point in covering Root-Bernstein's testimony.

Root-Bernstein was an excellent witness for the defence, polished and assured. He testified firmly that HIV does not cause AIDS. In order for AIDS to occur, there must be an additional "triggering mechanism," he said.

He did not go so far as some of his colleagues, who believe that HIV has no connection whatsoever to AIDS, but he insisted the virus was not the primary cause of the fatal illness. AIDS becomes established when a person's immune system weakens, Root-Bernstein maintained, and immune systems falter for many reasons.

DAY TWENTY: *Wednesday, June 23, 1993*

Geoff Beasley's cross-examination of Robert Root-Bernstein was a stinging exchange. The Crown lawyer presented the professor with a series of scientific papers, all of which pinpointed HIV as the cause of AIDS. Root-Bernstein was unmoved. Those studies, he said, were the result of careless scholarship and were not conducted under rigorous conditions. As Beasley continued to hack away at his statements, Root-Bernstein yielded so far as to say that HIV was not an insignificant virus. Satisfied, Beasley said he was finished.

Though the Crown lawyers initially had not been troubled by the prospect of Root-Bernstein's testimony, they had grown uneasy that it might indeed be crucial. "I thought that Root-Bernstein was the only expert who would be a threat to the prosecution," Bruce Long later commented. "Root-Bernstein bothered us. It gave us some trouble when he came along with his theory, but then he backed off so much in cross-examination we didn't really worry so much. Geoff did a good job. Root-Bernstein has very limited knowledge about the actual process. He's not a clinician."

DAY TWENTY-ONE: *Thursday, June 24, 1993*

The day began with Robert Root-Bernstein on the stand again for a few final questions from Fletcher Dawson, who had the physiologist touch up his previous testimony that HIV is not a direct cause of AIDS. Root-Bernstein happily repeated that he believes the development of AIDS requires such co-factors as intravenous drug use or exposure to other viruses.

Then Dr. Klaus Kuch, associate professor of psychiatry at the University of Toronto medical school and the Crown's key expert witness on the Section 16 defence, took the stand for an intriguing battle of wits. Geoff Beasley conducted the examination as the psychiatrist established himself as a leading authority on post-traumatic stress disorder, with twenty years of work in the field. He declared quietly that Robert Wood Hill and Ronald Langevin were wrong.

Kuch was clearly uncomfortable in the court setting, which was unfamiliar for him. He took pains with his answers and often sounded anxious. He testified that he found Ssenyonga to be emotionally distressed and depressed, but not suffering any mental disorder in the clinical sense. Most significantly, he said that Ssenyonga had not experienced the kind of stress in his life that could cause post-traumatic stress disorder.

If Ssenyonga really did suffer PTSD as a result of learning that he was HIV-positive, Kuch said he would have avoided the cause of his infection, namely sexual intercourse. "If a person is traumatized in a sexual context, then reminders of the trauma will bring out symptoms...of intense distress and fear," Kuch testified.

Fletcher Dawson for the first time in the trial was short-tempered with a Crown witness. He thought Kuch's hesitant and careful style of responding indicated a crafty mind, and it made him furious.

What Dawson wanted from the PTSD authority was admission that people suppress memories of painful experiences. Kuch resisted him firmly. "The hallmark of post-traumatic stress disorder," he said, "is the inability to get away from the memory of the experience. If they could [suppress it], they wouldn't have a problem."

Kuch then said that Ssenyonga had spoken of his wish to marry, an indication to the doctor that he was carrying on his life fairly normally.

Dawson was sarcastic about the brevity of the tests Kuch had administered. Whereas Robert Wood Hill spent twenty-seven hours with Ssenyonga, Kuch had reached his conclusions after only four and a half hours. Kuch replied with equanimity that the length of the testing procedure was not important; what mattered was the accuracy.

DAY TWENTY-TWO: *Friday, June 25, 1993*

The last day of evidence was brief. Klaus Kuch was in the stand all morning, stolidly repelling Fletcher Dawson's assaults on his methodology, and then the judge adjourned the trial to July 5 for opposing lawyers to present their closing arguments.

The three Crown lawyers, together with Beth Pimm, Terry Hall, and Chris Lewis of the Ontario Provincial Police, were in a celebratory mood as they repaired to their stark temporary office. The prosecution had gone wonderfully and they felt sure of a conviction.

"Dr. Kuch was a godsend," Bruce Long commented. "He was such a dear man. He was not a hired gun, he had never testified before. Langevin's psychiatric evidence made us sweat bullets, but then we got Dr. Kuch's report and we were okay again."

Beasley agrees that Kuch was "an extremely good witness." He said, "Some might think he was evasive on the stand, but I would characterize it as caution."

Simon Johnson and Fletcher Dawson had nine days to prepare summations, the last kick at the can for prosecution and defence.

Meanwhile, worldwide attention had focused on London. That week the esteemed British medical journal *The Lancet* ran a long article on the Ssenyonga trial, concluding, "Although some tolerance must be given to those who have unwittingly contracted the disease, the fate of those who cavalierly spread it should be seen less sympathetically... In common law countries there is no clear consensus. Some punish offenders whereas others counsel. Since common law is based on precedent, the Ontario verdict, expected shortly, will be viewed with no little interest."

Simon Johnson set to work as never before in his life. "It was all day, every day, into the night," he says. When he finished writing his summation, it covered forty-nine pages.

"We couldn't even get him to stop and have a beer," Long complained.

"Putting together a closing argument is a matter of marshalling the facts," Simon explains. "I ended up with thousands of pages of notes. For instance, I wanted to attack Ssenyonga's credibility because I thought that was key to the insanity defence." He searched the notes he had made of all the testimony, looking for the contradictions. An obvious one was Francine Dalton's account of the scene in her kitchen when Ssenyonga said he wasn't infected. Ssenyonga, on the other hand, testified that he told her he *was* HIV-positive. "Which version is more likely?" Simon asked himself. "Would she have continued on with him if *just after she learned she was HIV-positive* he told her he was too, and thus she would realize he gave it to her knowingly?"

He made a decision not to spend much time challenging Root-Bernstein's evidence. "Bernstein obviously was a good witness," Simon felt. "He had a depth of knowledge, but what we are dealing with here is a legal situation. This is negligence causing bodily harm. What causing bodily harm means is a matter of law, not medicine."

Long and Beasley agreed with Johnson that Fletcher Dawson probably would argue that transmission of HIV doesn't amount to bodily harm as a matter of law. They expected that the defence lawyer would say that the relationship between HIV and AIDS is not understood, and therefore the cause of AIDS is by no means certain. So how can anyone be punished for passing along a virus that has dubious risk? To that line of reasoning, Johnson would declare "we don't have to know how HIV is involved, only that it is a contributing mechanism." Simon thought a small expansion on that point should be sufficient to establish that, in any language, bodily harm had been inflicted.

DAY TWENTY-THREE: *Monday, July 5, 1993*

London was suffering a hazy, hot day, and the Ssenyonga trial regulars were grateful for the frostiness of the air conditioning in Courtroom 18. Buzz Girden arrived early on Mondays to switch on the air conditioners and rid the courtroom of the weekend's buildup of summer heat. Outside in the corridor two lawyers on their way to work elsewhere paused to chat with Geoff Beasley. One of them asked, "Who is going to present the Crown's argument?"

Beasley replied with a wide grin, "Simon. He's the brains of this operation."

Connie Neill and Charles Ssenyonga walked quickly through the cluster of people outside the courtroom door. Ssenyonga was changed, much thinner than the week before. He had shaved his beard, revealing sores on his cheeks, and was wearing a long, collarless shirt of a brilliant orange pattern, with sandals on his bare feet.

Nancy Gauthier was disgusted. "He's acting like some kind of bushman," she snapped. "He's trying to look like someone from another culture. That's not the man I met in a laundry room wearing a $200 sweater."

After some initial skirmishing among Fletcher Dawson, Simon Johnson, and the judge about the niceties of the legal meaning of negligence in criminal negligence charges, Fletcher Dawson began in his orderly, quiet manner. He started his summation by pointing out that the Supreme Court of Canada has not been clear about the definition of criminal negligence, whether the test should be subjective or objective, whether it should pertain to acts of omission or acts of commission.

"The Ontario Court of Appeal is not doubtful," Judge Dougald McDermid interjected in a pleasant tone.

Dawson agreed, adding quickly that Ontario was waiting for the Supreme Court to sort it out.

"Your position is that the Crown has to prove that there was intent to cause bodily harm?" the judge asked. Dawson said yes.

Another issue in the case was the degree of risk for a woman having sex with an HIV-infected man. While doctors had moved a great distance from the belief that women are not at risk when they have vaginal sex with an HIV-infected man, even the experts don't agree on how much risk is involved. Dawson pointed out that two doctors who testified had put the figure at one in a thousand to ten thousand, and Dr. Janet Gilmour one in three hundred, so she was out-numbered "two to one."

"There has to be a very high chance of causing bodily harm or death," Dawson argued. "There has to be a very high degree of risk ... My submission is the real question, a serious question, is that a risk of one in ten thousand is not the type of risk-taking that would make one liable for crim-inal negligence."

Dawson's next point was that the women consented to sexual intercourse with his client. "Why don't we prosecute directors of tobacco companies for causing cancer?" he asked. "Because we take into account that smokers know the risks of smoking." Then he turned to Root-Bernstein's evidence and declared, "We can't impose criminal liability on the basis of populist notions on the causation of the dis-ease ... Overall we have evidence that this is a very difficult virus to transmit."

The judge did not appear to be impressed. "There is ev-idence that your client was told quite clearly of the risks to partners," he commented.

Dawson jolted spectators with a comment that there was no evidence that his client had infected Jennifer Anderson, Linda Booker, or Katie Newman. Some other man might have infected them, Dawson declared. "The basic compo-nent is missing," he insisted. Bruce Long groaned inwardly. Montpetit had made the match in all three cases but did not testify to it because those women, infected before Ssenyonga tested positive, were not complainants.

Dawson continued, "It can't be said beyond a reasonable doubt the transmission of HIV by my client has caused the complainants [Francine Dalton, Joan Estrada and Nancy Gauthier] any bodily harm" unless AIDS developed. This skipped over Cheryl Wagner's testimony that Francine

Dalton had full-blown AIDS. Subsequently, Dawson reviewed Root-Bernstein's evidence and said, "It hasn't been established in science that HIV causes AIDS."

"He did concede that he felt there was some connection," the judge observed with no inflection, looking at Dawson over his reading glasses.

"But we don't *know*," Dawson replied stubbornly.

"Could it not be argued that it put in motion the event that ends in bodily harm?" McDermid asked.

Dawson had an adroit reply. He observed that people who die from drowning always have CO_2 in their blood, but no one says that the CO_2 in the blood causes the drowning.

The judge continued as if thinking aloud. "There is evidence in this case that at least one of the complainants has AIDS," he said. "Are you saying your client didn't cause that?"

Dawson didn't hesitate. "We can't say beyond a reasonable doubt," he insisted.

Later the judge asked, "Isn't HIV bodily harm in itself?" and Dawson replied, "No. We don't know its role in relationship to anything that comes later." He added, "Even if we have theories, even if we have theories that are probably correct, we do not have proof beyond a reasonable doubt... What would happen if we found out six months from now, two years from now, three years from now, that we've really been off on the wrong track?"

In the break that afternoon, Long said cheerily to Johnson and Beasley, "Well, we haven't heard Fletcher's conspiracy theory yet." They didn't have long to wait.

When court resumed Dawson opened with an elaboration on the post-traumatic stress disorder defence. Ssenyonga lacked "appreciation of the physical consequences of his act," he said. "His thinking was disordered and that information [that he was infected] wasn't available to him. He didn't appreciate that he could cause bodily harm."

"Your previous argument," the judge observed placidly, "was that he wasn't a danger to these women."

Dawson was startled but pushed ahead firmly. "We can't say it was established in a legally relevant way."

"Your position is that he wasn't legally a danger to them?" asked the judge with lifted brows.

"Right."

The tapping of the judge's computer could be heard as he made a note of this while Dawson turned pages in the loose-leaf binder on his lectern. Dawson's speech mannerisms had become more noticeable under the strain of the judge's unsettling questions. To give himself time to think, he ended sentences with "and so on and so forth" or began them with, "In my respectful submission . . ."

The three Crown lawyers, absorbed in note-taking, were taken by surprise towards the end of the day when Dawson launched into a description of the methodology in the London testing lab, where, he said, dozens of vials of blood samples were uncorked and side by side. Someone could have jostled the specimens, he said; Ssenyonga's blood sample could have been contaminated by another person's.

Fletcher Dawson then introduced the conspiracy theory, as the Crown lawyers disdainfully had been calling it. He reviewed the evidence of meetings and telephone calls between the infected women and Dr. Cheryl Wagner, which he suggested showed a degree of collusion about their testimony. He then characterized each of the complainants as less than prudent or virtuous.

"He even went after Joan Estrada," Nancy protested afterwards. "And she's Miss Squeaky-Clean!"

The Crown's post-mortem that night lasted longer than usual. "How did Fletcher come up with blood slopping around?" Beasley asked disgustedly.

Long replied, looking on the bright side, "Well, we didn't hear about Ssenyonga's blood sample left in the cooler on Bendheim's porch."

The discussion centred on how to respond to the unexpected elements Dawson had introduced. The decision was to ignore the uncorked vials as too frivolous a concern but to respond vigorously to the conspiracy theory.

"Dawson raised that at the prelim," Long recalled with exasperation. "He tried to show that contacts between Linda, Jennifer, and Francine were all orchestrated by Cheryl Wagner, who drew in Joan and Nancy. That didn't fly at the prelim. There was no evidence of that at all." He threw up his hands. "How can anyone possibly infer a conspiracy from Wagner, a sweet, gentle thing?"

Bruce sternly instructed Simon, "Insert a little righteous indignation, Simon."

DAY TWENTY-FOUR: *Tuesday, July 6, 1993*

This was Simon Johnson's day. It fell to him to meet Dawson's arguments and summarize the prosecution's case. He tackled the responsibility with poise and decisiveness. His pauses this time to accommodate the judge's typing speed were smoothly integrated into his speaking style. Simon's most compelling point was that Ssenyonga simply didn't care whether he infected others. Citing example after example of Ssenyonga's indifference to the well-being of the women, Simon commented that the accused man's actions were "characterized throughout by a focus on himself." Only self-interest would explain Ssenyonga's apparent lack of concern, the lawyer said.

"There is an explanation to the behaviour that you see here," he said. "It is entirely consistent with a person who was aware of his infection, a person who was aware of the risk he posed in having unprotected sex, and simply didn't care."

Johnson maintained that the defence had not met the burden of proof in claiming that Ssenyonga suffered from post-traumatic stress disorder. Ssenyonga had maintained a normal lifestyle, whereas PTSD is "very disruptive of a person's life . . . the hallmark of PTSD is intrusive recollections." Ssenyonga, however, had never avoided the subject of AIDS. Simon found it odd that a man suffering from repression would be able to recall in detail the experiences in Africa that were supposed to have traumatized him and yet at the time the trauma was supposed to have occurred, he showed no signs of anxiety. Ssenyonga had addressed a student rally and behaved in a clear-headed way in making his escape. "If he is so obsessed with death," Johnson asked, "why didn't he get tested when Dr. Mackie suggested it?"

He then cited a stream of references and precedents relating to "wanton or reckless disregard" for the well-being of others. "It is proved that the accused infected the complainants," he said. "He was the only sexual partner who carried the HIV over a certain period of time, the only sexual partner they had in common during that relevant period, and there is the DNA match." Without question, he declared, it was impossible for the defence to evade the fact that Ssenyonga infected the complainants.

Johnson was critical of Ssenyonga's behaviour during cross-examination, particularly the witness's frequent response that he didn't remember. He catalogued the times when Ssenyonga had been caught in a lie, and his persistence in having unprotected sexual intercourse after being advised by many people of the need for safe sex. Johnson's tone was especially contemptuous in reviewing Ssenyonga's admission that he didn't wear a condom when he had sex with Joan Estrada because it was "uncomfortable."

Towards the end of the afternoon, exhaustion overtook the young lawyer. His voice dropped almost to a whisper. The judge asked him to speak up, adding sympathetically that he knew it was late in the day. When court adjourned, Johnson, a perfectionist, was depressed.

"You never feel like you've done a good job," Bruce Long, a perfectionist himself, consoled him. "You always wish you had done it differently." He smiled and patted the young man's shoulder. "Simon, I couldn't have done it as well and you couldn't have done it any better."

Later Bruce commented, "You could see Simon getting better as he progressed. He was a bit hesitant and non-committal at the prelim, but he was neither of those when dealing with the summation. He just gained in strength and assurance."

Fletcher Dawson shook hands with Ssenyonga as they parted. Their relationship had not been a smooth one, Dawson admits, but he genuinely cared about the man. "He was not an easy man to know," he commented tactfully some months after the trial, avoiding comment about their frequent clashes. "But by the time the trial was over the relationship was good." He added, "I think Charles felt his point of view, the alternative view with respect to HIV and AIDS, had been presented. My feeling is that he was content."

DAY TWENTY-FIVE: *Wednesday, July 7, 1993*

The trial was ending. Simon Johnson finished what he had to say in an orderly, crisp presentation, and Fletcher Dawson made some biting rejoinders. Then Judge Dougald McDermid looked down at them and inquired, "Are we finished?" They were.

"I have plenty of other things to do," the judge said with a thin smile. He consulted his schedule to set a date when he would render a decision. He chose August 4, but said he might be later than that. Bruce Long was surprised. He thought the judge would need at least two months.

18

CHARLES SSENYONGA DIED on a beautiful summer morning, Tuesday, July 20, 1993, in a private room at the yellow-brick Listowel Memorial Hospital, which is near a tranquil park and just over a bridge fringed with marigolds. Connie Neill was alone in the room with him when it happened. She was sitting on his bed, lifting his oxygen mask to wipe bubbles from his mouth. His lungs were filling. In the hour since he had left the emergency department, Ssenyonga had not spoken. He appeared a vacated shell. Suddenly his body jerked in one final convulsion and he stopped breathing.

Connie ran into the hall to get help. A nurse herself, she thought he could be resuscitated. The staff nurse said she was under orders to do nothing. Ssenyonga had made an agreement with his doctor that there would be no medical intervention to prolong his life. Connie returned to the room to weep over the body. Charles Ssenyonga was gone, taking his enigmas with him.

His conduct during his final few days of life suggest that he wished to die. According to Connie Neill, the deterioration was rapid. Just about two weeks earlier the couple had been in the mountains north of the Ontario-Quebec border. It was the happiest camping trip of their two summers together, marred only by mosquitos. Charles suffered a multitude of bites, which festered in large, hot welts. He developed headaches and a raging fever that strong medication didn't touch.

On their return to the farmhouse, Charles was unable to keep down even the liquid vanilla-flavoured food supplement Connie provided. His digestion was so unsettled he would vomit after sipping water. Connie, worried about dehydration, urged him to see a doctor, but Charles insisted he would be fine. Just some flu bug, he said, he would recover soon. She argued, but he was adamant.

On Friday, July 16, he was confined to his bed, his fever rising. Late that afternoon he finally yielded to her entreaties to get help. She telephoned the Listowel family physician who had become Ssenyonga's regular doctor, but the doctor was gone for the weekend. Charles would not hear of her calling the replacement.

On Saturday he pulled himself from bed to bring the horses into the barn. Their landlord appreciated finding them there on Sunday mornings. Charles appeared even sicker on Sunday, but still he insisted on waiting for his regular doctor's return. Connie is sorry she listened to him.

"That's another guilt I went through," she says, "but Charles was very determined. And I always did what he wanted me to do."

Charles's condition became alarming on Monday. He permitted Connie to notify the doctor, who suggested he go at once to the hospital in Listowel. Charles refused, maintaining that he would be better in the morning.

During the night Charles had two seizures. Connie overcame his protests about calling an ambulance by assuring him that he would be in hospital only two days. "Just let them rehydrate you, renourish you, and you'll be home again," she promised.

The ambulance and paramedics arrived some time after dawn, just as Ssenyonga had a massive seizure. Charles made a gesture of reaching out to Connie and then life went out of his eyes. "It was as though his soul had left him," she recalls. "He wasn't himself any more. He couldn't speak. It was like a stroke."

She drove her jeep behind the ambulance and arrived at the Listowel Memorial Hospital emergency department around seven. Ssenyonga's doctor had been summoned but had not yet arrived: Listowel's eighty-five-bed hospital and nursing home has no resident physicians.

Administrator James Van Camp, a genial man who was born in the hospital he now runs, was notified that an unusual patient had arrived. When Ssenyonga's doctor came into the emergency room, Charles was not communicating. His eyes were fixed on a vanishing point in the distance.

Connie speculates that Charles wanted his own doctor there, and not the weekend substitute, because of the Do Not Resuscitate agreement between them. "The doctor knew he wanted no medicine, no IV, nothing," she says. Van Camp will say only that the hospital was aware that Ssenyonga wished to be "made comfortable," a euphemism for non-intervention.

The dying man was provided with oxygen to ease his laboured breathing, and he was transferred to a room on the second floor where medical and surgical beds are located. An hour later, he stopped breathing.

When she could collect herself, Connie made a telephone call to Jeanine LeRoy in London. Jeanine was in court that morning but Michael Thompson, another lawyer in Fletcher Dawson's firm, took the call. Thompson could not find Dawson, who was on vacation. Jeanine heard the news when she returned to the office around noon and she immediately called Connie Neill to offer comfort. Her next consideration was for the women Ssenyonga had infected. She didn't want them to learn of his death by reading a newspaper, so she telephoned the office of the Crown. Bruce Long was on vacation and Simon Johnson was in Toronto on business, but Geoff Beasley was there.

He was devastated. Dismayed at what he saw as the end of the case, more than two years of work for nothing, Geoff called Judge Dougald McDermid to tell him what had happened. The judge commented that he had written 125 pages of his decision. Beasley thought he seemed "miffed" that his efforts were in vain, but McDermid maintained decorum. He suggested a meeting in his chambers to decide what to do next.

Everyone knew the case was over: the death of an accused person ends a trial. When reporters called Beasley, his response was that disposing of the case "was just a formality now." He told Alan Barnes of the *Toronto Star*, "You can't prosecute a ghost."

Geoff reached Dr. Cheryl Wagner at her cottage. The cause of death was not yet known, Geoff said, though rumours were circulating about a heart attack. Was it possible that he died of an AIDS-related cause? At the time Cheryl wasn't sure. Although Ssenyonga had full-blown AIDS, judging from his appearance in court, it was her opinion that he had "a couple of years left." Geoff told her about the infected mosquito bites. Could that be connected to Ssenyonga's death? She thought it far-fetched, and certainly not something common with HIV, but maybe he died of encephalitis, an inflammation of the brain. Ssenyonga's suppressed immune system might have contributed to that.

Cheryl felt badly for the women, her patients and the others, who had gone through so much invasion of their privacy to bring Ssenyonga to justice. They would feel cheated, she thought.

That was Francine Dalton's first reaction. She decided Ssenyonga must have committed suicide. "I figured he killed himself to avoid going through what lay ahead," she said.

The rumour about a heart attack came from the first reporter who called the Listowel Hospital for information, reaching a flustered nurse who said a possible cause was heart attack. That was a lapse of medical confidentiality, and inaccurate as well, but after that the hospital yielded no information. Administrator Van Camp is proud that his staff subsequently stood up to a barrage of attention that centred on his normally quiet institution. "We had calls from all over the place," he comments, "even one from Africa. Everyone wanted to know the cause of death and what his last minutes were like."

Debora Van Brenk was working at her computer in the *London Free Press* newsroom when she learned of Ssenyonga's death. She dropped everything and drove to the modest home of Nancy Gauthier. It wasn't the kind of news one delivers over the telephone.

"It's about Ssenyonga," Debora began when Nancy answered the doorbell.

Nancy hastily stepped out and closed the door behind her. "I have some guests," she whispered. "They don't know I'm infected."

When Debora told her that Ssenyonga was dead, Nancy felt only numbness. She bit her lips and murmured, "I went through hell for nothing. I feel overwhelmed . . . It's just a reminder for me, a reminder that my life is over too."

Later, in tears, she called Debora. "He shouldn't be allowed to die in dignity," she wept. "I'm hoping the judge says something so it doesn't all get lost."

Nancy was certain he must have killed himself, though it was plain that he was deteriorating over the months of the trial. "He was just withering away," she says.

Her feelings for Ssenyonga are still muddled. She has never understood the contradictions of his nature. Sometimes she talked of revenge and said she loathed him for heartlessly infecting her with a disease that will kill her, but often she spoke of Ssenyonga with loving admiration. "He was a really good person, he was a classy guy," she commented only weeks after Ssenyonga's death. She gave her head a vigorous shake. "But I have to separate the two sides of him. He's also no better than a serial killer."

Geoff Beasley reached OPP Inspector Terry Hall on the golf course. To the annoyance of the inspector's wife, he takes his beeper with him on vacation. Terry's first thought on hearing the news was disgust. "The son of a bitch got off easy," he thought. Geoff told him it looked like a heart attack. That didn't seem right to Terry. He immediately ordered an autopsy. "He went too quick," he explained. "It could have been from an injection. I was concerned that a few years from now people might say one of the victims had him killed."

Debora Van Brenk, doing her job, called around for reactions in preparation for the next day's front-page story. She reached Jessica Msamba Lewycky, Ssenyonga's former partner in The African Store, and, as tactfully as such things can be done, told her that Ssenyonga was dead.

Jessica said, "Oh, my god. Oh, my god." A long pause followed. Then she asked, "Did he do it himself? He never would have accepted what was happening to him."

Debora said it was a suspected heart attack. Jessica rejected the possibility. "No," she said firmly, "that wouldn't be it at all."

Simon Johnson could not be reached in Toronto on the day Ssenyonga died, despite Geoff Beasley's efforts. That night he heard about Ssenyonga's death when he talked to his mother-in-law on the telephone. She said, "So what is going to happen now that Ssenyonga is dead?" When what she had said sunk in, Simon's first thought was, "Two and a half years of work down the tubes."

He speculated on the possibility of finding legal grounds for the judge to render his decision anyway. Simon had never heard of such a situation. "In Britain," he said, "all trials at the level of Ssenyonga's are jury trials. There is no case where an accused dies between the time the judge charges the jury and the jury returned with the verdict, which is sometimes only hours later." He decided he would search American precedents and see what he could unearth. "Once again," he sighed, "this case is legal history."

Bruce Long, vacationing in Quebec, heard the news later that day. So did Rick Galli, called by Beasley. Michael Montpetit got word from his wife, who saw an item about it on television news just before Beasley called. "Geoff told me that this meant the court case in many ways didn't exist," Montpetit comments. "I felt great disappointment. I felt sad for the victims."

He regretted he would never get the blood sample Ssenyonga had agreed to provide. Two days later he had a pleasant surprise. Rick Galli called to say the sample had arrived in his lab. Ssenyonga had provided a vial just before leaving on that last camping trip.

The only person close to the trial who by nightfall on July 20 still did not know about the death was Ssenyonga's lawyer, Fletcher Dawson. The next afternoon, idly turning the pages of the *Globe and Mail* with no real intention of reading anything, he flipped right by the headline "Ssenyonga Dies Before Verdict." Then he registered what he had seen and stopped in mid-turn. Minutes later he was talking to Jeanine LeRoy, who told him what she knew.

He commented gravely, "It's very sad when anybody dies. There is a great deal of tragedy associated with this case."

Dr. Richard Schabas was depressed when he heard the news. He was keenly interested in finding out if Section 22 of the public health protection act was unconstitutional. If so, then either the province needed a new section or public health should stop trying to deal with people like Ssenyonga and give up the ground completely to the criminal courts. Now Fletcher Dawson would not be pushing for a ruling and the question was back in limbo.

The London region coroner, Keith Johnston, took charge of Ssenyonga's body, which was taken to Toronto for a full forensic autopsy on July 21. Pathologists there were not able to make an immediate decision as to cause of death. The liver and spleen were enlarged and so were some lymph glands, but nothing provided a conclusive explanation: the pieces just didn't fit. Ssenyonga's lungs showed fungal infection, a possible cause, but not to a degree that made a diagnosis obvious. Terry Hall was intrigued by the report of an invasion of fungus. Katie Newman also died of a fungal infection, hers in the brain.

Doctors removed certain body parts for further analysis. Days later they decided from fluid in Ssenyonga's lung that he might have died of a pneumonia. The final diagnosis, however, was cryptococcosis, a fungus associated with AIDS which can spread throughout the body and, in his case, caused meningitis. Ssenyonga's condition was treatable by well-proven methods, if he had chosen to have intervention.

The remains were released to Connie Neill as the official next-of-kin. She ordered cremation and placed Ssenyonga's ashes in five containers, one a calabash she hung on her kitchen wall, the others assorted urns and jars she placed on a cupboard in the living room. She had plans for them all. She would scatter the ashes from one of them in a place special to them both. Another, a small bronze jar, she would take to Uganda and present to his parents, if she could raise the money to travel. She would keep the ashes in a tall oriental jar; the littlest container was reserved for "someone I expect to hear from," whose identity she keeps to herself.

Ugandans crowded around to express their sorrow. At the urging of the Ugandan community, memorial services for Charles were held in London, Listowel, and Toronto. Connie's small farmhouse thronged with people. Fletcher Dawson and Jeanine LeRoy attended with their spouses.

George Seremba, the actor-writer, went to the Toronto service. He was struck by the outpouring of genuine grief. When Connie asked for donations to enable her to go to Uganda with Ssenyonga's ashes, many people contributed. (Francine Dalton, hearing of the collection, said derisively, "Even after his death he's mooching off people.")

Seremba says, "People gathered to say farewell as they would for anybody from the Ugandan community, but some were sincerely sorrowful. Only a few said, 'Why should we contribute for someone who snubbed us, who didn't call?'"

Connie had mixed feelings about the rush of support. She found herself wondering where Charles's friends had been since his arrest. "You're trying to make it up to me," she thought sadly, "but I'm not the one to make it up to."

She admits she had to fight to control her anger. At the church service, she found herself musing, "What are you people mourning for? Wouldn't it be easier if you did nothing? You did nothing before." She says, "I was afraid to speak because I might say something they wouldn't want to hear."

On the other hand, she has to agree that Charles pushed away the Ugandan community. "It is true, he didn't want them around," she admits. "He felt they were judgemental of him, and they had no right to be judgemental."

Francine Dalton, despite her outrage that Ssenyonga had died before facing his guilt, sent a message of sympathy to Connie by way of Jeanine LeRoy. A similar exchange across the lines was made by Simon Johnson. Aware that Jeanine had become Ssenyonga's friend, he called with his condolences. "That was a beautiful thing for him to do," she says.

Two days after Ssenyonga's death, Nancy Gauthier was recovered enough to make telephone calls herself. She left messages for Bruce Long and for Fletcher Dawson that she expected the Crown to continue to represent her and also that she "expects the judge to have the balls to finish what he started."

Geoff Beasley, preparing to go on vacation, was torn with indecision about what to do next. He wondered if the Ontario Court of Appeal might be persuaded to order McDermid to render a decision. On the other hand, if the judge did give a verdict it could not be appealed in the absence of an accused person. That would be fine with Geoff if the verdict was guilty but if the judge acquitted Ssenyonga, "then we're stuck with it." It would stand on the books and affect all other AIDS cases.

The Crown had appealed Ssenyonga's acquittal on the aggravated sexual assault charges. Geoff wasn't sure whether that action could go forward; perhaps the Court of Appeal would render a decision because of the need for clarification in criminal charges involving AIDS. Who knew? Considering the huge backlog of cases, it seemed unlikely the judges would welcome a thorny problem they could easily dump.

When later interviewed, the judge who presided at the preliminary hearing, Deborah Livingstone, had strong doubts that the Court of Appeal would push the matter. "Without an accused to face the jeopardy of a conviction one wonders how a Court of Appeal can deal with the issue."

Bruce Long, desolate at the strange twist of one of the biggest trials of his life, commented gloomily, "We could ask the Court of Appeal to make a determination because of the public interest factor, but the rule is that when a party is dead, that's it."

Fletcher Dawson returned to London and on July 28 went with Simon Johnson to see the judge. Dawson declared that the case was closed. There could be no verdict with a dead accused. Johnson was still hoping to find a way to give the judge room to render a verdict. McDermid encouraged him to search for legal precedents, but he made it clear he would not budge unless the precedents were persuasive. When Dawson delicately fished for a hint of what the judge was thinking, saying that "people are wondering" which way the decision would have gone, McDermid said coldly that he would not respond to such a question.

Dawson was quite confident that the judge would confide in no one about his verdict. "The case is moot," he said. "It is unlikely we'll ever know what the judge was going to say. McDermid will never leak it to anyone. He is an extremely competent, principled judge."

Simon Johnson hit the books again. He still could find no similar situation that would allow the judge to speak but he wasn't giving up.

It was in the midst of the uncertainty in Ontario that the Court of Appeal in Newfoundland startled the country by increasing the sentence of Raymond Mercer from thirty months to eleven years and three months. The three-judge appeal court (Chief Justice Noel Goodridge, J.W. Mahoney and W. Marshall) declared, "Mr. Mercer's crimes were of monumental proportions." The forty-two pages of reasons, written by Marshall, were withering in their contempt for Mercer.

"By any standard the consequences of Mr. Mercer's conduct for these two young women must be viewed as catastrophic and dreadful," the court declared in describing a situation that was a replica of Ssenyonga's. "Dr. [Ian] Bowmer's evidence attests to the reality of untimely deaths for both of them and lives of misery and anguish in their contracted life spans. The evidence indicates that they live in awareness of these realities. There is, therefore, no way to either gainsay or rationalize the enormity of the consequences of Mr. Mercer's acts . . .

"There is clear evidence here that, conscious of the probable consequences of his actions, Mr. Mercer deliberately disregarded warnings and engaged in unprotected sexual relations with his victims. Moreover, his deceitful assurances in the initial sexual contact with each of his partners that protection was unnecessary heightens the deliberate aspect of his criminality as, indeed, does the whole pattern of his deceptive conduct throughout. These calculated actions, evidently undertaken to satisfy his own predilections and desires, put the degree of his culpability at a very high level. This must tell against him in assessing his punishment...

"Individuals who have proven themselves capable of paying no heed whatsoever to competent and authoritative medical instruction as to the measures absolutely essential for the protection of others from HIV infection represent a grave danger to society and they cannot be allowed to circulate freely in it for fear that they will continue to knowingly infect other unwitting partners with impunity... The consequences are too grave for society not to take every means at its disposal to curb such conduct and the court has a duty to protect the public accordingly."

The court had no confidence that Mercer would abstain from unprotected sexual relations with unwitting partners if he had the opportunity. "He has the capacity to act with calculated contempt for any warnings as to the danger of his actions... purely to satiate his amorous desires and appetites... rehabilitation is not a viable option in these circumstances."

Some protested that the sentence was too harsh. Mercer's lawyer, Michael Crystal, announced that the decision would be appealed. "This case really cries out for some sort of direction from the Supreme Court of Canada," said Crystal.

In the spring of 1994 the Supreme Court of Canada decided it would not hear the appeal. The rejection was taken as confirming lengthy sentences in cases involving the transmission of HIV.

Bruce Long had great admiration for the Newfoundland decision. He wondered if Judge McDermid's would have been similar.

DAY TWENTY-SIX: *Wednesday, August 4, 1993*

Courtroom 18 was more crowded than on any previous day of the trial, mostly because of a throng of media people. Geoff Beasley cut short his vacation to attend. Bruce Long was away and Geoff was unwilling to leave Simon Johnson alone. Fletcher Dawson and Jeanine LeRoy emerged from the elevator together and threaded their way through the gaggle of reporters.

When Judge Dougald McDermid seated himself and booted up his computer, Dawson rose to enter into the court record the information that Charles Ssenyonga had "passed away" on the twentieth of July. The judge asked for proof of death, which Beasley said would be provided.

"What position does counsel take?" the judge asked.

Beasley first wanted to compliment Jeanine LeRoy for notifying the Crown quickly so that victims would not get the news through the media. As for the Crown's position, he went on to say, there was some hope that the Court of Appeal would provide direction "if Your Honour should consider giving a verdict . . . in this extremely unusual situation."

He asked for an adjournment until autumn to give time for study. "I haven't been able to find a precedent for a trial judge to render judgement," Dawson protested. "I am not opposed at all [to the delay] but I don't have a client to tell me what position to take."

The judge nodded understandingly. "There is no precedent I can find except at the appellate level," he agreed.

"My present feeling is it would not be proper to deliver reasons in this case, much as I would like to and much as others may wish." He acknowledged that the public had an investment in the outcome, both from the standpoint of the amount of money spent on the investigation and trial and from the perspective of the implications for future cases. If the Court of Appeal ordered it, he would be willing to deliver his reasons, but he had a problem with delivering a verdict against someone who could neither be vindicated nor punished.

"I will adjourn," he concluded.

Beasley remarked, as a pointed reminder to the media, that the publication ban on the names of the victims was still in existence.

"Very much so," the judge said sternly.

Connie Neill arrived alone and left alone. She was planning to move from the farmhouse; it would be too lonely to stay there over the winter. One of the containers of Ssenyonga's ashes already was buried during a tree-planting ceremony. She was resisting pressure to give the coroner permission to allow Michael Montpetit to examine Ssenyonga's lymph gland. Montpetit was anxious to study the evolution of Ssenyonga's HIV, but she firmly refused to cooperate. She didn't want Charles's body parts scattered that way.

Nancy Gauthier, striking in a white suit, looked distraught. "I'm having a bad day," she confessed. "I put my heart and soul into this case and I got nothing out of it."

Together with Francine Dalton and Joan Estrada, she had shed tears over the preparation of the victim-impact statement. If Ssenyonga had lived and been found guilty, all three would have had the opportunity before sentencing to tell the judge what his crime had done to their lives. The three women spent many days that summer in the expectation that they would stand in court on August 4 and tell the judge — and Ssenyonga — about their pain.

Francine Dalton "cried buckets" while composing her victim-impact statement. She imagined the scene: herself in the witness box and Ssenyonga, crushed by the verdict of guilty, forced to listen. "I wanted him to know that people see him as a bad person," she said. "He didn't think he was a bad person. He just didn't get it. I really wanted to say it to his face. It would have been a great moment, but it is lost now."

Nancy Gauthier began her statement with a bleak observation: "When I was first diagnosed HIV-positive, I was told that I had seven to ten years before I might become ill with the disease. It's been two years now — does this mean I have five years left before I get sick? Will I in five years not have the energy to cook supper, play with my child? Will I lose my hair, go blind?"

She continued, "My daughter has suffered terribly. At Christmas I noticed she doesn't colour in red. Even Rudolph the Red-Nosed Reindeer had an orange nose. When I asked her why, she said red was painful and it looked like blood. She knows something happened to her mummy that was terrifying, and it had to do with blood...

"Once she had a dream that her mother was dead in the apartment, her dad didn't come and get her, and she died in the apartment because there was no food for her. I know this dream was caused by the fear she senses in me...

"My life is destroyed. Ssenyonga has sentenced me to death, and he enjoyed himself when he did it."

Joan Estrada's statement consisted of four pages in her schoolgirl handwriting. "I am sitting on a deserted beach as I write about what my life has become," it begins. "There is a storm coming in and I am left all alone to ponder, to cry and to write the most difficult statement of my life. The irony of this situation is all too perfect. I once used to be a very happy person with many friends, many dreams and so much to offer. When this whole nightmare began, I was barely twenty-one with my whole life ahead of me..."

"I cannot plan a future for I do not have one. I now have been reduced to an individual with no spirit, no happiness, and no will to survive. I live my life as a recluse...I shall never again be able to show affection or love a man without endangering his life...I am dying and I can't do anything about it. I am so afraid. It's like a countdown."

Joan concluded the statement with an entry from her diary written in 1991 soon after her diagnosis: "I really wish I had a gun to end all of this. I would do it. I swear I would. It would be quick and easy. I hate all of this. I hate life. Charles Ssenyonga has taken my life from me."

19

ON AUGUST 11, 1993, Joan Estrada and Nancy Gauthier appeared in London before the Criminal Injuries Compensation Board to ask for the maximum compensation of $25,000 available to them as victims of a crime. This tribunal consisted of two people, Mohammed Sharmarke, who mostly was silent, and the tribunal's chair, Anne Stanfield, who is vice-chair of the compensation board. Stanfield, a complacent woman, oozed with patronizing platitudes and appeared to have an invincible ignorance of the law. Thousands of such patronage-ridden quasi-judicial tribunals exist everywhere in Canada, few of them monitored by any authority and many with untrammelled powers to do harm and injustice without public scrutiny.

Both women were aghast at the insensitivity they encountered. Stanfield said she was not certain that a crime had been committed since there was no verdict, a position at odds with the reality of her mandate.

"Is this really a health issue or is it a criminal issue?" she asked with a smile. "The question is, has there been a crime? Has there been a court in the land that has found this to be a crime?"

Joan Estrada burst into tears and was advised by Stanfield to go to the washroom and splash cold water on her face.

The same two-person tribunal was assigned to hear the third claimant, Francine Dalton, at a hearing in Toronto. Francine arrived with her lawyer, Jacquie Chic, who was articling at Parkdale Community Legal Services. Stanfield, commenting that she had no confidence that the media would respect a publication ban, considered banning reporters from the hearing. She asked each reporter to give reasons why she should not do so. When it was the turn of Tracey Tyler of the *Toronto Star* to respond, the reporter coldly declared that she would be consulting her paper's lawyer. Stanfield hastily backed down and contented herself, for mysterious reasons of her own, with collecting the reporters' tape recorders.

Francine told the story of the relationship with Ssenyonga and ended with the victim-impact statement she had written for Ssenyonga's conviction. It began, "I have full-blown AIDS." Incredibly, as she began to cry, Stanfield clucked indulgently. Francine rallied and continued, "I measure my life in weeks and months, not years...I can't concentrate. There are never any good days any more, there are only days that are better than others...My hopes and dreams have been devastated by Charles Ssenyonga. He has robbed me of all that was rightfully mine, namely my future."

When Francine finished her tearful testimony, she was followed by witnesses: nurse Marylin McConnell; Dr. Cheryl Wagner who spoke of Francine's advanced illness; a lawyer from the attorney-general's office who proffered much-needed legal advice to the chair; and Dr. Ken Citron, a specialist in psychological and psychiatric problems related to HIV and AIDS in the Mount Sinai Hospital HIV clinic.

Citron, who has hundreds of HIV-positive people on his caseload, testified that Ssenyonga's behaviour was "atypical." He observed that Ssenyonga's "lack of concern is not reassuring. It indicates a great deal of denial of what the illness meant. He didn't want to accept that. If he accepted it he would have to alter his behaviour." He added sombrely, "I don't know him but he seems very callous to me." In his two years of involvement with infected people, the doctor had never encountered such behaviour. It seemed to him more than denial. "It is outright lying that seems very deliberate to me. It's a different kettle of fish than denial... He is someone who bends the truth for his own means without any guilt about it."

Francine Dalton emerged badly shaken. She told Kathleen Griffin of the *Toronto Sun*, "I just have this sense of disbelief that they're wondering whether a crime was committed. I was afraid I'd end up feeling victimized all over again by this and sure enough I do."

At the time of the hearings before the Criminal Injuries Compensation Board, Connie Neill was going through devastating shocks. She was making discoveries about Charles Ssenyonga that rocked her confidence in her own judgement and inclined her to bitterness. Over his ten years in Canada Ssenyonga had kept every letter, even postcards, and made copies of his own correspondence. Sorting through Ssenyonga's effects, she found evidence of a devious man who had lied to her on many matters. She was shattered to find that Charles had more women in his life than she had imagined. Once, appalled by something she found, she dumped a box of letters outside in the rain. When she relented and retrieved the container days later, everything was soaked and mildewed. She prefers not to talk about what she learned of his past.

"Lots of other women emerged," she says bleakly. "I am rethinking my decisions. I am not sure that I was right. Francine and Joan and Nancy came to court for a reason and I was on some sort of crusade, thinking, 'What do all these women want?' I'm not so sure about things now. We all learn something every day, don't we?"

She had an urge to call Francine. "I was finding out all these terrible things," Connie explains. "Of all the women in the case, I think she's the one I probably could get along with." But even a year later she still had not made the call. She was feeling too confused.

"I've made a lot of sacrifices," she comments. "I just want to get on with my life. I'm questioning whether I should go to Uganda. Maybe I'll just mail the ashes." She never refers to the probability that she is infected with HIV. She continues to believe that infection doesn't matter because a healthy lifestyle will protect her from AIDS.

Connie invested more than two years of her life in Ssenyonga and gave him love and loyalty when few others would come near him. Her support never wavered, not even when he was abusive to her. It was desolating for her to doubt herself, to wonder if she had been wrong about him. "Sometimes I think it was selfless love," she says with painful candour, "sometimes I think it was a crusade of some kind, sometimes I think it was just the mother in me. It was so many different things."

She comforts herself by remembering that Ssenyonga was an extraordinary man. "He had magnetism," she says wistfully. "He lit up when he talked to people. He stopped performing for me, that was part of my attraction for him that he could do that. But he loved the intensity, the rush of a new relationship."

It was a haunting echo of something Lois Swift had said. Lois, the businesswoman who was Ssenyonga's platonic friend, once observed, "A part of Charles always wanted to be normal, to fit into the group. But he was always an outsider. He didn't fit anywhere. He was acting normal in order to be normal. The part of him that was fantasy was about ninety percent. The part of him living in reality was ten percent. He had lots of control. He was an absolute survivor. He knew he was a really terrible person but he kept trying to be charming."

A controversy raged in the media about whether McDermid should give his decision. One view was that the significance of the case would be lost without a verdict. Another opinion, voiced by Ottawa lawyer Lawrence Greenspon, was opposed to forcing a verdict. Greenspon asked, "Have we come so far down the path of disguised hatred that we are prepared to hang the corpse?"

Geoff Beasley arranged for the three complainants to be examined by Dr. Keith Travis of Burlington, a consulting psychologist and author of *Critical Incident Stress and the Interruption of Behaviour*. What Beasley had in mind was to present Judge McDermid with evidence that failure to render a verdict would cause emotional damage to the complainants. Travis conducted an examination of each of the women and presented Beasley with a report.

"It is clear that none of the complainants could afford this ordeal to start with," he wrote. "The quality of [their] life has been reduced, and will almost certainly deteriorate if no verdict, or other public facsimile, is not forthcoming. More seriously, failure to deliver a verdict would likely potentiate the traumatization process which has been underway, detract substantially from the meaning of their lives, and militate against working out a meaningful, dignified death."

Travis said even a verdict of not guilty would be "less problematic" than no verdict at all.

DAY TWENTY-SEVEN: *Wednesday, October 13, 1993*

Mr. Justice Dougald McDermid prepared himself to hear legal arguments, possibly involving the Charter of Rights and Freedoms, on whether a trial judge can deliver a verdict after the death of an accused. Bruce Long began by asking the judge to set aside two days to hear the arguments and gave notice that "a lawyer from Toronto" would be seeking intervener status on behalf of the complainants. Francine Dalton, he had learned, was considering having a lawyer appear on her behalf. Further, Bruce said, he would be presenting a report or testimony from Dr. Travis.

All this clearly caught the judge off guard. McDermid had expected to hear arguments that day. Long explained that such a presentation was coming, but not yet. At a future date he would be putting the Crown's position that there was a "compelling societal interest" in a verdict.

Fletcher Dawson, still staunchly representing the interests of his deceased client, protested. If the Crown wanted to call Travis to testify to the state of mind of the victims, he asked sarcastically if he should not be allowed to call the coroner to testify to the condition of Mr. Ssenyonga at the end of his life. And a doctor to discuss how much stress Mr. Ssenyonga was experiencing during the trial. His point was that it was absurd to continue to drag out the Ssenyonga case. "There has to be some finality, in a sense, to the proceedings," he said. It seemed to him that "we are opening the biggest Pandora's box that we have ever seen in a trial situation... Cases could just go on interminably."

A much annoyed judge commented, "What I am hearing this morning is certainly not what I anticipated... My reaction to prolonging this matter is, I may say, very negative in terms of having further people testify, having people intervene. I *am* prepared to deal with it on the basis of legal argument."

McDermid appeared weary. He said he would be commencing a trial expected to last from six to eight weeks and he would not be available until December. Dawson, too, was about to begin another trial.

After conferring over their crowded schedules, the judge and lawyers agreed tentatively on December 16. The notion of extending the ordeal by bringing in witnesses quietly evaporated.

DAY TWENTY-EIGHT: *Friday, December 17, 1993*

The day was crisp and clear in London, with morning frost on the grass, and the mood in Courtroom 18 was one of a festive reunion. Simon Johnson was there without his court gown: he had been hired by a prestigious Toronto law firm and was attending as a spectator. The media regulars were out in force, bolstered by camera crews waiting in the courthouse lobby. Debora Van Brenk, who had been posted to Chatham by the *London Free Press*, was elated to have a reprieve to finish the Ssenyonga saga she began more than two years earlier. Fletcher Dawson hurried into the courtroom, looking more distracted than usual. Francine Dalton and Nancy Gauthier arrived with Ruth Rutherford of the court's victim-witness assistance program. Crown lawyers Geoff Beasley and Bruce Long were accompanied by a newcomer, Tom Wickett, the lawyer from the attorney-general's department who worked on the Section 101 application. Wickett intended to ask for intervener status on behalf of the Ministry of Health. Connie Neill, seeming very alone, slipped quietly into a seat near the back of the courtroom. Pat Vooy was there representing the OPP. The Ssenyonga investigation and trial dragged on for so long that, like Cheryl Wagner, she had managed to have two babies during it all.

Next to Fletcher Dawson was an eloquent empty chair.

Judge Dougald McDermid entered, his expression severe and impatient. He turned on his computer and gave Bruce Long a sharp look. Long explained that Tom Wickett wanted to be heard first. He was seeking "a procedural avenue" to having standing in the hearing.

Dawson would have none of it. Wickett worked for the Crown, which already was represented by Long and Beasley, he said, and his presence therefore was redundant.

The judge agreed. He said, "The Crown speaks for the public at large...I don't know why we need intervention when we already have a Crown."

"This is an exceptional case," Long argued. He said it was a Catch 22 situation. "This trial is waiting on the Court of Appeal and the Court of Appeal is awaiting on the outcome of this trial."

Not so, Dawson interjected swiftly. He had checked. The Court of Appeal as yet did not have the death certificate. So far as the appellate court was concerned, Ssenyonga was alive.

The judge thought it would be an "impossible" situation if everyone who wanted intervener status got it. Wickett bowed acknowledgement of his dismissal and took a seat away from the counsel table.

Dawson then said in a brisk tone of voice that court had "no jurisdiction to hand down a decision."

Bruce Long maintained that the court did have jurisdiction. "There was a full and complete trial," he argued, stepping back from the lectern, gesturing with a pencil in his left hand. "The accused heard all the case against him." Ssenyonga's death, he said, in a startling turn of phrase, amounted to merely "the evaporation of the sub-strata."

Fletcher Dawson, moving restlessly behind his lectern, snapped, "We're here to punish a man who is now dead." The court, he said, would be venturing "into the legislative field" if a decision was rendered. He concluded in measured tones, "A lot of people have put a lot of time on this case... but there should be no judgement."

Bruce Long, in rebuttal, said that there was no intent to punish the deceased. The issue was "the education of the living and the clarification of a legal issue."

The judge called a recess. He would return with his decision in fifteen minutes, he announced, and departed with his computer disk in hand.

Jeanine LeRoy, occupied until then with another case, turned up to watch the end of the story. Francine Dalton had moved to sit beside Connie Neill, who smiled at her tremulously. No one wanted to leave the room. People milled around aimlessly.

The judge returned. He began with a recital of the issues before him. He noted, in part, "The case has sparked some interest in the community at large and is of particular interest to the three complainants who have applications pending before the Criminal Injuries Compensation Board arising from the events surrounding the charges before me. As well, the Crown submits that because there has been no judgement in this case they are suffering physical and psychological stress, of which I have no doubt...

"Mr. Ssenyonga is now beyond the reach of this court and there can be no doubt that the issues in this trial are moot... Admittedly, this situation is most unusual and perhaps even unique."

The bottom line arrived. He said, "The circumstances militate against my delivering judgement... I find that the trial has abated due to the death of the accused."

Sadness fell on the room; the lack of conclusion made people feel bereft. They listened numbly as the judge gracefully complimented the defence and the Crown on a case that was "vigorously prosecuted and vigorously defended." McDermid said, and clearly meant it, that the trial had been conducted on both sides "in the finest tradition of the bar."

Gail McGilvray distributed impeccable copies of the judge's decision, prepared on his computer. "Nice to have a judge who can type," she commented wryly.

The Crown lawyers who worked on the case remain dejected by the absence of completion: Ssenyonga's long trial had ended without being finished. "I still feel empty," Bruce Long said months later. "We all do. It used to be that I spent an entire day on Ssenyonga. No question in my mind, he was going to be found guilty." He would have asked the judge for a sentence of eight years. "There has to be a lesson to the public and other people who may offend as well," he explained.

Fletcher Dawson is not so sure that the judge was planning to find Ssenyonga guilty. "Frankly, I think we had a real chance," he says. "I don't see it as a long shot."

Dougald McDermid's ruling that the case was closed seemed final, but Ssenyonga's legacy of legal tangles was not played out. Three more avenues were left to those who wanted to see some kind of resolution. One was the civil action, launched by Nancy Gauthier in May, 1994, against the Middlesex-London public health unit for failing to protect her from being infected by Ssenyonga after the unit was aware that he was infected and sexually active. The second was the possibility that the Ontario Court of Appeal would review McDermid's decision to drop the aggravated sexual assault charges. The third was the Criminal Injuries Compensation Board decision. There was even a fourth, a wild speculation that an inquest might be called into the death of Katie Newman.

One of those avenues vanished a few months after Ssenyonga's death: the Ontario Court of Appeal said it would not be looking at the Crown's motion on the dismissal of the sexual assault charges.

The three complainants put their hopes instead on the compensation board, anticipating some level of validation from that source and counting on the maximum award of $25,000 each. Nancy, bouncing with confidence, consulted real estate agents. She planned to use her payment to make a down-payment on a house, something substantial to leave her daughter when she died. Francine Dalton, by far the sickest of the three, fighting heavy night sweats and debilitating infections, also had plans to use her compensation money to move. Joan Estrada was thinking of securing the future of her beloved younger brother.

Jim Chapman, a radio talk-show host on CJBK in London, asked listeners to comment on whether victims should receive compensation. Nancy Gauthier, who heard the show, was shocked that almost all the callers were opposed to the women receiving any money at all. She asked Chapman to allow her to put her side of the story.

On October 7, 1993, she tremulously described what had happened to her life. Only one caller attacked her, a woman who said, "You got infected and you are asking society to pay for it. My children are being asked to pay for your mistakes." Nancy wept.

At the end of January, 1994, the women finally had word of the compensation board's decision, the first in Canada involving AIDS. Attached to the order mailed to each was a cheque for $15,000, a full $10,000 less than the board could have granted. The board explained that the amount was reduced because the women were in part responsible for their infections. "The board does not consider it reasonable to entrust one's life to an almost complete stranger on such a brief acquaintance," the order reads. "Given the dangers of unprotected sexual activities, a reasonable person would require a much longer period of trust building... The applicant's behaviour in engaging in unprotected sexual intercourse was behaviour which contributed to the injury she sustained."

The board agreed to provide an additional $3,500 towards the cost of each woman's funeral when that became necessary.

(In the summer of 1994, Danielle Fitzgerald applied to the Criminal Injuries Compensation Board and was granted the full amount allowable, $25,000. The tribunal felt that she was more victimized than the other applicants because she was raped.)

The most eloquent outcry against the reduced payment to the three women came from Michele Landsberg of the *Toronto Star* after a meeting with Francine Dalton. On February 19, 1994, Landsberg wrote, "Charles Ssenyonga was deliberately committing slow murder with his penis... To my mind, the board's comments are an ugly throwback to blaming the victim in rape trials... I think the board owes her [Francine] full compensation and a public apology for its coarse and repugnant woman-blaming." The column concluded with the telephone number of Ontario's attorney-general, Marion Boyd, and the suggestion that readers ask her to take some action.

Jeanine LeRoy sent an angry letter to the *Star* objecting to Landsberg's use of the word murder. "As junior counsel for Ssenyonga at his trial," she wrote in the letter, published March 9, 1994, "I heard every moment of the testimony. I have nothing but compassion for the women fighting for their lives. But ever since the first sexually transmitted disease was discovered, women and men have had to take responsibility and precautions. The members of the compensation board simply reminded the public of that. They repeated a warning offered on airwaves and billboards everywhere: Be careful. Landsberg's strong views on this matter do not give her the right to convict Ssenyonga of a charge he did not even face."

Following a meeting with lawyer Gail Cadieux from the Parkdale Community Legal Services, Ontario's attorney-general, Marion Boyd, decided to appeal the decision of her own tribunal. When asked about this exceptional motion by Richard Brennan of the *Windsor Star*, she commented, "We do not believe that [the decision] is a fair representation of the case as it is, and so we are appealing to divisional court so that a judge will make that determination." The case was heard in Toronto's Osgoode Hall on November 17, 1994, before an imposing panel of three judges headed by the Chief Justice himself, Roy McMurtry, flanked by Justices John O'Driscoll and William Jenkins. The complainants, Dalton, Gauthier and Estrada, were described as Jane Doe, Jean Doe and Joan Doe.

McMurtry, a former Ontario attorney-general, faced a perplexing situation. The Crown appeared to be at war with itself. The opposing lawyers both represented the attorney-general. One, Eleanor Smith, was there on behalf of the Criminal Injuries Compensation Board to defend its decision to make a reduced award, and the other, Leslie McIntosh, also appointed by the attorney-general, would attack the decision.

Observing in a friendly manner that the legal representation was "unusual, probably without precedent," McMurtry asked for assistance in sorting it out. McIntosh, a small, authoritative, crisp woman, undertook to reply. She pointed out that the board had a right to "respond fully" to arguments that it had erred.

That settled to the satisfaction of the judges, McIntosh set out in a calm, uncluttered style the attorney-general's position that the board was mistaken in this case when it exercised its statutory right to reduce compensation in circumstances where the victim's behaviour contributed to the harm. The award of $15,000, she pointed out, was a reduction from the permissable amount of $25,000 by forty percent, and the board had given no rational reasons for being so punitive. The explanation that the women should have protected themselves was not acceptable, she said, because as recently as 1991 women were being informed by experts that they had no reason to fear AIDS. Further, the board's comment that the women should have waited longer in the relationship before having sex with Ssenyonga was not borne out by the evidence. However long they delayed having sex, the outcome would have been the same. Ssenyonga would have maintained that he was healthy. "They thought they were dealing with an honest person," she said, "who was concerned and cared about them."

In order to justify such a reduction in their compensation, the lawyer said, Jane Doe, Jean Doe and Joan Doe would have had to indulge in "flagrant, reckless and foolish disregard" for their own safety, which none of them did.

Malcolm Bennett, a man with a narrow, anxious face and dark hair curling at the back, spoke next. He was appearing for Nancy Gauthier, their often tempestuous relationship being in remission. He introduced a catalogue of other tribunal rulings where the permissable level of compensation had not been reduced. Then Eleanor Smith, a solid, grey-haired woman with long experience in tribunal justice, gave the defence of the board's action. She spoke of the "foolishness" of the women not to insist on condoms.

It is unwise to make assumptions on the basis of what is said during legal arguments, but it seemed to spectators that the judges were sympathetic to the women. McMurtry said at one point, that "given the severity of the injuries" even the full amount of $25,000 seemed paltry. He also said, glossing over the fact that the Ssenyonga trial ended without a verdict, "His conduct was criminally negligent...no question about that." The judges reserved their decision and retired to think it over.

Meanwhile, only the day before the appeal in Toronto, Nancy Gauthier fought in a London courtroom to keep her civil suit against the Middlesex-London health unit alive. The unit went to court to claim that her action was spurious since she had filed the suit after the six-month limitation period. Anne Marie Frauts, retained by Gauthier for this matter, suggested that the issue of lateness should be decided by the trial judge at the time the case is heard. At the end of a tedious day of arguments, Gauthier was delighted when Justice Michael Meehan decided not to quash the suit.

Ssenyonga's death left a flatness, a sense of incompletion, that will haunt all those close to the trial for the rest of their lives. Dr. Richard Schabas, chief medical officer of health for Ontario, takes from Ssenyonga the lesson that "public health has got to be much more forceful in its counselling of people with HIV infection, much clearer in explaining to them what appropriate behaviours are, what risks they may pose to others. I think there has been a lot of confusion, and it is not unique to the Ssenyonga case, in the counselling that has been given to HIV-infected people."

He hasn't made up his mind about public health stepping out of the way to let criminal law deal with future Ssenyongas. He notes with a sigh, "There are no easy answers." The criminal action took two years to bring Ssenyonga to trial and spent maybe a million dollars doing it; will any Crown attorney want to do that again? "In the long run," Schabas says, "the most powerful strategies are public education strategies."

Many AIDS organizations agree. Clarence Crossman, Education Coordinator at the AIDS Committee of London, says the first step is counselling. "Legal restrictions are a very clumsy way to change behaviour," he says. "A combination of education and counselling strategies are more effective. It is human nature: if we are told 'don't do that' we are less likely to respond."

Dr. Janet Gilmour believes that the notion of counselling making a change in behaviour is too idealistic. "I don't think four months, four years, of counselling would impress someone who didn't care, someone who consciously infects people. It all comes down to who a person is."

Much was written in legal and medical journals at the time of the Ssenyonga trial about the need for a special law in the Criminal Code against knowingly infecting an unaware person with AIDS. With his death, discussion of a new law evaporated. Even a year later, no case like Ssenyonga's had emerged. The absence of arrests and court cases does not mean that no one in Canada is deliberately putting someone else at risk of HIV. Rather, it is a reflection of the manifest difficulties of bringing such a person to justice, as the Ssenyonga trial amply demonstrated. Without the combination of a dedicated investigation, intense legal resources, Ssenyonga's unique virus, and Michael Montpetit's groundbreaking DNA match, it will be almost impossible and, certainly, staggeringly expensive to prove guilt.

Public health laws, therefore, remain the country's main protection against the reckless transmission of the AIDS virus. Even these raise troubling questions about the efficacy of counselling and the legality of ordering someone to be celibate. Theresa Dobko, an experienced counsellor in the field of AIDS, is wary of the absence of legal safeguards for accused people. Fletcher Dawson thinks a court someday will strike down public health restraint orders, such as the one served on Charles Ssenyonga, as unconstitutional. "No sex order is worth the paper it is written on," he says with a shrug.

Canada is not the only country to wrestle with the dilemma that Ssenyonga posed for authorities. In November, 1994, Israel was dealing with the implications of the behaviour of Yeshayahu Demner, an engineering professor who went on an AIDS "spree" with "many dozens of men," as the police described it, until someone shot him. Within days, an "AIDS prevention law" was tabled in the Israeli parliament.

In the absence of any coordinated approach, Canadian courts continue to deal with AIDS-related situations in a random and inconsistent manner. In the summer of 1993 in Edmonton, charges of common nuisance were laid against a man who infected two men with HIV, having failed to wear a condom or to tell them that he was infected. A Toronto man was sentenced in February, 1994, to 45 days in prison on a charge of sexual assault for removing his condom during sex, after which his sex partner, a woman, withdrew consent in vain. In August, 1993, a Montreal doctor was suspended from practice for having anal and oral sex with patients, although he knew he was infected. At the time of his suspension, no criminal charges had been laid. A HIV-infected man in St. Stanislas de Koska, Quebec, who broke a bottle during a bar fight, cut his wrist and smeared blood on his opponent, went to jail for three years on a ludicrous charge of attempted murder.

The most important message to emerge from the Ssenyonga tragedy is that women can be readily infected with HIV: sexually active women of every age and social class are vulnerable. The incidence of HIV infection is rising faster in North American women than it is in men. A United Nations study in Europe, Africa, and Southeast Asia found that sexually active teenaged women are the next "leading edge" of the epidemic; they have higher rates of HIV infection than older women or young men. Women already are beginning to make up half the world's new AIDS cases.

Sex with a new partner in the nineties means sex with a condom. The recommended practice with a new relationship is that condoms be used without fail for six months of a new affair, after which both partners should have HIV tests. If both are negative for the AIDS virus *and* if both are monogamous, they run no risk of an HIV infection from intercourse.

Cheryl Wagner wanted Ssenyonga's story told in the hope that women everywhere will know they risk death when they have unprotected sex with a new partner. The women who testified at Ssenyonga's trial feel the same: none of them knew their lives were at stake when they had sexual intercourse with Charles Ssenyonga. They want other women to be more wary.

Betty Anne Thomas, Executive Director of the AIDS Committee of London, comments of the Ssenyonga trial, "I hope it increases the awareness that everyone is at risk. The heterosexual population does not believe itself at risk. University students have been growing up with this and they seem to be more aware, but heterosexuals older than twenty-five really don't perceive this being a problem for them." She sighs. "And high school students think they are invincible, immortal. It would be a big thing to have change in behaviour there."

Rick Galli and Michael Montpetit say that science was a winner in the Ssenyonga trial. "The Ssenyonga case was very interesting from an epidemiological standpoint," Galli said. It gave scientists an unprecedented opportunity to observe how the same virus mutates differently in different people. One of Ssenyonga's earliest victims, Linda Booker, had no symptoms of AIDS eight years later, while two women with more recent infections, Katie Newman and Barbara Williams, already were dead. "The fact we can now map the differences in their viral makeup and compare the differences is very significant."

Michael Montpetit will be working on the Ssenyonga virus for years to come. He is hoping to isolate the whole virus. Late in 1993 he had isolated about five hundred out of the ten thousand bases in one HIV. When he does isolate ten thousand bases of Ssenyonga's virus, he will contribute the work to the international data bank so that people all over the world will have complete information of Ssenyonga's peculiar strain. As an additional benefit, Montpetit will be following the development of the virus in the women Ssenyonga infected.

"It's another piece of the puzzle," he explained. "Working on this case means that we now have better tools for some of the puzzle work."

Late in 1994 Montpetit and Cheryl Wagner saw one another for the first time. Though they had talked on the telephone dozens of times over the years, they had never met. Montpetit was in Toronto for a discussion with Cheryl and Dr. Evan Collins about establishing a research project based on the uniqueness of the Ssenyonga circumstances. Nowhere else, with the possible exception of the people infected by the Florida dentist, is it possible to study the progression of one person's virus in a variety of individuals, each of whom had different reactions.

The plan is to find as many people as possible who were infected by Ssenyonga and obtain repeat blood samples from them for virologic and immunologic analyses. The expectation is that valuable insights into the development of HIV will be obtained. Both Dr. David Ho, director of the Aaron Diamond AIDS Research Center in New York, and Dr. Ken Rosenthal of McMaster are participating out of fascination in the potential for such a study. Montpetit therefore is anxious that yet-unidentified people infected by Ssenyonga contact him to assist in this important research. He can be located in Ottawa at the AIDS Laboratories of Health and Welfare Canada. Confidentiality will be protected. The results, omitting identifying information, will be presented in scientific papers and at international gatherings.

Connie Neill lives with Ssenyonga's ashes and very mixed feelings. Despite the unpleasant truths she learned from reading his papers, she still is inclined to love him. It is too painful to accept that he was a shallow, selfish man who used and abused her. She prefers to think he was a good person, if confused, and that he truly loved her. She tells friends that he cried in her arms just before he died. "The last couple of days he seemed to be feeling very guilty," she recalled sadly. "He was sort of trying to make it up with me."

Charles Ssenyonga, the AIDS-carrier, remains in death the complex, ambiguous man he was in life. The man who charmed women to death was unknowable, even to himself; he didn't seem to know if he was a good man or an evil one. Some thought he was waiting for a judge to tell him. Or perhaps he died because he didn't really want to hear what the judge had to say.

INDEX

INDEX

Vera Hay

604. 291- 6884.